le

2012

Hope you enjoy praying
with the Kings!
Wear the CROWN!

Love, Mom

PRAYING
WITH THE KINGS

Books By Elmer Towns

How God Answers Prayer

Knowing God Through Fasting

How to Build a Lasting Marriage

Praying the Scriptures Series

Praying Genesis

Praying Your Way Out of Bondage: Prayers from Exodus and Leviticus

Praying for Your Second Chance: Prayers from Numbers and Deuteronomy

Praying with the Conquerors: Praying Joshua, Judges, and Ruth

Praying the Heart of David

Praying the Book of Job

Praying the Psalms

Praying the Proverbs, Song of Solomon, and Ecclesiastes

Praying the New Testament

Praying the Gospels

Praying the Book of Acts and the General Epistles

Praying Paul's Letter

Praying the Book of Revelation

Praying for Spiritual Breakthroughs for Your Children

Praying for Spiritual Breakthroughs for Your Marraige

Available From Destiny Image Publishers

PRAYING

WITH THE KINGS

PRAYING FIRST AND SECOND KINGS AND SECOND CHRONICLES

Praying the Scriptures Series

Elmer L. Towns

DESTINY IMAGE® PUBLISHERS, INC.

P.O. Box 310, Shippensburg, PA 17257-0310

"Speaking to the Purposes of God for This Generation and for the Generations to Come."

This book and all other Destiny Image, Revival Press, MercyPlace, Fresh Bread, Destiny Image Fiction, and Treasure House books are available at Christian bookstores and distributors worldwide.

For a U.S. bookstore nearest you, call **1-800-722-6774.**

For more information on foreign distributors, call **717-532-3040.**

Reach us on the Internet: **www.destinyimage.com.**

Trade Paper ISBN 978-0-7684-3267-1

Hardcover ISBN 978-0-7684-3485-9

Large Print ISBN 978-0-7684-3486-6

Ebook ISBN 978-0-7684-9098-5

For Worldwide Distribution, Printed in the U.S.A.

1 2 3 4 5 6 7 8 / 14 13 12 11 10

CONTENTS

Preface 9

Introduction 11

1 Adonijah Attempts Take-over of David's Throne 17

2 King David's Final Instructions to Solomon 25

3 King Solomon Receives Wisdom, Riches, and Honor 35

4 Solomon Prepares to Build the Temple 41

5 Solomon's State Officials 45

6 Building the Temple of God 51

7 Other Building Projects of King Solomon 59

8 The Ark of the Covenant Is Brought Into the Temple 67

9 The Lord Appears to Solomon a Second Time 77

10 The Queen of Sheba Visits King Solomon 83

11 King Solomon Turns Away From the True God 89

12 Rehoboam Ignores Wise Counsel of Older Men 97

13 The Man of God From Judah 105

14 Ahijah's Prophecy Against Jeroboam 113

15 Abijah Becomes King After Rehoboam 119

16 Abijah Rules Over Judah 125

17 Asa Defeats the Ethiopians 129

18 Asa Relies on Man, Not God 135

19 Baasha Rules Over Israel 139

20 Jehoshaphat Rules Over Judah 145

21 Yahweh Takes Care of Elijah 149

22 Elijah Confronts King Ahab 155

23 Elijah Runs Away to Mount Horeb 165

24 Syria and Israel at War 171

25 The Vineyard of Naboth 179

26 The Prophet Micaiah Predicts Ahab's Defeat 185

27 Jehoshaphat Appoints Judges 193

28 Jehoshaphat Defeats the Moabites and the Ammonites 197

29 Elijah Predicts Death of King Ahaziah 203

30 Elijah Taken up to Heaven 207

31 Moab Rebels Against Israel 213

32 Elisha Helps a Widow 219

33 Naaman Cured of Leprosy 227

34 An Iron Ax Head Floats 233

35 Open Windows of Heaven 241

36 The Shunemite Woman Returns 245

37 Jehu Is Privately Anointed King of Israel 251

38 Ahab's Descendants Are Killed 257

39 Joash Becomes King 263

40 King Joash Rules Over Judah 269

41 Jehoahaz Rules Over Israel 273

42 Jeroboam II Rules Over Israel 279

43 Amaziah Rules Over Judah 283

44 Uzziah Rules Over Judah 287

45 Ahaz Rules Over Judah 293

46   Hoshea Rules Over Israel 299

47   Hezekiah Rules Over Judah 307

48   The Passover Feast Is Celebrated 315

49   The Priests and Levites Receive Provisions 321

50   The Assyrians Threaten Jerusalem 325

51   King Hezekiah Seeks Advice From Isaiah 331

52   Yahweh Heals King Hezekiah 339

53   Manasseh Rules Over Judah 345

54   Josiah Rules Over Judah 351

55   King Josiah Enforces God's Laws 355

56   The Passover Observed 363

57   Jehoahaz Rules Over Judah 369

58   The Fall of Jerusalem 375

59   Cyrus Allows the Jews to Return to Jerusalem 381

Preface

WRITING THE KINGS

The Books of First and Second Kings are perhaps the most consistent historiography found in Scripture. The author (the identity of whom is discussed in the Introduction) tells how faithful each king was—or was not—to the law of Moses. The author continually condemns kings for allowing idol worship of all kinds.

Described are the "revival" kings and how each one removes the high places of worship, destroys idols, and cleanses the Temple. But because Israel went back to idolatry when an evil king took the throne, this tells us the problem was not the idols in "high places," but the idolatry in the hearts of the people. And it was not the physical Temple that needed cleansing, but the people needed to keep clean the inner person.

The Books of Kings reveal that God will consistently punish His people when they disobey the commandments and rebel against Him. Obviously, the author was alive during the final days of the earthly kingdom, because that's when the narrative ends.

Back when I was in the Junior Class at Eastern Heights Presbyterian Church in Savannah, Georgia, my teacher, Jimmy Breland, told me all the 22 kings of the northern tribes were lost, so we didn't have to memorize them. I didn't. Therefore as you read, notice how their sins are condemned because they continued *"in the sin of Jeroboam who made all Israel sin"* (1 Kings 14:16).

I had to memorize the kings of Judah—the southern kingdom—because many of them were good kings. Jimmy Breland told me to memorize their names because I would meet them in Heaven. I did, and no doubt I will meet them.

Of course some kings in the south were evil, but I learned them as well. Only two kings received great recognition—Hezekiah and Josiah *"did what was right in the sight of the Lord, according to all that David his father did"* (see 2 Kings 18:3; 22:2).

We are commanded, *"Pray...plead God's mercy upon them and give thanks. Pray this way for kings"* (1 Tim. 2:1-2 TLB). So as we read the good examples of the Old Testament kings, let's pray for our rulers to lead the same way today, and thank God when they do. But let's not forget the negative kings. Let's ask God to deliver us from evil leaders.

This is the fourteenth book in the series, *Praying the Scriptures.*

Previous volumes are:

Praying Genesis
Praying for Your Second Chance
Praying the Heart of David
Praying the Psalms
Praying the New Testament
Praying the Book of Acts
Praying the Book of Revelation

Praying Your Way Out of Bondage
Praying with the Conquerors
Praying the Book of Job
Praying the Proverbs
Praying the Gospels
Praying Paul's Letters

There will be three more volumes forthcoming in this series:

Praying When God Speaks:
Praying Isaiah, Jeremiah, Lamentations, and Ezekiel

Praying When You Come Back to God: Praying Daniel, Ezra, Nehemiah, Esther, Obadiah, Haggai, Zechariah, and Malachi

Praying Minutia: Praying the Minor Prophets

My prayer is that you will touch God as you are *Praying With Kings*, but more importantly than that—may God touch you through this volume.

Written from my home
at the foot of the Blue Ridge Mountains,
Elmer Towns

Introduction

A LOOK AT KINGS

A king is more powerful than a United States president or a prime minister of any Parliament. In biblical times, a king ruled for God and was almost absolute in authority. He controlled every aspect of government and had enormous power over the lives of his people.

David was by far the godliest of the kings, for he was "a man after the heart of God." Solomon began his reign with wealth, glory, and power, and seemed to fulfill what Benaiah said of him at the beginning of his reign, "May King Solomon be an even greater king than you (David)!"

Solomon began with godly wisdom and spiritual insight when he built and dedicated the Temple. But Solomon compromised some of the most sacred spiritual principles to achieve political ends (the end justifies the means).

Then the kings after Solomon were a vacillating lot. Some followed God, but most did not. Those kings who abandoned God and His commands were described as "evil." Those kings who followed the worship of the God of Israel were called "good."

In this manuscript you will pray with the kings who sought the Lord. For God has promised He would be found by those who honestly seek Him. You will also pray for wisdom to not follow the example of some kings who gave themselves to evil. *Lord, may this manuscript give the readers strength so they will not compromise in the areas of their lives that eventually destroyed both Northern and Southern Israel.*

There are three lessons this book teaches. First, human values are faulty, even when they do good some of the time, or even when they do good most of the time. *Lord, may I learn from their mistakes.*

11

Second, God continually rules His people in spite of the weaknesses or failures of His leaders and His people. *Lord, help me look beyond human foibles to see Your power.*

Third, God's power and glory is manifested in those who obey God. But also, God's power is manifested in His judgment of those kings who disobeyed God and chased after idols and gave themselves to corruption. *Lord, I will learn obedience as I read about Your punishment of those who disobeyed You. Amen.*

Who Wrote Kings?

Originally, First and Second Kings were one book in the ancient Hebrew manuscripts. But when they were translated into Greek in the Septuagint (the Hebrew language has no vowels, but Greek does; taking more space), the books were divided into two manuscripts. First and Second Samuel were the first two books of the Kings. What we today call First and Second Kings were actually "third and fourth kings."

No one knows for sure who wrote First and Second Kings. We know the author was faithful to the commands of God, especially to God's directives for the king to obey the writings of Moses.

The author begins with the death of David and ends with the deportation of Judah to Babylon; therefore, the author had to be alive then. Jeremiah lived at the end when the Jews went into captivity, so he probably wrote these books. The passage in Second Kings 24:17 to 25:30 is repeated in Jeremiah 52, giving a stronger suggestion Jeremiah was the author of First and Second Kings. The Old Testament *Talmud: Baba Batha* 15a attributes the authorship to Jeremiah.

One more thing, prominence is given to the prophets Elijah and Elisha, plus Isaiah is mentioned, suggesting the prophetic standpoint of the author. Even though Jeremiah was born into the line of the priesthood, God called him into a prophetic ministry (see Jeremiah 1).

Jeremiah was the weeping prophet who shed tears over the sin of Israel and the destruction of Jerusalem. Surely, he wept over all the kings who did evil that led to God's punishment.

Jeremiah got much of his information about Solomon from the *Book of Solomon Events of Israel's Kings* (14:19 ff). Finally, Jeremiah makes 15 references to the book *Historical Record of Judah's Kings* (14:29 ff). Although Jeremiah used documentary research to write the Scriptures, this does not suggest the books were not plenary inspired, nor verbally accurate. "*All Scripture is given by inspiration of God*" (2 Tim. 3:16). See Luke 1:1-4 where Luke says he consulted many sources, yet wrote by the Holy Spirit, *anothen* "from above."

Who Wrote Chronicles?

The author is unknown according to the scholars, so we should call him "the chronicler." We know he wrote after the 70 years of captivity in Babylon because the chronicler ended with the decree of Cyrus, the Persian (remember Persia defeated Babylon), then some Jews returned home in 538 B.C.

First and Second Kings have already been written when the chronicler wrote his sacred history that parallels Kings. Why did he write a second history? Think of what he experienced. Jerusalem was in shambles, the walls in ruins. Very few returning Jews were faithful to God and they were vulnerable to attacks from their enemies. The spiritual life of the Temple had collapsed.

So the chronicler wrote to restore Israel to the Davidic Covenant. He wrote to show the religious sins of all Israel had political and military results. He did not want Israel to re-experience the judgment of God on the nation again, so he told how Israel's original disobedience was punished by God.

The chronicler writes history with an emphasis on the priesthood and the Temple, whereas the Books of Kings were written from the viewpoint of kings, the military, and the warnings of the prophets. The chronicler wrote to show how God hated idol worship, so Israel wouldn't fall back into idolatry after she returned to the land.

Originally, Chronicles was one book when written in Hebrew. But when it was translated into Greek (the LXX Septuagint), it became two books. As mentioned previously, the Hebrew grammar had only consonants, whereas Greek had both consonants and vowels; the lengthened book was too large for one scroll.

Originally, the Chronicles were called "The things omitted," meaning he included the things about the priesthood and Temple worship that were left out of Kings. But the early church father, Jerome, described it as, "A Chronicle of all sacred history," and the title *Chronicles* stuck.

Because the chronicler wanted to emphasize the spiritual, he left out the personal failings of David and Solomon, as well as the stories of Absalom, Amnon, and Adonijah. He wasn't trying to whitewash David and Solomon; he assumed the readers would know of their sins from First and Second Kings.

Genealogies are important in First Chronicles. When the Jews returned after their Babylonian captivity, it was important to determine who was qualified to be a priest for God. Since many of the records were destroyed when Nebuchadnezzar destroyed the Temple in 586 B.C., the records needed to be reestablished and verified. The returning Jews had a compelling reason to worship rightly, being led by legitimate priests.

But there was a greater reason to reestablish a correct Jewish lineage. Since God had promised to send the Messiah through Abraham, the genealogy in Chronicles begins with Adam—includes Abraham—and traces the Messianic line. This was the basis that was used in Matthew 1:1-17 and Luke 3:23-38 to trace Jesus' connection to the Old Testament prophecies.

In this volume, not every passage in Chronicles is included if the material is included in the Kings account. The aim is to give a complete and accurate chronology of the Kings from both First and Second Kings and Second Chronicles.

When you read and pray these sources of Scripture with the kings of the Old Testament, remember your Christian foundation. Christ is your King (see 1 Tim. 1:17). Christ lives within you (see Gal. 2:20, Col. 1:28), so the Lord Jesus Christ can make these prayers within your heart.

But there's a second stage. Christ is your High Priest in Heaven. *"He [Christ] everliveth to make intercession for you"* (Heb. 7:25 ELT). Therefore, pray with Christ as He prays for you.

> *Lord, it's my desire to let Jesus pray through me, so I now yield to His power of prayer in me. But also, I want Jesus to intercede for me as He stands at Your right hand. Amen.*

May you meet King Jesus as you read and pray this book (see 1 Tim. 1:17), and may He sit on the throne of your heart. One day, He will sit on the throne in Jerusalem in the Millennium, but today you have the privilege of inviting Him to sit on the throne of your life.

1

ADONIJAH ATTEMPTS TAKE-OVER OF DAVID'S THRONE

First Kings 1

At that time, King David was very old and his servants covered him with blankets, but he could not keep warm. So they said, "We will find a young woman, a virgin, to take care of you. She will lie close to you and keep you warm." So they looked everywhere within the borders of Israel for a beautiful young woman and found a girl named Abishag from the Shunammite people. The girl was very beautiful and took care of the king and served him. But King David did not have sex with her.

Adonijah was the son of Haggith and King David. He was born next after Absalom. Adonijah was a very handsome man who exalted himself, saying, "I will be the next king." So, he got for himself a chariot and horses and 50 men to run ahead of him. Now, David had never interfered with him by questioning what he did.

Adonijah talked with Joab, the son of Zeruiah and with Abiathar the priest. They told Adonijah that they would help him. But several men did not join Adonijah—Zadok the priest, Benaiah the son of Jehoiada, Nathan the prophet, Shimei, Rei, and King David's special guard (probably the 600 soldiers mentioned in First Samuel 25:13; 27:2).

Then Adonijah killed some sheep, cows, and fat calves for sacrifices.
(This was a solemn occasion intended to inaugurate himself as
king, the way that Absalom had done [see 2 Sam. 15:12].) He
made these sacrifices at the Stone of Zoheleth near En-Rogel
Spring. He invited all of his brothers, the other sons of King
David, to come. He invited all the rulers and leaders of Judah,
too. They were servants of the king. But Adonijah did not invite
Nathan the prophet, Benaiah, his father's special bodyguard,
or his half-brother Solomon. (The motive behind Adonijah's
banquet was purely political; he wanted to curry the favor of
certain people to support his "claim" to the throne of David.
Since Adonijah was David's oldest surviving son, Adonijah
thought that he should surely be the next king, even though
Adonijah knew that David had chosen Solomon. Solomon was
not invited to this banquet, which was to precede his attempted
coup d'état. If the rebellion of Adonijah had succeeded, Solomon
would be among the first to be executed by "King" Adonijah.)

Solomon Is Appointed King

When Nathan heard about this, he went to Bath-Sheba, the mother
of Solomon. Nathan asked, "Have you heard what Adonijah,
Haggith's son, is doing? He had made himself king. And, our
real king, David, does not know it. Your life and the life of your
son Solomon may be in danger. But I will now tell you how to
save yourselves. Go to King David and say, 'O my master and
king, you made a promise to me that my son Solomon would be
the king after you. You said that he would rule on your throne.
So, why has Adonijah become king?' While you are talking to
him, I will come in and tell the king that what you have said
about Adonijah is true."

So, Bath-Sheba went in to see the king in his bedroom. He was very old; and Abishag, the girl from Shunam, was taking care of him there and Bath-Sheba kneeled and bowed down in front of the king.

He asked, "What do you want?"

She answered, "My master, you made a promise to me in the Name of Yahweh your God. You said: 'Your son Solomon will surely become king after me. He will rule on my throne.' But now, Adonijah has become king. And, you did not know it! Adonijah has killed many cows, fat calves, and sheep for sacrifices, and invited all of your sons. He has also invited Abiathar the priest and Joab the general of your army. But he did not invite Solomon, your son, who serves you. O my master and king, all the people of Israel are watching you. They are waiting for you to decide who will be the next king after you. (There was the absolute right of the king to designate that one of his sons would be his successor.) As soon as you die, Solomon and I will be treated as criminals."

While Bath-Sheba was still talking with the king, Nathan the prophet arrived. (When Nathan entered the chamber, in accordance with oriental ideas of propriety, Bath-Sheba left the room.) The servants told the king, "Nathan the prophet is here." So, Nathan went to the king and bowed face down on the ground before him, then said, "O my master and king, have you said that Adonijah will be the king after you? Have you decided that he will rule on your throne after you? Today, Adonijah has gone down and sacrificed many cows, fat calves, and sheep, and invited all your other sons, the commanders of the army, and Abiathar the priest. Right now they are eating and drinking with him. They are saying: 'Long live King Adonijah.' (The usual way of acclaiming a new king.) But Adonijah did not invite me your servant, Zadok the priest, Benaiah the son of Jehoiada, or your son Solomon who serves you. Did you do this? We are your servants. Why didn't you tell us whom you chose to be the next king after you?"

Then King David said, "Tell Bath-Sheba to come in." So, she came in and stood in the presence of the king. Then the king said, "The Lord has saved me from all troubles. As surely as the Lord lives, I make this oath to you: today I will do what I promised you in the past. I made that oath in the Name of Yahweh, the God of Israel. I promised that your son Solomon would be king after me. I promised that he would rule on my throne in my place."

Then Bath-Sheba bowed face-down on the ground before the king. She said, "May my master, King David, live forever."

Then King David said, "Summon Zadok the priest, Nathan the prophet, and Benaiah the son of Jehoiada here to me." So they came into the presence of the king. Then the king said to them, "Take my officers with you and put my son Solomon on my own mule. (This was symbolically tantamount to being the co-regent of David. The rabbis tell us that it was death to ride on the king's mule without his permission.) Take Solomon down to the Gihon Spring. Let Zadok the priest and Nathan the prophet pour olive oil on Solomon there and make him king over Israel. Then blow the trumpet and shout: 'Long live King Solomon!'

"Then follow him back up here, where he will sit on my throne and rule in my place. I have chosen him to be the ruler over Israel and Judah." (This was a public proclamation of David's official choice of the new ruler.)

Benaiah the son of Jehoiada answered the king, "This is good. 'Amen,' says the Lord, your God! The Lord has always helped you, our king. May the Lord help Solomon, too. May King Solomon be an even greater king than you!"

So Zadok the priest, Nathan the prophet, and Benaiah the son of
Jehoiada went down with the Cherethites and the Pelethites (the
king's bodyguards) and put Solomon on King David's mule and
led him to Gihon Spring. And, Zadok the priest took along with
him the container of olive oil from the Tabernacle. He poured the
olive oil on Solomon's head (to show that Solomon was the new
king). Then they blew the trumpet (signifying that a "coronation"
was in progress). And all the people shouted: "Long live King
Solomon!" Then all the people followed Solomon into the city.
They were playing flutes and shouting with great joy. They
made so much noise that the ground resounded (an oriental
hyperbole).

At this time, Adonijah and all the guests who were with him were
finishing their meal. They heard the sound from the trumpet.
Joab asked, "What does all that noise from the city mean?"

While Joab was speaking, Jonathan, the son of Abiathar the priest,
arrived. Adonijah said, "Come in! You are an important man, you
must be bringing good news?"

But Jonathan answered Adonijah, "O no! Our master, King David, has
just made Solomon the new king! King David sent Zadok the
priest, Nathan the prophet, Benaiah the son of Jehoiada, and
all the king's bodyguards with Solomon. And, they have put
Solomon on the king's own mule. Zadok the priest and Nathan
the prophet have poured olive oil on Solomon at Gihon Spring
to make him king. Then they went up from there into the city,
rejoicing. Now the whole city is excited. That's the noise you
hear. Solomon is now sitting upon the throne of the kingdom.
All the king's officers have come to congratulate King David,
our master. They are saying: 'May your God make Solomon even
more famous than you. And, may your God make Solomon an
even greater king than you!'" Jonathan continued, "And, King
David bowed himself down on his bed to worship God. And

thus David said: 'Praise the Lord, the God of Israel. Today God has made one of my sons the king and permitted me to see it.'"

Then all of Adonijah's guests were afraid, and they got up and left, each going his own way. Adonijah was also afraid of Solomon. So, Adonijah went and took hold of the corners of the altar. (This was a place of asylum. The "horns" of the altar were vertical projections at each corner of the brazen altar where blood sacrifices were made for sin.)

Then someone told Solomon: "Adonijah is afraid of you. He is at the altar, holding on to its horns. He says: 'Tell King Solomon to promise me today that he will not kill me.'" So, Solomon answered, "Adonijah must show that he is a man of honor. If he does, then I promise that he will not lose even one hair from his head. But if he does anything wrong, then he will die." Then King Solomon sent some men to get Adonijah and bring him from the altar to King Solomon. So, Adonijah came into the presence of King Solomon and bowed himself down. Then Solomon said to him, "Go home." (Either this was a full pardon or a direct order to retire from public life, no longer interfering with the kingdom.)

My Time to Pray

Doing the Right Thing Rightly

There let Zadok the priest and Nathan the prophet anoint him King over Israel; and blow the horn, and say "Long live King Solomon!" (1 Kings 1:34)

God loves symbols and God communicates to us with symbols because they are outward things that represent inward truth. Aren't baptism, communion, and the cross cultural symbols that reflect inward spiritual truth? Therefore, when faced with an extreme problem—Adonijah's usurping the throne—David instructed his closest team to use the following symbols that would convince the people that Solomon was king. Then public acceptance would eliminate Adonijah. First they took Solomon to the Tabernacle where sins are forgiven and where God dwelt. Second, they were to anoint Solomon with holy oil from the Tabernacle. Third, Solomon was to ride David's mule (equivalent to riding in the presidential jet Air Force One), then parade Solomon in public and sit him on David's throne. Next they blew the trumpet (a shophar) and proclaimed Solomon king. The people responded with the triumphant shout, "Long live King Solomon!" Note carefully, Adonijah didn't use any of the proper symbols in proclaiming himself king. *Lord, I will follow Your symbols in the church to gain Your authority.*

Why did Adonijah bypass the imperative symbols? Maybe he didn't know what to do, which means he was unqualified for the job. Also, Adonijah recruited the wrong people to help him. Maybe he didn't understand palace politics, again suggesting he was not qualified. Also, Adonijah left God and the Tabernacle out of the loop; he didn't go to the Tabernacle where the presence of God was located. And did he try to "buy" loyalty by feeding his followers at a banquet? *Lord, may I always go about Your work in the right way, at the right time, at the right place.*

Be careful of people who do things secretly. Notice, *"David our lord does not know it"* (1 Kings 1:11). David had previously announced publically that Solomon would be the next king. But David was sick and people expected his death at any time. Perhaps Adonijah thought with David out of the way, he could pull a coup and it would be accomplished once he got a multitude yelling, "Long live King Adonijah!" *Lord, may I seek the wisdom and approval of godly people when doing Your service.*

This story teaches us timing. If Adonijah's coup had not been challenged, then the illegal king might have pulled it off. Time was critical. While Adonijah was eating his coronation banquet, David instructed those closest to him to use the correct symbols to put Solomon in office. If Nathan and Bath-Sheba had waited a short period of time—one day—Adonijah might have pulled it off. Then think of the consequences—part of the people for Adonijah, the others for Solomon, civil war, political confusion at the beginning of the monarchy. Then the Philistines and other nations could have challenged and perhaps defeated God's people, as they did in Judges and First Samuel 31. *Lord, help me use time correctly. May I act quickly when a crisis approaches and may I wait patiently when time dictates problems will solve themselves. Then, Lord, teach me how to interpret the differences between these two periods of time.*

Did you see how Adonijah used questionable counselors in contrast to the godly counselors who put Solomon on the throne? *"There is no wisdom or understanding or counsel against the Lord that will not fail"* (Prov. 21:30 ELT). *Lord, give me good, godly, and smart counselors. I will listen to them to find Your plan for my life.*

God had a threefold anointed office in the Old Testament. There was the anointed prophet who was represented by Nathan. Second, there was the anointed priest, who was represented by Zadok. Third, was the king's office. Solomon entered that office by anointing. Adonijah forgot about the anointing, which suggests the Holy Spirit was not upon him and he didn't have the Spirit's leading because oil was not used to inaugurate him into office. Remember, oil is a symbol of the Holy Spirit. *Lord, anoint me with Your spirit of wisdom, power, and service. I seek the Holy Spirit and I want His anointing in my life. I will not try to serve You in the flesh. Fill me today.*

The Hebrew word *Messiah* means "anointed one," which is translated into the Greek word *Christ*. This means Jesus fulfilled the three-fold anointed office of prophet, priest, and king. *Jesus, You are my anointed King, lead me. Jesus, You are my anointed Prophet, speak to me. Jesus, You are my anointed Priest, thank You for Your sacrifice for my sins. Now You are the High Priest at the right hand of God the Father, interceding for me. Amen.*

2

KING DAVID'S
FINAL INSTRUCTIONS TO SOLOMON

First Kings 2

The time of David's death was getting closer. So, David gave his last commands to Solomon, his son. (This private speech is different from the farewell address that was delivered in public some time before [see 1 Chron. 28:2-10].) David said, "The time of my death is very near. You must be strong. Be a man. (Solomon was only about 20 years old at this time.) Obey everything that the Lord your God commands. Live by His ways. Obey all His laws, rules, and decisions—do whatever He told us. Obey whatever is written in the Law of Moses. If you do these things, then you will be successful in everything you do, and wherever you turn. And, if you obey the Lord, then He will keep the promise that He made to me. This is what He promised: 'Your descendants must live as I tell them. They must have complete trust in Me. If they do this, then a male from your family will always be king over the people of Israel.'

"Also, you know what Joab the son of Zeruiah did to me. He killed the two generals of Israel's armies. (The Law of Moses said that the whole land was defiled as long as a murder remained unpunished [see Num. 35:33].) Joab murdered Abner the son of Ner and Amasa the son of Jether. He killed them as if they were at war with him. But that was in a time of peace. He assassinated innocent men, and their blood spurted on his belt that was around his waist and the sandals that he wore. You should punish him in the way you think is the most wise. (General Joab was very popular in the military.) But do not let him die peacefully of old age.

"And, be king to the descendants of Barzillai the Gileadite. Allow them to eat from your royal table. They helped me when I was retreating from your brother Absalom.

"And, remember, Shimei the descendant of Gera is still here with you. He is from the people of Benjamin in Bahurim. Don't forget that he cursed me (that was a capital offense, and, even King David had no power to forgive such an offense) in the most terrible way that he could on that day when I left for Mahanaim. Later, he came down to meet me at the Jordan River. I vowed to him by the Lord that I would not kill him by the sword. However, you should not let him go unpunished. (Don't treat Shimei as if he is an innocent man, because he is not.) You are a smart man. You will know what you ought to do with him. But, you must be sure that he is put to death."

David Dies

Then David died, and he was buried in the City of David, Jerusalem. David had ruled over Israel for 40 years. (From 1010 to 970 B.C. Jewish writers almost always omit the fractions of a year. Seven of those years were in Hebron. The exact length was seven years and six months [see 2 Sam. 5:5]. David ruled in Jerusalem for 33 years.)

Now Solomon became king after David, his father, and Solomon was in firm control of his kingdom.

Adonijah, Still the Rebel

At this time, Adonijah, the son of Haggith, went to Bath-Sheba, Solomon's mother. Bath-Sheba asked, "Do you come in peace?" (She was suspicious of Adonijah because of his earlier, attempted coup.)

Adonijah answered, "Yes. This is a peaceful visit. I have something to say to you."

"You may speak," she said.

Adonijah said, "Do you remember that, at one time the kingdom was to be mine? (Adonijah as the oldest living son of David.) All the people of Israel thought that I was about to become their king. However, things changed. Now my half-brother is the king, because the Lord chose him. So now, I have only one thing I'd like to ask from you. Please do not deny me."

Bath-Sheba answered him, "What do you want?"

Adonijah said, "I know that King Solomon will do anything that you ask him. So, please ask him to give me Abishag, the Shunammite woman, to be my wife."

"All right," she answered, "I will speak to the king on your behalf." (Bath-Sheba was unaware of Adonijah's cunning abilities. Perhaps, since Bath-Sheba did not consider that Abishag was indeed a concubine of David, she did not perceive any real danger in Adonijah's request. Nevertheless, Adonijah was using Bath-Sheba to get to King Solomon.)

So, Bath-Sheba went to King Solomon to talk to him on behalf of Adonijah. When Solomon saw her, he stood up to meet her. (This act showed great respect for his mother.) He bowed himself down to her, then he sat back on his throne. He told some servants to bring another throne for his mother. She sat down at his right side.

Bath-Sheba said to Solomon, "I have just one small favor to ask of you. Please don't refuse me."

The king answered, "Ask, mother. I will not refuse you."

So she said, "Please permit your half-brother Adonijah to marry Abishag, the Shunammite woman."

King Solomon answered his mother, "Why are you asking me to give him Abishag? Why not ask for him to become the king of the kingdom? (Solomon interpreted this initiative as the first move in an elaborate plot, which was supported by Abiathar and Joab, as well.) He is my older brother." (If Adonijah could be perceived as possessing part of David's royal harem, then he might be widely regarded as a legitimate successor to David's throne. Abiathar the high priest and Joab the son of Zeruiah will support his bid to become the new king. Apparently, Abiathar and Joab were involved in further treachery.)

Then King Solomon vowed by the Name of Yahweh, saying, "I swear that Adonijah will pay dearly for asking this thing of me. May God punish me terribly if it does not cost Adonijah his life. (Solomon's previous pardon of Adonijah was conditional.) The Lord has established me and given me the throne that once belonged to my father David. The Lord has kept His promise and given the dynasty to me. And now, as surely as the Lord is alive, Adonijah will be executed today." So, King Solomon gave orders to Benaiah the son of Jehoiada. And, Benaiah went out and executed Adonijah. Adonijah died.

Solomon Puts Abiathar Out of Office

Then King Solomon said to Abiathar the high priest, "I should kill you. (Abiathar was an accomplice of Adonijah.) However, I will not execute you today. Instead, I will permit you to go back to your home in Anathoth. You carried the Holy Ark of the Lord Who Is Always Present while marching ahead of my father David. And I know you went through all of those tough times with my father." So, Solomon removed Abiathar from being high priest to the Lord. This made what the Lord said come true. God had predicted that Eli the priest and his family in Shiloh would come to an end.

When the news came to Joab, he was afraid. He had supported Adonijah's scheme, though he did not support Absalom's revolt. So Joab ran to the Tabernacle of the Lord and grabbed hold of the horns of the altar. (This was a place of asylum.) Someone told King Solomon that Joab had run to the Tabernacle of the Lord: "Joab is holding the horns of the altar." So Solomon ordered Benaiah the son of Jehoiada: "Go and execute him."

Benaiah came into the Tabernacle of the Lord and said to Joab, "The king says: 'Come out.'"

But Joab answered, "No, I will surely die here."

So, Benaiah brought back Joab's answer to the king. Then the king commanded Benaiah, "Do as Joab says. Execute him right there on the spot. Then bury him. I and my father's household will be set free from Joab's past blood-guilt. Joab is guilty of killing innocent people. Joab murdered two men who were better than him. They had more integrity than Joab. They were Abner the son of Ner and Amasa the son of Jether. Abner was the general of Israel's army, and Amasa was the general of Judah's army. My father David did not know that Joab planned to murder them. So the Lord will pay Joab back for murdering those innocent men with a sword. Benaiah, you will always hold Joab and his family responsible for the deaths of those two men. However, there will be peace from the Lord for David, his family, his descendants, and his throne forever."

Then Benaiah the son of Jehoiada went up, struck him down, and killed Joab. And, Joab was buried near his home in the desert. Then Solomon appointed Benaiah (Benaiah had been the commander of David's bodyguard), the general of the army, instead of Joab. Solomon also made Zadok the new high priest, instead of Abiathar.

The Blasphemy of Shimei Is Finally Judged

Then the king sent someone to summon Shimei. The king said to him, "Build a house for yourself here in Jerusalem. Live in that house, and do not go anywhere else. (King Solomon wanted to restrict Shimei's possible conspiracy with any remaining followers of Saul.) If you ever leave the city and cross the Kidron Brook, you can be sure that you will most certainly die. And that will be your own fault." (Your blood will be on your own head.)

So Shimei answered the king, "What you have said is good. I will obey you, O my master and king." So Shimei stayed inside Jerusalem for a long time. However, three full years later, two of Shimei's slaves ran away. They went to Achish the Younger (Achish the Elder was a contemporary of David), the king of Gath. Shimei heard that his runaway slaves were in Gath. So, Shimei got up and put a saddle on his donkey and left Jerusalem. He went to Achish in Gath to find his slaves. After he found them there, he brought them back to his home in Jerusalem.

Someone told Solomon that Shimei had traveled from Jerusalem to Gath and that he had returned to Jerusalem. So Solomon summoned

Shimei, and said to him, "I caused you to swear by the Name of Yahweh not to leave Jerusalem. I warned you that if you ever went anywhere else you would surely die. You agreed to what I said. And, you said that you would obey me. Why did you break your vow to Yahweh? (Insincerity was treated as sacrilege.) Why did you not obey the order that I gave you?" The king continued speaking to Shimei, "You know all the evil that you planned against my father David. Now the Lord is about to bring all your evil upon your own head. Nevertheless, the Lord will bless me. (King Solomon believed that he would be blessed for removing any curses from the royal household.) And, the Lord will cause the throne of David to be established in His presence forever."

Then the king ordered Benaiah the son of Jehoiada to execute Shimei. Shimei died. Now Solomon was in full control of his kingdom.

My Time to Pray

Unfinished Business

Now the days of David drew near that he should die, and he charged Solomon his son, saying…"be strong, therefore, and prove yourself a man" (1 Kings 2:1-2).

There were three negative items of unfinished business that David told Solomon to deal with after he died. The first was Joab's murder of two men. Second, Shimei had blasphemed the office of King and David himself. Third, Abiathar had supported Adonijah. Then there was a positive item. Barzillai helped David when he fled from Absalom, and David wanted his family rewarded. *Lord, I will take care of Your business.*

Joab was a study in contradictions. He won wars for David when others couldn't, and he captured Jerusalem, and he counseled David to go review the troops after the battle against Absalom; if it hadn't been for Joab, David may have lost his army and never regained the throne. This proves bad people can do good things, and can be used of God in the divine scheme of things. But Joab murdered Ner and Amasa. People must be held accountable to God for the evil they do. *Lord, I bow to You who will judge all people.*

Will we see Joab in Heaven? No one knows for sure. It's not his good deeds that will get him into Heaven. Just because he murdered doesn't mean he will automatically be kept out. Look at Paul the apostle who was responsible for the death of believers, even if he didn't deliver the death blow. Joab will be in Heaven if he had faith in the blood of a sacrificed lamb for his sins. Remember, *"the blood of Jesus Christ God's son cleanses us from all sin"* (1 John 1:7). *Lord, I don't deserve to be in Heaven, but Your Son Jesus has justified me (just as if I'd never sinned). I will go to be with You because I believe in Jesus and have Him in my heart.*

David was a gracious man to forgive Shimei, but apparently Shimei had never taken care of this sin before God. Solomon gave Shimei every chance to demonstrate loyalty to the crown. But when Shimei couldn't obey Solomon's decision, it reflected the rebellion of Shimei's heart. *Lord, I will obey Your commands to demonstrate I have repented of the sins of my past.*

The sins of a servant in the priesthood have greater consequences than the sins of the average believer. Abiathar's sin in promoting Adonijah was greater than the others who attended Adonijah's feast and yelled out, "Long live King Adonijah!" *Even today, Lord, You judge Your preachers harshly. I will live clean and be loyal to You.*

Apparently, Adonijah planned a second attempt to become king. He wanted to marry Abishag. That meant when he had one of David's concubines he had a claim to the throne. A careful reading of the text suggests both Joab and Abiathar were part of this plot, just as they had been part of the first attempt to put Adonijah on the throne. Solomon acted decisively. He fulfilled David's challenge to him, *"prove yourself a man"* (1 Kings 2:2). *Lord, I will be decisive in dealing with sin, rebellion, and divisiveness in my heart. Forgive me! Cleanse me! Give me strength of resolve!*

In decisiveness, Solomon established his rule in the place of David. Solomon was no weakling, nor did he give in to court politics. *"The kingdom was established in the hand of Solomon"* (1 Kings 2:46). *Lord, make me decisive for You, use me in Your service. Amen.*

3

KING SOLOMON
RECEIVES WISDOM, RICHES, AND HONOR

First Kings 3

Solomon made an alliance (this political marriage secured peace
with Egypt, the Hebrew verb meant "to make oneself a son-
in-law") with Pharaoh, the king of Egypt, by marrying the
Pharaoh's daughter. Solomon brought her into the City of
David, Jerusalem. At that time, Solomon was still building (King
Solomon did not begin building the Temple until the fourth
year of his rule [see 1 Kings 6:1]) his own palace, the Temple
of the Lord, and the wall surrounding Jerusalem. In those days,
the Temple where God would put His Name had not yet been
completed. So, the people were still offering sacrifices on high
places. (High hills, some of these sites were old places for
worshiping Baal. God did not want the Israelites to use pagan
altars to worship Him [see Num. 33:52; Deut. 7:5; 12:3]. God
commanded them to have just one central place for offering
sacrifices [see Lev. 17:8-9; Deut. 12:5,11;13-14;26-27; Josh.
22:29]. Eventually, their worship on high places led to their
complete apostasy [see 2 Kings 17:7-18; 21:2-9; 23:4-25].)
Solomon loved the Lord and followed the commands that
his father, David, had given him. However, Solomon was still
offering sacrifices and burning incense on the high places.

The king went to Gibeon (God's tabernacle and the brazen altar were still there) to offer a sacrifice there, because it was an important high place. (Prior to the construction of the Temple, it was considered "normal" to worship at a variety of places.) Solomon offered 1,000 burnt offerings on that altar. While Solomon was at Gibeon, the Lord revealed Himself to him in a dream, during the night. God said, "Ask for anything you want. I will give it to you."

Solomon answered, "You have been very kind to Your servant, my father David. He obeyed You. He was honest and lived uprightly. And, You showed great loyalty to him by allowing me to be king after him today. Yes, O Lord, my God, You have caused me to be king in my father David's place. I am only a young man; I do not have the experience necessary. I am here among Your chosen people. They are a great people—there are too many of them to even count. So, I ask that You give me wisdom. Then I can govern Your people in the right way. Only then can I tell the difference between what is fair and what is unjust. Without wisdom, it would be impossible to govern this great people who belong to You."

When Solomon asked the Lord for wisdom, this pleased the Lord. So, God said to Solomon, "You did not ask for a long life for yourself. You did not ask for riches for yourself. And, you did not ask for the death of your enemies. Instead, you asked for insight to make the right decisions. Because you asked for wisdom, I have given you what you asked for. I have given you a wise and discerning mind. There has never been anybody like you in the past. And, no one will ever be like you in the future. I have given you what you did not ask for. You will have riches and honor, too. And, during your lifetime—among the kings—there will be no king as rich and famous as you will become. If you follow me and obey My laws and My commands, as your father David did, then I will also give you a long life."

Then Solomon woke up and realized it was a dream. Then he went to Jerusalem and stood in front of the Lord's Holy Ark of the Covenant. Solomon offered whole burnt offerings and peace offerings to the Lord. Then he gave a banquet for all of his officials.

King Solomon Uses the Wisdom that God Gave Him

Then two women who were prostitutes came to stand in front of Solomon. One of the women said, "O my master, this woman and I live in one house (a brothel). I gave birth to a baby while she was there in the same house. Three days later, this woman also gave birth to her baby. There was no one else in the house with us. We were the only two adults there. One night, this woman rolled over on top of her baby, and it died. So, in the middle of the night, while I was asleep, she got up and took my son who was next to me. Then she put her dead baby in my bed. And, she carried my baby to her bed. The next morning, when I got up to feed my son, I saw that he was dead. Then I examined him more closely. And, I could see that he was not my son I had given birth to."

But the other woman said, "No, the living baby is my son. That dead baby is your son."

But the first woman said, "No, the dead baby is yours, and the one who is alive is mine." So, the two women continued arguing in front of the king.

Then King Solomon said, "Each of you women claims that the living baby is your son. And, each of you claims that the dead baby belongs to the other woman." Then the king said, "Bring me a sword!" So, his servants brought a sword into the presence of the king. Then the king said, "Cut this living baby in half! And give each woman one-half of the baby."

The real mother of the living baby boy was full of genuine love for her son. She said to the king, "O my master, do not kill him. Give the baby to her."

But the other woman said, "Neither of us will have him; go ahead and cut him in two."

Then King Solomon answered, "Give the live baby to the first woman. Do not kill him; she is his mother."

When the people of Israel heard about the king's decision, they respected him so much, because they could see that Solomon did have the divine wisdom to make the right decisions.

My Time to Pray

You Usually Get What You Seek

Delight yourself also in the Lord, and He shall give you the desires of your heart (Psalm 37:4 ELT).

What impression did Solomon have of his father, David? Probably, Solomon knew his father David was a warrior for God, but that was not Solomon's desire. Probably, Solomon knew David was the passionate singer of Israel who wrote psalms to bless Jehovah. Again, that was not Solomon's cup of tea. Solomon probably saw the wisdom of David, especially David's accumulated wisdom of serving God for over 60 years. That was probably the thing Solomon wanted most of all. So when God invited Solomon in a dream, *"Ask what I shall give you"* (1 Kings 3:5), young Solomon asked, *"Give me wisdom"* (1 Kings 3:9 ELT). He asked for the right thing. *God, give me everything I need to serve You and worship You. Like Solomon, I know I'm weak and human. Give me Yourself.*

Almost immediately a story is told of the prostitutes who argued over the possession of one baby boy. Solomon knew the mother would "love" her baby, so when he commanded "cut the baby in half," Solomon knew how the real mother would respond. It was one thing for Solomon to know God had given him wisdom, but this story demonstrates, *"All Israel heard of the judgment...they saw that the wisdom of God was in him..."* (1 Kings 3:28). *Lord, that's what I want, I want others to see Your work in me. Not I, but Christ.*

Notice what Solomon didn't ask. He didn't ask for riches, or to be victorious over his enemies. How many of us would have asked for wisdom, before we ask for money to do God's work, or money to make us rich? How many of us would have asked for victory over satan and victory over sin around us? Maybe God wants to do something *in* us, before He wants to do something *for* us. *God, give me wisdom. I will study, I will memorize Your Word; I will review often. For my work, help me be smart. But that's only the beginning, I want Your indwelling Holy Spirit to speak to me and help me understand Your will for my life. Give me wisdom.*

Another thing to get your prayers answered—be humble. Solomon thanked God for his father who taught him many things. Solomon realized God had chosen him and led him to that very house. Next, Solomon confessed, *"I do not have the experience necessary to lead this people"* (1 Kings 3:7). Finally, he looked at his task in life, to lead God's people. Solomon confesses the job was too big and there were too many people to count. *"So, I ask that You give me wisdom"* (1 Kings 3:9). *Lord, I pray like Solomon. Thank You for leading me to this hour, I am not fit to serve You with my limitations. Give me wisdom. Amen.*

4

SOLOMON PREPARES
TO BUILD THE TEMPLE

Second Chronicles 2

Solomon was commanded to build the Temple for the Name of the Lord.
He also decided to build a palace for his kingdom. He chose
70,000 men to carry things. He chose 80,000 men to supervise
the workers.

Then Solomon sent a message to Hiram, the king of the city of Tyre.
(This was the capital city of Phoenicia.) Solomon said: "Help
me as you helped my father David. You sent him cedar logs,
so that he could build himself a palace to live in. I will build a
Temple for the Name of the Lord, my God, and, I will dedicate
this Temple to the Lord. There we will burn sweet-smelling spices
in His presence. We will set out the showbread (the bread of
His presence) regularly. And, we will offer whole burnt offerings
every morning and every evening. We will worship on Sabbath
days and New Moons. And, we will celebrate the other scheduled
festival days of the Lord, our God. This will be the rules for Israel
to obey forever.

"The Temple I build will be great. This is because our God is greater than
all gods. But no one can really build a Temple for our God. Not
even the highest heavens of the heavens can contain God. How

then could I build a house for Him? I can only build a place to burn sacrifices to God.

"Now send me a man who is skilled in working with gold, silver, bronze, and iron. He must also know how to work with purple, red, and blue fabrics. He must know how to make engravings. He will be working with my skilled craftsmen in Judah and Jerusalem. These are the men my father David provided. Also, send me cedar, pine, and red sandalwood logs from Lebanon. I know your servants are experienced at cutting down the trees in Lebanon. My servants will help them. Send me plenty of lumber. The Temple that I am going to build will be large and wonderful. I will give your servants who cut down the trees 100,000 bushels of crushed wheat. (This amount was such a high price that it was bankrupting Solomon's kingdom. Later, Solomon had to cede part of his territory to settle the 20-year debt.) And, I will give them 100,000 bushels of barley, 110,000 gallons of wine, and 110,000 gallons of oil."

Then Hiram, the king of Tyre, answered Solomon with this letter: "O Solomon, the Lord loves His people. That is why He chose you to be the king over them." Hiram also said: "Praise the Lord, the God of Israel. He made the heavens and the earth. He gave King David a wise son who has wisdom and understanding. He will build a Temple for the Lord and a palace for his kingdom. I have sent you Huram-Abi, a skilled and knowledgeable man. His mother comes from the tribe of Dan. And his father came from the people of Tyre. Huram-Abi has skill in working with gold, silver, bronze, iron, stone, and wood. He has skill in working with purple, blue, and red fabrics, and expensive linen. And, he is skilled in making engravings. He can make any design that you show him. He will help your craftsmen and the craftsmen of your father David. Now send my servants the wheat, barley, oil, and wine that you promised. We will cut as much wood from

Lebanon as you need. We will use rafts to float it by sea to Joppa. Then you may transport it to Jerusalem."

Solomon counted all the foreigners living in the land of Israel. This was after the time when his father David counted the people. There were 153,600 foreigners inside the country. Solomon assigned 70,000 of them to carry things. He assigned 80,000 of them to cut stones in the mountains. And, he appointed 3,600 of them to supervise the workers. They were to keep the people working.

My Time to Pray

Attention to Detail

So my dear brothers and sisters...be sure everything is done properly and in order (1 Corinthians 14:40 TLB).

D id you read how carefully and orderly everything was done to build God's house? No matter what is done for God, whether we do it in our ministry, or we do it through our Christian organization, we must give attention to timing, details, and carefully using the resources God has given to us to handle. *Lord, help me organize my life so I can do more for You, and do it better. I will give attention to details, help me see Your hand in the minutia of life.*

Can you imagine how long it took Solomon to get everything ready to build the Temple? We're talking about vast resources—stone, wood, people, infrastructure. For a task as large as Solomon's Temple, it took years to get everything together. And don't forget David. He was gathering money—gold, silver, jewels, etc.—to build the Temple long before Solomon became king. *Lord, teach me how to respect the gift of time and how to use my time profitably.*

Solomon needed resources that were not available in Israel. He needed timber from Lebanon; the cedars of Lebanon were famous. Solomon also needed experienced craftsmen to cut the stone and prepare the resources.

So wise Solomon partners with the king of Tyre (Lebanon) to get ready the necessary resources. *Lord, teach me to prepare to work, long before I begin the task of work.*

The issue of Huram-Abi (see 2 Chron. 2:13) becomes an issue. This chapter says he comes from the tribe of Dan, while First Kings 7:14 says he comes from the tribe of Naphtali. His father came from the people of Tyre. The critics are quick to cry "mistake," but they do so because they are anti-supernatural. They don't believe a perfect God would produce a perfect book so people can confidentially put their trust in the message of salvation in the Bible. *Lord, I believe You exist, so I believe You gave me an authoritative message in the Bible that I can trust.*

The answer is there if you want it. One answer, Dan was close to Naphtali, so the mother's line could have been from the tribe of Dan, but her family could have lived in Naphtali. A second answer is that she is called "a daughter of Dan," meaning she lived there, but her family lineage was from Naphtali. *Lord, I don't understand everything in Scripture, but I trust You as the Author, and I know there is an answer for everything I don't understand.*

There's another principle about gifted people. Some are gifted to build, some were equipped to haul, or carry, and others were able to be supervisors or personal managers. God uses people according to their usability. Are you serving where you use your best gifts in the best way for the efficiency of God's work and for the glory of God? *Lord, I yield my gifts to You. Use me when and where I can do the most good for Your Kingdom and bring the most glory to You. Amen.*

5

SOLOMON'S STATE OFFICIALS

First Kings 4

King Solomon ruled over all Israel. Here are the names of his officials:

Azariah the grandson of Zadok (who was getting old) was the high priest.

Elihoreph and Ahijah the sons of Shisha were the scribes (secretaries of the state).

Jehoshaphat the son of Ahilud was the historian.

Benaiah the son of Jehoiada was the general over the army.

Abiathar, banished by King Solomon at the beginning of his rule, and Zadok had each been the high priest.

Azariah the son of Nathan supervised the governors of each district.

Zabud the son of Nathan was an official and an advisor to the king.

Ahishar was responsible for everything in the palace.

Adoniram the son of Abda was in charge of the forced labor.

Solomon put 12 governors over all the districts of Israel. (King Solomon mapped out his country into 12 administrative zones to support his elaborate building programs and military ventures. These regions were somewhat different from the old tribal borders.)

Their job was to supply the king and his family from their districts. Each governor was responsible for giving provisions to the king for one month out of every year. These are the names of the 12 governors:

Ben-Hur was the governor over the hill-country of Ephraim.

Ben-Deker was the governor over Makaz, Shaalbim, Beth-Shemesh, and Elon-Beth-Hanan.

Ben-Hesed was the governor over Arubboth, Socoh, and all the land of Hepher belonged to Arubboth.

Ben-Abinadab was the governor over Naphath-Dor. (He was married to Taphath, the daughter of Solomon.)

Baana the son of Ahilud was the governor over Taanach, Megiddo, and all of Beth-Shean, which is next to Zarethan. This was below Jezreel from Beth-Shean to Abel-Meholah beyond Jokmeam.

Ben-Geber was the governor over Ramoth-Gilead. His territory was all the towns of Jadir in Gilead. Jadir was the son of Manasseh. Ben-Geber was also over the Argob region in Bashan. It had 60 large, walled towns that had bronze bars on their gates.

Ahinadab the son of Iddo was the governor over Mahanaim.

Ahimaaz was the governor over Naphtali. He was also married to Basemath, the daughter of Solomon.

Baana the son of Hushai was the governor over Asher and Bealoth.

Jehoshaphat the son of Paruah was the governor over Isaachar.

Shimei the son of Elah was the governor over Benjamin.

Geber the son of Uri was the governor over Gilead. Gilead was the country where Sihon the king of the Amorite people had lived.

Og the king of Bashan had also lived there. And, there was one governor in the land of Judah.

The Riches of King Solomon

There were so many people in Judah and Israel, as many people there as the grains of sand on the ocean beaches. The people ate and drank freely; they were happy.

Solomon ruled over all the kingdoms—from the Euphrates River to the land of the Philistine people. His kingdom went as far as the border of Egypt. Those areas brought Solomon the payments that he required, and they served him as long as he lived.

This is how much food was needed for Solomon's royal court each day: he required 185 bushels of fine flour and 375 bushels of meal. He also required 10 bulls that had been fed in stalls by the best grain, 20 bulls that had been fed on pasture-land, and 100 sheep. He also required male deer, gazelles, roebucks, and fattened domestic birds.

Solomon ruled over all the areas that were west of the Euphrates River—from Tiphsah to Gaza. He was over all the kings west of the Euphrates River. And Solomon had peace on all sides of his kingdom.

During Solomon's life, Judah and Israel—from Dan to Beersheba— about 150 miles—lived in safety. Each man was able to sit under his own fig tree and his grapevine (symbols of prosperity and peace).

Solomon had 4,000 stalls for his chariot horses. And, he had 12,000 chariot-horsemen. Each month, one of the district governors gave King Solomon all the supplies that Solomon needed. This was enough food for every person who ate at the king's table.

The governors always made sure that Solomon had everything he wanted. They also provided to the king their quotas of barley and straw for the workhorses and the fast horses. Each governor brought this to the required places.

The Wisdom of Solomon

God gave much wisdom to Solomon. Solomon could understand many things; his insight was as difficult to measure as the sand on the ocean beaches. His wisdom was greater than all the wisdom of all the men of the East—greater than all the wisdom of the men of Egypt. Solomon was wiser than any other human being on earth. He was even smarter than Ethan the Ezrahite, or Heman, or Calcol, or Darda. They were the sons of Mahol. King Solomon became famous in all the surrounding countries. During his lifetime, Solomon spoke 3,000 proverbs (many of them are preserved in the *Book of Proverbs*). He also wrote 1,005 songs. (Solomon wrote Psalm 72, Psalm 127, Psalm 132, and the Song of Solomon.) He lectured about many different kinds of plants—everything from the great cedar trees of Lebanon to the common hyssop that grows out of the walls. He also lectured about various animals, birds, crawling things, and fish. People came from all nations to listen to King Solomon's wisdom. All the kings of the earth who had heard of Solomon's immense wisdom came to listen to him.

My Time to Pray

The Wealth of Wisdom

If any of you lacks wisdom, let him ask of God, who gives to all liberally and without reproach, and it will be given to him (James 1:5).

This chapter shows the wisdom of Solomon in many areas of life. It can be seen easily in his administrative ability, for he organized and managed his kingdom in an efficient way. The wealth and land conquered by David was administered and enjoyed by Solomon. Notice Solomon had time to write 3,000 proverbs and 1,005 songs. He couldn't have done this if he were involved in daily administrative duties. Solomon was smart enough to delegate. *Lord, teach me to do what only I can do, and delegate to others what others do best.*

Each of us does what comes from the heart. "David was a man after God's own heart." David was a spiritual man who wrote much of the Book of Psalms. These are written to draw us close to God. He wanted us to know God intimately, and worship Him wholeheartedly. *Lord, I worship You when I read the Psalms of David.*

Solomon prayed for wisdom and God granted his request. Out of his heart comes intellectual understanding and brilliance. People came to hear Solomon and marvel at his wisdom. He doesn't write Psalms, because that is not his nature, Solomon's wisdom is reflected in his 3,000 proverbs. He wrote these to improve our life and help us live wisely; better living with wise understanding. *Lord, teach me to live wisely as I read Solomon's proverbs.*

Since we live in a world created by God, no one can have complete wisdom without knowing God who is the source of all things in the world. Some people with Ph.D. degrees have great wisdom in their area of specialty, but they don't have complete wisdom. Even those who have a Ph.D. in religion from the best institutions don't have complete understanding in all things. People are finite, only God is infinite. *Lord, I don't know all things, and I never will. Teach me what I need to know, and guide me where I need to go. Meet my needs when the time is necessary, and even when I can't learn what I need to know; work all things together for Your good. Amen.*

6

BUILDING THE
TEMPLE OF GOD

First Kings 5 and 6

Now Hiram was the king of Tyre who had been an admirer of David
for a long time. Hiram had heard that Solomon had been made
king in David's place. So, Hiram sent his servants to congratulate
Solomon. Then Solomon sent back this message to Hiram: "You
knew that my father David had to fight many wars against his
enemies around him. That is why he was never able to build a
Temple to worship the Name of the Lord his God. David was
waiting for the time when the Lord defeated all David's enemies.
Now the Lord, my God, has given me rest. There is peace on all
sides of my country. We have no enemies now, and my people
are in no danger.

"Listen, the Lord made a promise to my father David: the Lord said, 'I
will cause your son to be king in your place after you. He will
build the Temple for My Name. I plan to build that Temple for
the Name of Yahweh, my God. So, King Hiram, I ask for your
help now. Send your men to cut down cedar trees for me from
Lebanon. My servants will work closely with your servants. I will
pay your servants whatever wages you decide. We do not have
anyone who knows how to cut down timber."

When Hiram heard what Solomon was asking, he was very happy. Hiram said, "Blessed by the Lord today. He has given David such a wise son to rule over this great nation."

Then Hiram sent back this message to Solomon: "I have received the message that you sent to me. I will supply you with all the cedar and pine trees that you want. My servants will haul the wood from Lebanon down to the Mediterranean Sea. Then I will tie the logs together. Next, I will float them down the shore to wherever you direct. (The harbor at Joppa was about 40 miles from Jerusalem.) There I will separate the logs, and you can take them away. As payment to me, you will supply food to all those in my royal household." So, Hiram was supplying Solomon with as much cedar wood and pine wood as Solomon wanted. And, Solomon paid Hiram about 125,000 bushels of wheat each year. It was enough to feed all those who lived with Hiram. Solomon also paid him about 115,000 gallons of pure olive oil every year.

The Lord gave wisdom to Solomon, just as He had promised. And, there were peaceful relations between Hiram and Solomon. These two kings made a treaty between them.

So, Solomon began to build the Temple for the Lord. This happened in the 480th year after the people of Israel had left the land of Egypt. (The exodus occurred in 1446 B.C., and this is substantial agreement with Genesis 15:13; Exodus 12:40-41; Judges 11:26; and Acts 13:20.) This was the fourth year (966 B.C.) of King Solomon's rule over Israel. It occurred in the second Jewish month, the month of Ziv (our month of April.)

Now the Temple that King Solomon constructed for the Lord was 90 feet long, and 30 feet wide, and 45 feet high. The porch in front of the main room of the Temple was 30 feet wide and 15 feet deep. This room ran along the front of the Temple itself. Its width was equal to the width of the Temple. And, Solomon made narrow windows in the Temple. These windows were narrow on the inside, but larger on the outside. (Partly to let out the vapor of the lamps and the smoke of the frankincense, as well as to let light in.) Then, all around, Solomon built some side rooms against the walls of the main room of the Temple. These rooms were built on top of each other. The rooms on the bottom floor were 7½ feet wide. The rooms on the middle floor were 9 feet wide. The rooms above that were 10½ feet wide. The Temple wall that was on the side of each room was thinner than the wall in the room below. The rooms were pushed up against the wall, but they did not have their main beams built into the wall.

The stones were prepared at the same spot where they were cut out of the ground. These stones were the only ones used to build the Temple. So, there was no noise from hammers, axes, or any other iron tools at the Temple site.

The entrance to the bottom rooms built alongside the Temple was on the south side. From there, stairs went up to the rooms of the second floor. And from there, they went on up to the rooms of the third floor. Solomon put a roof on the Temple. It was made from wooden beams and cedar boards. So, he finished building the Temple. He also finished building the bottom floor that was beside the Temple. It was 7½ feet high. It was attached to the Temple by the cedar beams.

God Speaks to Solomon

Then the Lord spoke His word to Solomon: "Regarding this Temple that you are building, if you obey all My laws and My commands, then I will do for you what I promised to your father David. And, I will live (God promises to 'dwell' in the Temple, conditionally, unfortunately the nation came to put her trust in the Temple itself instead of in the God of the Temple [see Jer. 7:1-15]) among the children of Israel in this Temple. I will never abandon My people Israel."

The Temple Is Completed

Therefore, Solomon finished building the Temple. This is the way he built it: the inside walls were covered with cedar boards, from the floor to the ceiling. The floor was made of boards of pine wood. A room that was 30 feet long was built in the back part of the Temple. It was divided from the rest of the Temple by cedar boards, reaching from the floor to the ceiling. The sanctuary was called "The Holy Room." The main room—that is, the room in front of "The Holy Room"—was 60 feet long. Inside the Temple, there were cedar carvings. The wood was carved with pictures of flowers and plants. Everything on the inside was covered with cedar wood in such a way that a person could not see the stones of the walls.

Solomon prepared the sanctuary at the back of the Temple to contain the Lord's Holy Ark of the Covenant. This inner room was 30 feet long, 30 feet wide, and 30 feet high. (It was cube-shaped.) Solomon covered this room with pure gold; there was no seam. He built an altar of cedar and plated it with gold, too. Solomon covered the inside of the Temple seamlessly with pure gold. And, he put gold chains across the front of the inner room. (The thick curtain that separated "The Holy of Holies" from "The Holy Room" was probably hung from these chains [see 2 Chron. 3:14; Matt. 27:51; Heb. 6:19]. No one was to enter the Holy of Holies except the high priest, and even he only once per year on the Day of Atonement.) It was plated with gold. So, when it was completed, all the inside of the Temple was plated with gold. Also, he covered the altar in "The Holy of Holies" with gold. Solomon made two angels from olive wood. Each angel was 15 feet high. He put them inside "The Holy of Holies." Each angel had two wings, and each wing was 7½ feet long. So, it was 15 feet from the tip of one wing to the tip of the other wing. (Since their wingspan was 15 feet, their combined wings covered the whole room. In other words, as the two cherubs stood side by side and faced toward the front of the inner sanctuary, they touched the walls on either side of the Ark of the Covenant. Contrariwise, in the tabernacle of Moses' day, the two cherubs were turned toward one another and toward the mercy seat, and they were much smaller [see Exod. 25:18-20].) The second angel also measured 15 feet. The angels were the same size and shape. And, each angel was 15 feet tall. These angels were put beside each other in "The Holy of Holies." Their wings were spread out. So, one angel's wing touched one wall, and the other angel's wing touched the other wall. And, their wings touched each other in the middle of the room. Solomon also plated the two angels with gold.

All the walls around the Temple had carvings. They were carved with pictures of angels, palm trees, and flowers that bloomed. This was true for both the main room and the inner room. The floors of both rooms were also covered with gold.

Doors made of olive wood were put at the entrance to "The Holy of Holies." The doors were made to fit into an area with five sides. (The lintel was one-fifth of the width of the wall, and each door post was one-fifth of its height. Therefore, the opening was a square of 6 feet.) Solomon carved pictures of angels, palm trees, and blooming flowers on the two olive-wood doors. Then, he plated the doors with gold. (The doors had gold hammered to fit the forms of the palm trees, the cherubs, and the flowers that were carved upon them [see 1 Kings 6:35].) And, the angels and the palm trees were covered with gold, too. At the entrance to the main room, there was a door frame. It was square, and it was made of olive wood. Two doors were made of pine. Each door had two parts hinged in such a way that the doors folded. (Probably opening outward.) The doors were carved with pictures of angels, palm trees, and blooming flowers. And, all of the carvings were covered smoothly with gold—expertly plated.

Solomon built the inner courtyard and enclosed it with walls. The walls were made of three rows of cut stones and one row of cedar boards.

Work began on the Temple in the Jewish month of Ziv. This was during the fourth year that Solomon ruled over Israel. And, the Temple was finished during the eleventh year when Solomon ruled (959 B.C.). It was finished in the eighth month, the Jewish month of Bul. It was completed exactly as planned. Solomon worked seven years to build the Temple.

My Time to Pray

Our Intimate God

Then the word of the Lord came to Solomon saying, "...if you will keep all My commandments...I will dwell among the children of Israel" (1 Kings 6:11-13).

God said He would live among His people. He came to live in the Tabernacle in the wilderness. *"Then the cloud covered the Tabernacle of meeting and the glory of the Lord filled the Tabernacle. And Moses was not able to enter the Tabernacle of meeting because of the cloud"* (Exod. 40:34-35). This was not a "spiritual" presence of God, or just the influence of God. It was His *localized* presence because Moses couldn't go in the tent. *Lord, I know Your presence is in my life, and it's more than Your influence or "spiritual" presence. I know You're here in me.*

When we speak of the *transcendence of God*, it means He is high and exalted above us. When we speak of the *immanence of God* we are describing His closeness to us. God is both.

When we speak of the *omnipresence of God*, we mean He is everywhere present at the same time. When we speak of God's *localized presence*, it means the place where God manifests Himself at one time. It does not mean He is not at all other places. It's where God sits on His throne in Heaven, or God talks to Moses on Mount Sinai. Besides calling this the *localized presence* of God, many have called it the *manifest presence* of God.

The *indwelling presence of God* is when He comes to live in the life of a believer. The *institutional presence of God* is His living in His Church today (the Church is the Body of Christ), or in this case where God came to live in Solomon's Temple, it was His *institutional presence*.

There's one more phrase I use in revival and worship literature; it's the *atmospheric presence of God*. Revival is when God pours His Spirit or His presence on His people. I've been in church meetings where I seemed to feel the presence of God, and I've been in church meetings that are dead. Believe me, I'd rather be in an alive worship service where I experience or feel God's presence. Like you can feel atmospheric moisture in the air when it's not raining, you can also feel God's atmospheric presence when He's working in hearts in a church service because He's poured His Spirit on that meeting. *Lord, I know You're in my heart, and I have confidence in Your Word that teaches me Your indwelling. But I worship You best when I feel Your atmospheric presence.*

Just as God had a blueprint for His Temple, so God has a blueprint for the temple of our hearts and bodies. He has told us how to live, how to keep the temple clean, and how to serve Him in our bodies, the Temple of the Holy Spirit (see 2 Cor. 6:17-18). *Lord, may Your holiness and glory shine through my body. Amen.*

7

OTHER BUILDING PROJECTS OF KING SOLOMON

First Kings 7

King Solomon also built a palace for himself. It was finished at the end of thirteen years. And he built "The Palace of the Forest of Lebanon." (This name may have been given because the cedar pillars resembled the cedar forest in Lebanon where the trees originated.) It was 150 feet long, 75 feet wide, and 45 feet high. It had four rows of cedar posts. And, they supported the cedar beams. The ceiling was covered with cedar above the beams. There were 45 beams on the roof. Fifteen beams were in each row. There were three rows of windows, or in groups of threes (side by side) and they were facing each other. All the doorways and windows had square frames. The three windows at each end faced each other, too.

Solomon also built "The Hall of Pillars." (It served as a vestibule that was used as a waiting room for those who sought an audience with the king.) It was 75 feet long and 45 feet wide. Along the front of the hall, there was a covering supported by pillars.

Solomon also built "The Hall of the Throne," where he gave legal judgments. He called this "The Hall of Justice." (This was the Supreme Court, with the king acting as the presiding judge [compare 2 Sam. 14:3; 15:2]. An elaborate throne was made for this room [see 1 Kings 10:18-20].) The room was covered with cedar—from the floor to the ceiling. The palace where Solomon was planning to live was behind "The Hall of Justice." Solomon also built a similar palace for his wife. She was the daughter of the Pharaoh of Egypt.

All these buildings were made of huge blocks of fine stones that were expertly cut. Then they were trimmed with a saw in the front and the back. These fine stones went from the foundations of the buildings to the top of the walls. Even the great courtyard was constructed with huge blocks of stone. The foundations were made with huge blocks of fine stone. Some of the stones were 15 feet long. Others were 12 feet long. There were other cut blocks of fine stone and cedar beams on top of those stones. The palace courtyard, the courtyard inside the Temple, and the porch to the Temple were surrounded by walls. All of these walls had three rows of cut stone blocks and one row of cedar beams.

Completing the Bronze Work

King Solomon sent a messenger to Tyre; he brought Huram to Solomon. Huram's mother was a widow from the tribe of Naphtali. His father was from Tyre; he had been an engraver of things made of bronze. Huram was also very skilled and experienced in working with bronze. So, Huram came to King Solomon. And, Huram performed all the bronze work that Solomon wanted.

Huram made two large bronze pillars. Each column was 27 feet tall and 18 feet around. He also made two bronze capitals at the tops of the columns. Each of them were 7½ feet tall. Then Huram made a network of seven chains for each capital. They covered the capitals on top of the two columns. Then he made two rows of bronze pomegranates to go on the nets. They were designed to cover the capitals at the top of the columns. The capitals on top of the columns in the porch were shaped like lilies. They were 6 feet tall. The capitals were on top of both columns. They were above the bowl-shaped section and next to the networks. At that spot, there were rows of 200 pomegranates all around the capitals.

Huram put these two bronze columns at the porch of the Temple. He named the south column "Jachin" (this Hebrew name means "He Establishes" = stability). And, he named the north column "Boaz" (this Hebrew name means "In Him Is Strength" = power of endurance.) The capitals on top of the columns were shaped like lilies. So, the work on the columns was completed.

Then Huram made a large, round pool from bronze. (It took the place of the brass laver of the tabernacle [see Exod. 30:18-21].) It was 45 feet around, 15 feet across, and 7½ feet deep. There was a rim around the outer edge of the pool. Under this rim, there were two rows of bronze plants surrounding the pool. Every 18 inches, there were ten plants in two rows. They were made of one piece—that is, they were part of the pool itself. (There were about 300 gourds all around the brim of this metal pond.) The pool was sitting on the backs of the 12 bulls made of bronze. (This symbolized the unity of the 12 tribes.) They faced outward from the center of the pool—three bulls faced north; three bulls faced east; three bulls faced south; and three bulls faced west. The sides of the pool were about 4 inches thick. The rim was like the rim of a cup or like the bud of a lily blossom. The pool held about 11,000 gallons of water.

Then Huram made ten bronze stands. Each one was 6 feet long, 6 feet wide, and 4½ feet high. The stands were made from square sides and put on frames. On the sides were bronze lions, bulls, and angels. On the frames above and below the lions and the bulls there were designs of flowers that were hammered into the bronze. Each stand had four bronze wheels (symbolizing the mobility of God [see Ezek. 10:1-22]) with bronze axles. And, there were bronze supports for a large bowl at each corner. The supports had designs of flowers. There was a frame on top of the bowls. It was 18 inches high above the bowls. The opening of the bowl was about 27 inches deep. There were designs carved into the bronze on the frame. The frame was square, not round. The four wheels were under the frame. They were 27 inches high. The axles between the wheels were made of one piece with the stand. The wheels were like the wheels of a chariot. Everything on the wheels was made of bronze. The axles, the rims, and spokes, and the hubs were all made of bronze.

The four supports were at the four corners of each stand. They were made of one piece with the stand. There was a strip of bronze around the top of each stand. It was 9 inches deep. It was made of one piece with the stand. The sides of the stand and the frames were completely covered with carvings. They were carved with pictures of angels, lions, and palm trees. There were also pictures of flowers carved everywhere. This was the way that Huram made the ten stands. The bronze for each stand was melted and poured into a mold. And, all of the stands were the same size and shape.

Huram also made ten bronze bowls. There was one bowl for each of the ten stands. Each bowl was 6 feet across and could hold about 230 gallons of water. (These lavers, their stands, and the bronze pond were positioned outside the Temple in the inner courtyard.) Huram put five of the stands on the south side of the Temple. And, he put the other five stands on the north side. He put the large pool in the southeast corner of the Temple. Huram also made pans (used to boil the peace offerings), shovels, and small bowls.

So, Huram finished making everything that King Solomon wanted him to make. Here is a list of what Huram made for the Temple of the Lord:

Two columns;

Two large bowls for the capitals on top of the columns;

Two networks to cover the two large bowls for the capitals, which were on top of the pillars;

Four hundred pomegranates for the two networks. There were two rows of pomegranates for each network covering the bowls for the capitals on top of the columns.

Ten stands with one bowl on each stand;

The large pool with 12 bulls under it;

The pots, the shovels, and the small bowls, and all the dishes for the Temple of the Lord. (The pots were used to catch the blood of the animals that were sacrificed. The shovels were used to clean out the ashes from the bronze altar where the sacrifices were slaughtered. And, the bowls were used to carry away the ashes.)

Huram made everything that King Solomon wanted. They were all made from polished bronze. The king ordered these things to be cast in the plain of the Jordan River between Succoth and Zarethan (Recent archeological excavations now confirm that Succoth was indeed a center for metallurgy at that time—it had the best clay molds, which would not stick to the bronze). (They were made by melting and pouring bronze into clay molds.) Solomon never weighed the bronze that was used to make these things. There was too much of it to weigh. That is why they never knew the total weight of all the bronze.

Other Precious Objects for the Temple

Solomon also ordered them to make many things for the Temple out of gold:

The golden altar (the altar of incense);

The golden table where the special "bread of the presence" was placed;

The lampstands of pure gold (they contained little bowls into which olive oil was poured and burned, five on the right side and five on the left side in front of "The Holy of Holies");

The golden flowers, the lamps, and the tongs;

The pure gold bowls, the wick-trimmers, the small bowls (they were more like large vases containing the oil for the lamps, complete with spouts), the pans, and the pans that were used to carry coals;

And the hinges for the doors of "The Holy of Holies" and for the doors of the main room of the Temple.

So, the work that King Solomon did for the Temple of the Lord was finished. David, Solomon's father, had reserved silver, gold, and other dedicated things for the Temple. So Solomon brought these sacred things into the Temple, too. He put them into the treasures of the Temple of the Lord.

My Time to Pray

What's in the Temple

The temple...was built with stone finished at the quarry, so that no hammer or chisel or any iron tool was heard in the temple while it was being built (1 Kings 6:7).

The amazing story is told of the stones being cut perfectly at the quarry so no finishing was necessary at the Temple site. There had to be a perfect blueprint to make it happen (it was given to David by God). There had to be a perfect cut by the masons at the quarry, along with a perfect finishing job at the quarry. Then the stone had to be handled carefully and perfectly as it was transported to the Temple site. Even the way the stones perfectly fit together brought glory to God. *Lord, may the little things in my life fit "perfectly" to bring glory to You.*

When you think how perfectly all the many stones fit together, you sit back and marvel at the way God arranged for His Temple to be constructed. In the same way, we marvel at how God fits so many different people into His collectively perfect plan on earth. *"Oh, the depth of the riches, both of the wisdom and knowledge of God! How unsearchable are His judgments and His ways past finding out!"* (Rom. 11:33). *Lord, I marvel at Your marvelous ability to bring many people together to get Your work done.*

When it came to the furniture in the Temple, there was something "old" and something "new." Did you notice a new Ark of the Covenant was not constructed? They used the old one that Israel carried through the desert and it was the one carried around Jericho that brought the walls down. God had sat on that box (the word *ark* meant *box*) and He didn't want a new Ark. Why? Perhaps because of its plainness, God was satisfied with its simplicity. God didn't want, nor did He need, a more elaborate box-throne. After all, why a more elaborate Ark? Is not the One sitting on the Ark much more valuable than an old box? *Lord, help me look to You and not the things (the church) or people (preachers) where You dwell.*

No matter how elaborate the craftsmen could have tried to embellish a new Ark, it couldn't give more honor or glory to God. If anything, the embellishments of an Ark would take away from God who sat between the Cherubim. The only way to make God's box or throne more glorious by human standards was to bring glory to the One sitting between the pure gold, hand-carved Cherubim. We must glorify God, not the box. When we look, we must see God only, not the box. When we praise God who sits on the box, we give honor to the King of the throne that He wants. *"But You [God] are holy, enthroned in the praises of Israel"* (Ps. 22:3). *Lord, I worship You who sits upon the Mercy Seat, on top of the Ark of the Covenant.*

As each stone silently slipped together, the workmen were probably unconscious that they were worshiping God by their work. For everything done for God is worship. When we silently pray, we worship God. When another sinner is saved and silently takes his place in the Body of Christ, God is worshiped. Remember Ephesians 2:21-22 describes how new Christians are fitted together with older Christians, "in whom the whole building being fitted together, grows into a holy Temple in the Lord, in whom you also are being built together for a dwelling place of God." Just as workmen quietly placed stone to stone to build a Temple where God dwelt, we in the work of evangelism are putting new believers next to mature believers so God can dwell among us (His localized presence). *Lord, I marvel at the quiet way Your building is being put together on earth. Amen.*

8

THE ARK OF THE COVENANT
IS BROUGHT INTO THE TEMPLE

First Kings 8

Then King Solomon summoned all the elders of Israel, all the heads
of the tribes, and all the clan leaders of the people of Israel to
come in him in Jerusalem. He wanted them to bring up the
Lord's Ark of the Covenant from Zion (the older section of the
City of David). So, every man of Israel gathered together to
King Solomon. It was during the festival in the Jewish month of
Ethanim (Ethanim means "perennial," referring to living streams
of water, and corresponds to part of September and part of
October), that is, the seventh month. (Solomon finished building
the Temple in the eighth month [see 1 Kings 6:38], he delayed
the dedication ceremony for eleven months in order to coincide
with the scheduled, massive gathering for the annual Feast of
Tabernacles, also called the Feast of Ingathering.)

All of the elders of Israel arrived. Next, the priests picked up the Ark of
the Covenant and carried the Ark and the sacred things that were
in the tent to the new Temple. The Levites helped the priests carry
them. King Solomon and all the congregation of Israel gathered
together in the front of the Ark of the Covenant. They sacrificed
so many sheep and cattle that no one could count them all. Then
the priests put the Lord's Ark of the Covenant in its proper place.

This was in "The Holy of Holies" inside the sanctuary of the Temple. The Ark of the Covenant was put underneath the wings of the angels. (The ones made for Solomon's Temple, not the cherubs of Moses' time; those cherubs were on the lid of the Ark, the Mercy Seat.) These angels spread out their wings over where the Ark of the Covenant was resting. So, the angels covered it and covered the poles used to carry it. The carrying poles were very long. (Scholars believe that these poles were almost 30 feet long.) A priest standing in "The Holy Place" in front of "The Holy of Holies" could see the ends of the poles. However, no one could see them from outside "The Holy Place." The poles are still there today. (At the time this book was written, Solomon's Temple was still standing. It was destroyed in 586 B.C. by Nebuchadnezzar.) The two stone tablets of the Ten Commandments were the only things inside the Ark of the Covenant. (No one knows what happened to the pot of manna [see Exod. 16:31-34] or Aaron's rod that had sprouted [see Num. 17:1-11].) Moses had placed the two tablets inside the Ark of the Covenant at Mount Horeb. That occurred when the Lord made His covenant with the Israelites after they came out of the land of Egypt.

When the priests came out of "The Holy Place," the cloud filled the Temple (God was visibly showing that He accepted the Temple, just as He had accepted the Tabernacle [see Exod. 40:34].) The priests were not able to continue to serve there, because of the cloud; the glory of the Lord filled the Temple of the Lord.

Then Solomon said, "The Lord said that He would dwell in the 'thick' cloud. O God, I have certainly built a magnificent Temple for You. It is a place for You to dwell forever."

King Solomon Speaks to the People

While all the congregation of Israel was standing there, King Solomon turned around to face them. He blessed them and said: "Praise the Lord, the God of Israel. He has done what He promised to my father David. This is what the Lord told my father: 'Since the time that I brought My people Israel out of Egypt, I did not choose a city in any tribe of Israel where a Temple would be built for worshiping Me. But I did choose you, David, to rule over My people Israel.'

"My father David wanted to build a Temple for worshiping the Lord the God of Israel. But the Lord said to my father David, 'I know you want to build a Temple for worshiping Me. Your desire is good. However, you are not the one to build the Temple. It will be your son, the one who will come from your body. He is the one who will build My Temple.'

"The Lord has indeed kept the promise that He made. I am the king now in place of David my father. I am now the ruler of Israel, just as the Lord promised. And, I have built the Temple for worshiping the Lord, the God of Israel. I have provided a place in the Temple for the Ark of the Covenant. Inside that Ark is the Covenant (the Ten Commandments) that the Lord made with our ancestors when He brought them out of the land of Egypt."

Solomon Prays to Yahweh

Then Solomon stood facing the Lord's altar. All of the people of Israel were standing behind him. He spread out his hands toward Heaven and prayed,

"O Lord, God of Israel, there is no god like You—in Heaven above or on the earth below. You keep your promises and You show Your loyalty to those who truly follow You. You have kept the promise that You made to Your servant David, my father. You made that promise with Your own mouth. And, by Your great power, You have made it come true today. Now, O Lord, God of Israel, please honor what You told Your servant David, my father. You said: 'Your sons must be careful to obey Me as you have obeyed Me. If they do this, there will always be a male from your family to rule Israel.' Again, O God of Israel, I beg You, please continue to keep that promise that You spoke to my father, David, Your servant.

"But, O God, can You really live here on the earth? No! Look, even the sky and the highest place in Heaven cannot contain You. This Temple that I have built certainly cannot contain You, either. Nevertheless, O Lord, my God, please listen to my prayer and my request. I beg You to hear this plea and this prayer that I am praying to You today. In the past, You have said, 'I will be worshiped there.' So, I beg You to watch over this Temple night and day. Please hear the prayer whenever I pray to You in this direction. Heed my prayers and the prayers of Your people, Israel. Please hear us when we pray toward this place. Hear us from Your home in Heaven. And, when You hear us, please forgive us.

"If a person does something wrong against someone else, he will be brought near the altar in this Temple to swear an oath to tell the truth. If he swears an oath that he is not guilty, then listen to him in Heaven. Judge the man. Punish the guilty person for what he has done. And, declare that the innocent person is truly not guilty.

"In the future, Your people, Israel, will sin against You. Because of this, their enemies will defeat them. Then Your people will feel sorry and come back to You and praise You. In this Temple, they will pray to You and ask for things. At that time, please hear them from Heaven. Forgive the sins of Your people, Israel. Allow them to possess their land again—the land that You gave to their ancestors.

"Whenever they sin against You, You might stop the rain from falling on their land. Then they will pray toward this place. They will praise You. They will turn away from their sin because You will cause them to suffer. When this happens, please heed their prayer in Heaven. Then forgive the sins of Your servants, Your people Israel, so that You may teach them to do what is right, to go in the right direction. Then please send rain to Your land that You gave to Your people as their inheritance.

"Sometimes the land may become so dry that no food will grow. Or, a disease might spread among the people. Or, all the crops might be destroyed by blight (special fungus, Puccinia Graminis) or by locusts or by caterpillars. Or, enemies might attack our cities. Or, Your people might get very sick. Whenever any of these disasters occur, the people will know the pain of their own conscience. If any one of Your people, Israel, stretches out his hands in prayer toward this Temple, please hear his prayer. Hear it from Your home in Heaven. Then forgive him and help him. You are the only One who knows what each person in the human race is really thinking. So, judge each individual fairly. Do this so that Your people will revere You all the days that they live on the surface of this land that You gave to our ancestors.

"Foreigners—non-Israelites, who are not of Your people—that is, those who come from other lands for Your Name's sake—will also hear about Your greatness and sheer power. They, too, will come from far away to pray toward this Temple. Please heed their prayers from Heaven, where You live. Please grant whatever they ask of You. Then, non-Jewish people everywhere will come to know Your Name and revere You also, just as Your people Israel respect You. Then everyone will know that this Temple that I built has Your Name upon it.

"If You command Your people to go and fight against their enemies, then your people will pray to You in the direction of this city that You have chosen. They will pray, facing the Temple that I have built for Your Name. Whenever they pray, heed from Heaven their prayers and their requests. Please help them.

"Your people will sin against You—everyone sins. And You will become angry with Your people. Then, You will allow their enemies to defeat them. Their enemies will capture them and carry them away to their own countries, whether near or far. After Your people are taken as prisoners to another country, they might be sorry and repent because of their sins. They will pray to You in the land where they are held captive, saying: 'We have sinned; we have been committing immoral things.' In the land of their enemies who captured them, they may turn back to You with all their hearts and souls. Perhaps they will pray to You, while facing this land that You gave to their ancestors. They may pray to You in the direction of this city that You have chosen and toward this Temple that I have built for Your Name. If they do pray, then please listen to them from Your home in Heaven. Heed their prayers and their requests. Help them. Forgive Your people who will have sinned against You. And forgive them for turning against You. Cause those who will have captured them to show mercy to them. Why? Because they are Your people and Your inheritance. You brought them out of Egypt. It was as if You had pulled them out of a blazing iron furnace.

"Please direct Your attention to my request and the requests of Your people, Israel. Listen to their prayers whenever they call out to You for help. You selected them from all the peoples of the earth to be Your very own people. That is what You promised through Moses, Your servant, when You brought our ancestors out of Egypt, O Lord my God."

Then Solomon finished praying. He had prayed this whole prayer and made this plea to the Lord. He arose. He had been on his knees in front of the altar of the Lord. And his hands had been stretched out toward Heaven. (This rich, meaningful prayer was probably recorded immediately in the Book of the Acts of Solomon [see 1 Kings 11:41] or the Book of Nathan the Prophet [see 2 Chron. 6:20].)

King Solomon Blesses the People

Then Solomon stood up. And with a loud voice, he blessed the whole congregation of Israel. This is what Solomon said: "Praise the Lord. God promised that He would give rest to His people, Israel. And, He has done what He said He would do. The Lord has kept all the good promises that He gave through his servant, Moses. May the Lord, our God be with us. May He be with us as He was with our ancestors. May He never abandon us. May He cause us to turn toward Him and follow Him. May we obey all the laws and the commands and the judgments that He gave to our ancestors. May the Lord, our God, always remember this prayer that I have just prayed in His presence. May He always support me and uphold His people Israel every day in the future. That is how all the peoples of the earth will know that the Lord is the one true God. There is no other. Therefore, let your hearts be perfect with the Lord, our God. Live by His rules. Always obey His commands as you do today."

Sacrificing and Celebration

Then King Solomon, and all Israel with him, offered sacrifices in the presence of the Lord. Solomon slaughtered 22,000 cattle and 120,000 sheep as peace offering sacrifices. In this way, the king and all the Israelites were dedicating the Temple of the Lord.

Also on that day, King Solomon sanctified the courtyard in front of
the Lord's Temple. He offered whole burnt offerings and grain
offerings. He offered the fat from the peace offerings, too. He was
forced to offer all of these offerings in the courtyard because the
bronze altar in the Lord's presence was too small. It could not
hold all the offerings.

God Occupies the Temple

When Solomon finished praying, fire came down from the sky. It
burned up the whole burnt offering and the sacrifices. And, the Shekinah
glory of the Lord filled the Temple. The priests could not enter the Temple
of the Lord because the Lord's splendor filled it. All the people of Israel
saw the fire come down from the sky. They also saw the Lord's splendor
on the Temple. Then they bowed down on the pavement with their faces
to the ground. They worshiped and thanked the Lord Who Is Always Present with them. They said: *"The One Who Is Always Present is good; His love
continues forever"* (see 2 Chron. 7:1-3).

King Solomon, along with all the people of Israel, celebrated the other
festival that occurred at that time. People came from as far as
the entrance of Hamath in the north. And, they came from as far
away as the Brook of Egypt in the south. A huge gathering was
there. In the presence of the Lord, our God, they ate, drank, and
rejoiced for a total of 14 days. (The first seven days were spent
with the inaugural dedication, and the second seven days were
devoted to the Feast of the Tabernacles [see 2 Chron. 7:9]. And,
because of the Day of Atonement, there was some time set aside
between the two weeks.) On the next day, Solomon sent the
people away. They blessed the king and went home. They were so
happy because of all the good things that the Lord had done for
His servant David and for His people, Israel.

My Time to Pray

God's Approval

When Solomon finished praying, fire came down from the sky. It burned up the whole burnt offering and the sacrifices. And the Shekinah glory of the Lord filled the Temple (2 Chronicles 7:1).

Just as God showed His approval of the Tabernacle in the Wilderness, so He showed His approval for the new Temple. God demonstrated His approval by filling the Temple with His presence. The fire symbolized God's cleansing holiness; He burns up anything that is sinful or corrupting. The cloud symbolized the Holy Spirit who comes to make us spiritual. Yes, God approved the new Temple, but how will He approve of us when we offer anything to Him? God will show His approval by coming to fill our lives and live with us. *Lord, come in fire to burn up my sin, make me holy. Also send Your Spirit to fill the temple of my body, make me spiritual.*

When Solomon referred to the Temple as "this place," he was describing the point of contact between God and man. Israel would come to the brazen altar to offer their sacrifices for sin. It was there forgiveness was experienced. The Temple was a place of prayer, so naturally Israel would come to the Temple to pray. No wonder Jesus showed His anger at the money changers and salesmen in the Temple when He said, *"My house is the house of prayer, but you have made it a den of thieves"* (Luke 19:46). Today, we worship in a church building—not the same function as the Temple, but the same spirit—so let's go to our church building to pray. *Lord, I will pray in Your church building, because I will pray everywhere.*

This passage tells us our body posture should reflect our heart's disposition when we pray. Did you see that Solomon *"stood facing the Lord"* (1 Kings 8:22)? We usually stand in the presence of those we revere. Also, Solomon knelt before the Lord (see 1 Kings 8:54), to show his humility before God and his worship of the Lord. Shouldn't we do the same? Then notice, *"with his hands spread up to heaven"* (1 Kings 8:54). Since our prayers are directed to God in Heaven, shouldn't we also reflect it in our body gesture? *Lord, I will let my outward body posture reflect my inner reverence to You.*

When we leave the presence of God, we should be *"glad of heart for all the good that the Lord had done"* (1 Kings 8:66). Worship is not true biblical worship if we are not changed after leaving God's presence. What better results could we receive from God's presence than to be "glad of heart?" When we leave church on Sunday, we should be able to say, *"I was glad when they said to me, 'Let us go into the house of the Lord'"* (Ps. 122:1). *Lord, thank You for every time I've been able to enter Your presence in Your house.*

Did you notice how many times Solomon said "please" when asking God to answer his prayers? When was the last time you've said "please" when praying before God? When we say "please," we do more than ask for something, we are urgent and insistent. The word "please" has the weight of "begging." A beggar doesn't deserve anything, so the beggar pleads or urges his request. He begs. When is the last time you've begged God for something? God is everything and we are nothing, so we beg God to hear us and grant us our request. *Lord, I beg You for mercy because I know in my heart I'm a sinner. "Please" Lord, hear me. Amen.*

9

THE LORD APPEARS
TO SOLOMON A SECOND TIME

First Kings 9

So Solomon finished building the Temple of the Lord and his royal palace. He finished building everything that he planned to build.

Then the Lord appeared to him again, just as He once did at Gibeon. The Lord said: "I have listened to your prayer and heard what you were asking of Me in My presence. You built this Temple, but I have made it holy—I have put My Name there forever. I will always watch over it because My heart is there.

"However, you must serve Me as did your father David. He had an honest heart, and he was a good man. You must obey all of My laws and do everything I command you. If you do these things, then I will set up the throne of your kingdom to rule Israel forever. I made that promise to your father David when I told him that there would always be a male from his family to rule over Israel.

"But you and your sons must always follow Me. You must obey the laws and commands that I have given you. You must not serve different gods and worship them. If you abandon Me, then I will drive Israel off the land that I have given them. Though I have made the Temple holy for people for the sake of My Name—if you will not obey Me—I will turn away My face. Then Israel will become a proverb and a joke among all the nations. If this magnificent Temple is destroyed, everyone who sees it will be astonished. They will make fun of you and ask: 'Why did the Lord do this? Why did He do this terrible thing to this land and to this Temple?'

"Other people will answer: 'This happened because they abandoned the Lord, their God. He brought their ancestors out of the land of Egypt, but they decided to follow different gods. They worshiped and served them, instead of the Lord. That is why the Lord brought this whole disaster upon them.'"

Other Projects of King Solomon

By the end of 20 years, King Solomon had built both his own royal palace and the Temple of the Lord. Hiram, the king of Tyre, had helped Solomon by supplying materials for those buildings. Hiram had provided Solomon with all the cedar wood, pine, and gold that he wanted. In exchange, King Solomon gave to Hiram 20 towns in the northern region of Galilee. (As temporary collateral, until Solomon could replenish his supplies of gold. This gave Hiram right to tax those towns.) Hiram traveled from Tyre to see the towns that Solomon had given to him. But, after Hiram saw them, he did not like them. Hiram asked Solomon, "What kind of towns are these that you have given to me, my brother?" So, that land was named "The Land of Cabul" (means "unproductive land"). And, it is still known by that name today.

Hiram had sent to King Solomon about 9,000 pounds of gold! (During two decades of building activity, King Solomon had become more indebted to King Hiram than first anticipated in their original contract [see 1 Kings 5:6-11]. King Solomon really could not afford his own grandiose building schemes.)

King Solomon had forced slaves to build the Temple of the Lord and the king's palace. Then he had them build terraces on the east side of the city. And, he had them build the wall around Jerusalem. Solomon also had them rebuild the cities of Hazor, Megiddo, and Gezer. In the past, Pharaoh, the king of Egypt, had attacked Gezer and captured it. He set it on fire. He killed the Canaanites who lived there. Then he gave it to his daughter as a wedding gift. His daughter had married Solomon. So, Solomon rebuilt Gezer. Solomon built the towns of Lower Beth-Horon, Baalath, and Tadmor, which is in the desert of Judea. King Solomon also built all his towns where he could store grain and supplies. And, he built towns for his chariots and chariot drivers. Solomon built whatever his heart desired in Jerusalem, in Lebanon, and anywhere in the territory he ruled.

There were still some people in the land who were non-Israelites. They were the Amorites, the Hittites, the Perizzites, the Hivites, and the Jebusites. The Israelites had never been able to completely destroy those descendants from the land. So, Solomon forced them to work as slaves for him. (And, they are still slaves today.) But Solomon did not force any of the Israelites to be his slaves. The Israelites were his soldiers, his government leaders, his officers, his captains, his chariot commanders, and his horsemen.

And, there were 550 supervisors over different projects of Solomon. They were in charge of the men who did the work.

Now, Pharaoh's daughter moved from the old section of Jerusalem to her palace that Solomon had built for her. Then Solomon built more terraces (filled in earth) on the east side of Jerusalem.

Three times each year, (at the Passover, at Pentecost, and at the Feast of the Tabernacles) Solomon offered whole burnt offerings and peace offerings on the altar that he had built for the Lord.

PRAYING WITH THE KINGS

Solomon also burned incense on that same altar in the presence of the Lord. Thus, he fulfilled all the Temple obligations.

King Solomon also built a navy at Ezion-Geber. This town is near Elath. It is on the shore of the Red Sea (the Gulf of Agaba) in the land of Edom. With the fleet, King Hiram had sailors who had a great knowledge of the ocean. So, Hiram sent them to sail Solomon's ships, working together with Solomon's men. Solomon's ships sailed to the land of Ophir. (Many scholars believe that this place was in Eastern Africa, a rich source of gold.) From there, they brought back about 32,000 pounds of gold to King Solomon.

My Time to Pray

When God Comes a Second Time

The Lord appeared to Solomon the second time (1 Kings 9:2).

Has the Lord ever spoken to you a second time? Why was it important for God to appear to Solomon a second time? The first time God gave Solomon wisdom and he became the wisest man on earth. What else did God want to give Solomon? The second time God said, "If." God had a challenge for Solomon; God wanted Solomon to be *both* wise and godly. *Lord, I ask for wisdom from You (see James 1:5), but I also ask You to make me godly.*

God told Solomon, *"I heard your prayers"* (1 Kings 9:3), but the omniscient God who knows all things, saw the future when wives would turn Solomon's heart from God. So God appeared to Solomon a second time to say, *"If you will walk before me"* (1 Kings 9:4). God warned Solomon against serving other gods and worshiping them (see 1 Kings 9:6). *Lord, I will worship and serve You alone. When I am blinded by the world, the flesh, and the devil, convict me and show me the error of my ways. Keep me close to You.*

David sinned. He committed adultery with Bath-Sheba. His pride drove him to take a census of Israel for his pride. But David never served other gods or worshiped them. *Lord, may I never serve or worship other gods.*

Did you see God's warnings? *"I will cut off Israel from the land"* (1 Kings 9:7) and, *"I will cast you out of My sight"* (1 Kings 9:7). That's severe punishment for worshiping other gods. But God did it when Israel went a whoring after other gods. Remember what the second commandment says, *"I am a jealous God, visiting the iniquity of the fathers upon the children to the third and fourth generations"* (Exod. 20:5). Then God said those who worship other gods *"hate me"* (Exod. 20:5). *Lord, I love You with all my heart. I know I have a nature that is prone to wandering from You. Give me strength to keep my heart worshiping You.*

The Bible quickly jumps over much of Solomon's life by saying, *"At the end of twenty years"* (1 Kings 9:10). Solomon spent seven years building the Temple (see 1 Kings 6:38) and thirteen years building his own palace (see 1 Kings 7:1). Solomon is like us. We have to build our own "house," whether our "house" is a vocation, or a business, or anything else. Whatever we do, we must build our "house" in God's sight. What type of "house" are you building with your life? *Lord, I dedicated my "house" to You, I will build for Your glory. Amen.*

10

THE QUEEN OF SHEBA
VISITS KING SOLOMON

First Kings 10

Now the Queen of Sheba (Ethiopia) heard about the fame of Solomon
and his relationship with the Person of the Lord. So, she went to
test him with difficult questions. She traveled to Jerusalem with a
very large caravan of servants. There were many camels carrying
spices, precious gems, and much gold. She came to Solomon
and talked with him about everything that was on her heart.
And, Solomon answered all her questions. There was nothing
too difficult for him to explain to her. The Queen of Sheba could
see that Solomon was very wise. She saw the palace that he had
built, and she saw his many officials and the abundant food on
his table. And, she saw the palace servants and their very fine
clothes. She was shown the servants who served him at banquets
and the lavish whole burnt offerings that he offered in the Temple
of the Lord. All these things simply amazed her! (It overwhelmed
her.)

So she said to King Solomon, "I was skeptical in my country when I
heard about your accomplishments and your wisdom—but all of
it is *true!* I could not believe it then. But now that I have come
and seen it with my own eyes...I was not told even half of it!
Your wisdom and wealth are much greater than I first heard. Your

men and officers are very happy. They're so fortunate to *always* be able to hear your wisdom, while they constantly serve you. Praise the Lord, your God. He delighted in you to make you king of Israel. The Lord has a constant love for Israel. That is why He made you king—to administer justice and to rule fairly."

Then the Queen of Sheba gave the king about 9,000 pounds of gold. She also gave him many spices and jewels. Since that time, no one else has brought as many spices into Israel than what the Queen of Sheba gave to King Solomon.

Hiram's ships transported gold from Ophir. They also brought a huge amount of sandalwood (hard wood that had fine grain) and many precious jewels from Ophir. King Solomon used the sandalwood to build special railing for the Temple of the Lord and the royal palace. He also used it to make musical instruments—harps and lyres for the singers. Such fine sandalwood has not been imported or seen since that time.

And, King Solomon also gave the Queen of Sheba many gifts. It was customary for kings and queens to exchange gifts with one another. Solomon gave her whatever she wanted or anything else she requested. After this, she and her group returned to her own country.

The Riches of King Solomon

Every year, King Solomon received about 50,000 pounds of gold. Besides that, Solomon received gold from the traders and merchants. And, he also received gold from all the tributary kings of Arabia and the governors of the land.

King Solomon made 200 large shields of hammered gold. Each shield contained about 7½ pounds of gold. He also made 300 smaller shields of hammered gold. Each of them contained about 3¾ pounds of gold. The king put them in "The Palace of the Forest of Lebanon." (It was so called because the pillars came from the giant trees of Lebanon. It had the appearance of a forest.)

Then King Solomon built a large throne made of inlaid ivory. And, he covered it with pure gold. There were six steps leading up to the throne. The back of the throne was round at the top. There was an armrest on each side of the chair. And, next to each of the armrests, there was a statue of a lion. And, statues of 12 lions were standing on the six steps. There was one lion on each end of each step. There was nothing like this in any other kingdom. And, all of Solomon's drinking cups were made of gold. All of the containers in "The Palace of the Forest of Lebanon" were made of pure gold, too. Nothing was made of silver.

In addition, King Solomon had many trading ships at sea, along with Hiram's fleet of ships. Those ships returned every three years. And, they brought back gold, silver, ivory, apes, and peacocks. So, King Solomon had more riches and more wisdom than all the other kings on earth. (Opulence often leads to decadence.) People everywhere wanted to see King Solomon. They wanted to hear the wisdom that God had given him. Each year, everyone who came to Solomon brought a gift. They brought things made of gold and silver, along with expensive clothes, weapons, spices, horses, and mules.

Solomon had many chariots and horsemen (a violation of Deut. 17:14-17). He had 1,400 chariots and 12,000 chariot-soldiers. He kept some of them in special towns reserved for the chariots. And, he kept some units with him in Jerusalem. In Jerusalem, while Solomon was king, silver was as common as rocks (a strong hyperbole), and cedar trees were as common as the fig trees. Solomon also imported his horses from Egypt and Kue (modern Turkey). His exclusive land-bridge gave him a monopoly over the trade routes. His traders purchased their horses in Kue and brought them to Israel. A chariot could be imported from Egypt at a price of about 15 pounds of silver. And, each horse cost about 3¾ pounds of silver. Solomon's traders also sold horses and chariots to the kings of the Hittites and to the kings of the Syrians.

My Time to Pray

When Others See Your God

However I did not believe the words until I came and saw with my own eyes; and indeed the half was not told me. Your wisdom and prosperity exceed the fame of which I heard (1 Kings 10:7).

The Queen of Sheba (Ethiopia) had heard great things about Solomon, so she came to see for herself. What she heard about Solomon was only half the story. She saw twice what she expected. But notice the source of what she saw, *"The Queen of Sheba heard of the fame of Solomon, concerning the name of the Lord"* (1 Kings 10:1). The wisdom of Solomon was a divine gift from God. He asked for wisdom and God gave it to him. And Solomon used his wisdom to build the Temple for God and to glorify God with all his possessions. *Lord, I ask for wisdom (see James 1:5), may I glorify You with all the wisdom You've given me.*

The queen came to test Solomon with "hard questions"—riddles and puzzles. He answered all her questions. But most Bible scholars think she came to negotiate a trade agreement with Israel because Solomon had been trading with Ophir (see 1 Kings 9:28), a neighbor of hers. *Lord, may I use my business as a Christian testimony to outsiders, even as Solomon's business impressed the Queen of Sheba.*

The Queen was overwhelmed with Solomon's riches and grandeur. It was wealth that God had enabled Solomon to gain. But God has an even grander display. Jesus said, *"...even Solomon in all his glory was not arrayed like one of these [flowers]"* (Matt. 6:28-29). Let's remember beyond gold and glory, there is beauty and majesty in simplicity. *Lord, help me see Your majesty in small things like flowers.*

The question is often raised, "Was the Queen of Sheba saved?" She came to the conclusion, *"Blessed be the Lord your God, who delighted in you, setting you on the throne of Israel! Because the Lord has loved Israel forever, therefore He made you king, to do justice and righteousness"* (1 Kings 10:9). This may be a hint of her salvation, but the statement itself is not a confession of her becoming a proselyte of Israel and Hebrew salvation. She came from a polytheistic culture and they believed in many gods. Most kings and queens of other nations recognized the gods of their neighboring nations. Maybe the Queen of Sheba only recognized the Lord for "good luck" in case Jehovah had some "power," just as she recognized other gods because of political protocol. But she didn't repent or turn from her other gods. *Lord, I will be a good witness so others will see You are the greatest God...that You are the only God. Amen.*

11

KING SOLOMON
TURNS AWAY FROM THE TRUE GOD

First Kings 11

But King Solomon loved women—many foreign women—the daughter of Pharaoh, Moabite women, Ammonite women, Edomite women, Sidonian women, and Hittite women. The Lord had told the Israelites: "You must not intermarry with people of other nations. (See Exod. 34:16; Deut. 7:1-4,17; Josh. 23:12-13. There is a great spiritual danger in marrying those who are not of the same faith, and that holds true today [see 1 Cor. 15:33; 2 Cor. 6:14-7:1].) If you do, they will surely cause you to follow after their gods." Nevertheless, Solomon fell in love with these women. He had 700 wives (the purpose of these arranged marriages was to seal his international relationships with various kingdoms). He also had 300 concubines. His wives caused him to turn away from God. As Solomon grew old, his wives caused him to follow after different gods. (Their atmosphere of idolatry led Solomon into sanctioning syncretistic practices of other religions.) He did not follow the Lord his God completely, as his father David had done. Solomon even followed Ashtoreth (the goddess of fertility and war—worshiping her entailed doing extremely lascivious things [see 1 Kings 14:24; 2 Kings 23:7]), the goddess of the people of Sidon. And, he followed Molech, the disgusting idol of the Ammonites. So, Solomon did what was evil in the sight of the Lord. He did not follow the Lord completely, as his father David had done.

Then, on a high hill east of Jerusalem, Solomon built two places for worship: he built a place to worship Chemosh, the disgusting idol of the Moabites. And, he built a place to worship Molech, the disgusting idol of the Ammonites. Solomon did the same thing for each of his foreign wives. So they burned incense and offered sacrifices to their gods.

The Results of Solomon's Sins

The Lord had appeared to Solomon twice before. But Solomon turned away from following the Lord, the God of Israel. So, the Lord was angry at him. The Lord had instructed Solomon about this very thing—not to follow different gods. But Solomon did not obey what the Lord commanded. So the Lord said to Solomon, "This sin of idolatry is in you (a settled state of mind rather than a momentary lapse). You have chosen to break your covenant with Me. You have not obeyed My commands. Therefore, I hereby vow that I will certainly tear your kingdom away from you. And, I will give it to one of your own officers. However, I will not take it away while you are still alive. Why? Because of my love for your father David. I will tear it away from your son when he becomes king. But I will not tear away the entire kingdom from him. I will leave him one tribe to rule. I will do this for the sake of David, my servant, and because of Jerusalem (God's Temple was located there) the city that I have chosen."

Hadad

Now Hadad was a member of the royal family of Edom. And the Lord raised up Hadad the Edomite to become Solomon's enemy.

Earlier, David had defeated the country of Edom. Joab, the general of David's army, went over into Edom to bury the dead. While he was there, he killed all the males, especially the heirs to the Edomite throne (as retribution for the extreme cruelty of the Edomites earlier toward Israel). Joab and all the Israelites stayed in Edom for six months. During that time, they killed every male in Edom (every one that they could find). But, at that time, Hadad was only a young boy. He escaped to Egypt with some of his father's Edomite officers. They left Midian and went to Paran. In Paran, some other men joined them, and they all went down to Egypt to see Pharaoh, the king of Egypt. Then Pharaoh gave orders for Hadad to have a house, some land, and food to eat. (He wanted to strengthen his Egyptian kingdom against possible encroachment by Solomon's sprawling empire.)

Pharaoh liked Hadad so much that he gave Hadad a wife, the sister of Tahpenes, Pharaoh's queen. Tahpenes' sister gave birth to a son for Hadad; his name was Genubath. Queen Tahpenes allowed him to grow up in Pharaoh's royal palace, along with Pharaoh's own children.

While Hadad was in Egypt, he heard that King David had died. Hadad also heard that Joab, the general of the army, was dead. So Hadad said to Pharaoh, "Send me away, so that I may return to my own homeland!"

But the Pharaoh said to Hadad, "Look, why do you want to go back to your own country? Haven't I supplied your needs?"

Hadad answered, "Yes, everything. But please, let me go home."

Rezon

God also raised up another man to be an enemy to Solomon. It was Rezon, the son of Eliadah. Rezon had run away from his master,

Hadadezer (conquered by David), the king of Zobah. After David defeated the army of Zobah, Rezon gathered some men and became the leader of a small army of rebels. They went to Damascus and settled there, where Rezon ruled Damascus. Rezon ruled over Syria and he hated Israel. So, he was an enemy of Israel during the whole time that Solomon was alive.

So, both Rezon and Hadad caused trouble for Israel (interfering with Solomon's lucrative trade routes to the East).

Jeroboam

Jeroboam, the son of Nebat, was one of Solomon's own officers. He was from the Ephraimite people, from the town of Zeredah. His mother was a widow named Zeruah. Jeroboam turned against King Solomon. While Solomon was building up the supporting terraces on the east side of Jerusalem, he also repaired the wall of Old Jerusalem, the City of David, his father. It was then Solomon observed that Jeroboam was a good worker. So, Solomon put him in charge over all the workers from the tribes of Ephraim and Manasseh. (Jeroboam was therefore in a good position to learn of the smoldering discontent among those people because of Solomon's heavy-handed politics [see 1 Kings 12:4].)

About that time, Jeroboam was going out of Jerusalem. Ahijah, the prophet from Shiloh (Shiloh had been a beacon for God's Word for about 400 years), met Jeroboam on that road. Ahijah was wearing a new robe. The two men were in the field alone. Then Ahijah took his new robe that he was wearing and tore it into 12 pieces. Then he said to Jeroboam, "Take ten pieces of this robe for yourself, because the Lord, the God of Israel, says: 'Listen, I am about to tear the kingdom away from Solomon. Then I will give ten tribes to you. However, I will allow the family of David to control one tribe. I will do this for my servant David and for the sake of Jerusalem. Jerusalem is the city that I have chosen from among all the tribes of Israel. I will do this because they have abandoned Me. They worship Ashtoreth, the goddess of the Sidonians; and Chemosh, the Moabite god; and Molech, the god of the Ammonites. They have not obeyed Me. They have not done what I said is right. They have not obeyed My principles and My decisions. Solomon is not living the way his father David lived.

"'But I will not take all of the kingdom away from Solomon. I will let him be the ruler for the rest of his lifetime. I will do this for the sake of My servant David. I chose David, and he obeyed My commands and My laws. But I will take the kingdom away from his son. Jeroboam, I will allow you to rule over the ten tribes. I will allow Solomon's son to continue to rule over one tribe. I will do this so that David, My servant, will always have a king in My presence, in Jerusalem, the city where I have chosen to put My Name. Nevertheless, I will cause you to rule over everything you desire. You can rule over Israel (the northern ten tribes). And, I will always be with you, if you live by My ways, and do what I tell you is right. You must obey all My laws and My commands as My servant David did. If you do this faithfully, then I will build a dynasty for you, as I did for David. (The entire household of Jeroboam was destroyed by Baasha [see 1 Kings 15:29] because he chose to ignore the true God.) I will give Israel to you, IF...

"'And, I will punish David's descendants because of this. However, I will not punish them forever.'"

Later, Solomon tried to execute Jeroboam. (Jeroboam asserted himself in a failed coup. This bold step proved to be premature. King Solomon's power was still too firmly fixed to be shaken.) But Jeroboam got up and ran away to Egypt. He went to Shishak (a different Egyptian dynasty from the father-in-law of Solomon—

Shishak ruled from about 935 to 914 B.C.), the king of Egypt. And, Jeroboam stayed there in Egypt until after Solomon died.

The Death of King Solomon

The rest of what Solomon did was written down—including his intellectual accomplishments—in "The Book of the History of Solomon." Solomon ruled in Jerusalem over all of Israel for 40 years, then he died and he was buried in Old Jerusalem, the City of David his father. And, his son Rehoboam became king in Solomon's place.

My Time to Pray

For it was so, when Solomon was old, that his wives turned his heart after other gods; and his heart was not loyal to the Lord his God, as was the heart of his father David (1 Kings 11:4).

There are many things that tempt a child of God to turn away from God. Sometimes it's money—the lust of the eyes. Sometimes it's power, position, or the praise of others—the pride of life. But Solomon's downfall was sex and women—the lust of the flesh. *"King Solomon loved women"* (1 Kings 11:1). It was not a particular woman that was his downfall, like Delilah destroyed Samson. Solomon just liked women, all women; he liked sex. *"He had seven hundred wives and three hundred concubines"* (1 Kings 11:3). There is a reference in Song of Solomon that reflects his lustful passion, in this passage he says the Shulamite is better than *"sixty queens and eighty concubines, and virgins without number"* (Song 6:8). Solomon was a sex addict! *Lord, keep me from illegal sex, keep me from addiction. May I find my greatest love in You.*

It was Solomon's powerful kingdom that made it possible for him to gratify his sexual lust. So God said, "I'll take the kingdom from you. Your son will have one tribe, and another man—Jeroboam—will rule ten tribes." (The small tribe of Benjamin was included with Judah in the "one" tribe.) Be careful of putting anything between you and God, He may do two things to you. First, for those who serve something other than God, the Lord will make you an addict—a slave—to the thing you put in God's place. Would you rather be a slave to God, or a slave to sin? The second thing, God will take away the platform that gave you the ability to sin against Him. *Lord, I will be Your slave, I will serve You to the best of my ability.*

You should not let anything possess you in this life. Not money, not power, not physical comfort or pleasure. You should be possessed by God. How can you do that? You must seek Him with all your heart, you must run after God with all your strength. You must give yourself *wholly* to God with a passion to become *holy* for God. *Lord, I give You first place in my life. Sit on the throne of my life and rule me from the inside out.*

Solomon wrote three great books. When Solomon was young he wrote the *Song of Solomon*, the story of true love. When Solomon was a shepherd probably working for his father David in the fields, he met a Shulamite girl and fell in love with her. It was love from the heart, and physical love expressed in sexual intimacy. It's a wonderful picture of the love of Christ for His bride, and the intimacy a believer can have with His Lord. *Lord, may my love be pure for You, may I enjoy intimacy with You.*

The second book by Solomon was *Proverbs,* which reflects his wisdom. Solomon wrote *"three thousand proverbs: and his songs were a thousand and five"* (1 Kings 4:32). The thrust of Proverbs is, "Give yourself to knowledge, that you may gain wisdom." It was during these years Solomon acquired wives. Too bad he didn't take the Book of Proverbs to heart. He wrote Proverbs *"that they may keep you from the immoral women... her house is the way to hell, descending to the chambers of death"* (Prov. 7:5,27). *Lord, keep me sexually pure.*

The third Book is Ecclesiastes from the Hebrew *Koheleth* meaning "preacher" or "teacher." The King James version of the Bible describes

Solomon's view of life as an old man, who realizes all his wealth and sexual triumphs in life are "vanity of vanities" (Eccl. 1:2). The Living Bible describes it, *"Everything is meaningless...utterly meaningless"* (1 Kings 1:2). Isn't that true in all our lives, everything that takes the place of God is vanity, and our lives end up being meaningless. *Lord, I seek first Your kingdom and Your righteousness (see Matt. 6:33), all else is meaningless. Amen.*

12

REHOBOAM IGNORES
WISE COUNSEL OF OLDER MEN

First Kings 12

Rehoboam went to Shechem. (This was a centrally located city near
Mount Ebal and Mount Gerizim where all the Israelites
[Northern Kingdom] had gone to make him king. Solomon's
oppressive taxation favored the tribe of Judah and caused a lot of
jealousy. The northern tribes felt they were being discriminated
against.) Jeroboam, the son of Nebat, was still living in exile in
Egypt. He had gone there to escape from King Solomon. When
Jeroboam heard about Rehoboam being made king, Jeroboam
was ready to return from Egypt. So, the people of the north sent
for Jeroboam, summoning him. Then the whole congregation
of Israel and Jeroboam came to Rehoboam. They spoke to
Rehoboam:

"Your father forced us to work very hard. Now, therefore, make things
easier for us. Do not make us work as hard as your father did.
Then we will serve you."

Rehoboam answered them, "Go away and come back to me in three
days, and I will give you my answer." So the people left. Some
of the elders had previously served as advisers to Solomon,
Rehoboam's father during his lifetime. So King Rehoboam asked

them for their advice. He said, "How do you think I should answer these people?"

The elders told him, "You should be a servant to these people today. Serve them, and give them a kind answer. If you do this, they will always serve you." (Jesus said an effective leader must first be a good follower [see Matt. 20:20-28].)

But Rehoboam abandoned the wise counsel of the elders who advised him. Then he asked for the advice of the young men who had grown up with him. They were standing there in front of Rehoboam. He said to them, "The people said: 'Don't make us work as hard as your father did.' How do you think I should answer them? What is your advice?"

The young men answered him, "Tell those people who came to you and said, 'Your father forced us to work very hard. Now make our work easier for us....' This is what you should tell them: 'My little finger is bigger than my father's waist. My father forced you to work hard, but now, I will make you work even harder. My father beat you with whips, but I will beat you with hooks.'"

Rehoboam had told the people: "Come back to me on the third day." So, on the third day, Jeroboam and all the people returned to Rehoboam. At that time, King Rehoboam spoke to them in a cruel way. He abandoned the wise counsel that the elders had given to him. Rehoboam did what the young men had told him to do. He said, "My father forced you to work hard. So I will give you even more work. My father beat you with whips, but I will beat you with hooks" (leather lashes with metal spikes on the ends). So, the king did not listen to the people. This turn of events came from the Lord. The Lord did this to establish His word that He had spoken to Jeroboam, the son of Nebat, through Ahijah, the prophet from Shiloh.

When all the people of Israel saw that the new king refused to listen to them, they answered the king with this statement: "We have no share in David. We have no part in the son of Jesse. O people of Israel, go to your own homes. Now, let David look after his own household." So, the Israelites from the north went back home.

But Rehoboam still ruled over the Israelites who lived in the towns of Judah. (At this time, a number of pious Israelites emigrated southward from the kingdom of the north to the territory of Judah to remain under the rule of David's royal lineage [see 2 Chron. 11:16]. They wanted to worship the true God in the right way at Jerusalem.)

Adoniram was in charge of the people who were forced to work. King Rehoboam sent him among the people of Israel, but they threw rocks at him until they killed him. However, King Rehoboam hurried away to get into his chariot to escape to Jerusalem. Since that day until then, Israel has been in rebellion against the household of David.

They Made Jeroboam King Over Israel

All the Israelites heard that Jeroboam had returned from Egypt. So, they sent for him, calling him to a meeting. And, they made him king over all Israel—only the tribe of Judah continued to be loyal to the household of David.

When Rehoboam arrived back in Jerusalem, he gathered together all the people of Judah and the tribe of Benjamin. This was an army of 180,000 men to fight against the people of Israel. Rehoboam, Solomon's son, wanted to take back his former kingdom. But the one true God spoke His word to Shemaiah, the prophet of God. The Lord said,

"Talk to Solomon's son, Rehoboam, the king of Judah. Also, speak to all the leaders of Judah and Benjamin, and speak to the rest of the people of Judah and Benjamin, and speak to the rest of the people. (That is, northern Jews who had settled in the south, near the Temple of Solomon.) Tell them, 'The Lord says that you must not go to war against your brother, the Israelites. Every one of you should go back home. I made all these things happen.'" So, the men in Rehoboam's army obeyed the Lord's command. They all left, as the Lord commanded.

Jeroboam Turns Away From the True God

Then Jeroboam built up Shechem, and he lived there. It was among the hills of Ephraim. He also went out from there to the city of Penuel (a town of strategic importance to defend against a Syrian attack from Damascus; Penuel lay on the main caravan route from Gilead to Damascus) and rebuilt it, too.

Jeroboam thought to himself: *Now the kingdom will eventually turn back to David's household. The people will continue going up to the Temple of the Lord in Jerusalem to offer sacrifices. If they do, they will want to be ruled against by Rehoboam, the king of Judah. Then they will kill me and follow Rehoboam.* (Jeroboam decided to make the separation of Judah and Israel final.)

King Jeroboam asked his men for advice. So, he made two golden calves. (Pagan idols, perhaps Apis and Mnevis as symbols like the Egyptians, where Jeroboam had spent so much time.) He said to the people, "It is too difficult for you to go up to Jerusalem to worship. O Israel, here are your gods that brought you up out of the land of Egypt." King Jeroboam set up the golden calf in the city of Bethel. (This was their southernmost border; it was only about 12 miles north of Jerusalem.) And, he put the other one in the city of Dan (located in the far north of the land, near

Mount Hermon) and this thing was a sin. (It violated the second commandment of the Decalogue [see Exod. 20:4-6], and this caused the Jewish people to reject the only true God, Yahweh [see Exod. 20:3].) The people traveled to Dan to worship the calf there.

And, Jeroboam built shrines at the places of worship. And, he appointed priests from all the people. (They were not from the tribe of Levi, thus violating the exclusive right given to the Levites by Yahweh [see Num. 18:1-7; Heb. 5:1-4; 7:13-14].) Since the true Levites would not support Jeroboam's policies, undoubtedly Jeroboam confiscated all Levitical towns and land for his new state.) And Jeroboam made up a new festival. It was on the fifteenth day of the eighth month. This was like the festival held in Judah. (A substitute for the authorized Feast of Tabernacles that was observed from the fifteenth day to the twenty-first day of the seventh month [see Lev. 23:33-34]. Jeroboam wanted to get rid of any of the old associations with David's capital.) During that time, the king offered sacrifices on the altar to the set of calves that he had made in Bethel. He also ordained priests in Bethel to serve at the places of worship that he had made. So, Jeroboam made up his own festival for the Israelites. (Jeroboam overstepped his authority as king and appointed himself as the chief priest.) It was the fifteenth day of the eighth month. During that time, he offered sacrifices on the altar that he had built in Bethel. So, he invented for himself a new festival for the Israelites. And, he burned incense on the altar.

My Time to Pray

Turning Away From God

The King (Rehoboam) answered the people roughly and forsook the old men's counsel (1 Kings 12:13).

B right young people are infatuated with the things they know. Because they have finally come to a new fact that they themselves have recognized, they think they are right. No, let's go a step further, they think they are absolutely right And anyone who doesn't agree with them is wrong. That sounds like what the young men who counseled Rehoboam concluded. The problem with youth is that they haven't lived long enough to realize they were wrong at times in the past and the other opinion was right. So youth can give bad advice and not know it. They can come to wrong advice and not realize it because they haven't lived long enough to suffer the consequences of their bad decisions. *Lord, help me to listen to the advice of older people, give me the wisdom of the elders, and I will always measure it by the Word of God before I follow any advice.*

If we listen to young people, we are shut up to the mistakes of the young. Let's listen to counsel from the young, and the middle aged, and the elderly. Then we'll get a "long-life" perspective on the solution we seek. Solomon—the father of Rehoboam—said, *"In the multitude of counselors, there is wisdom"* (Prov. 11:14;15:22;24:6). When we ask a lot of people from various backgrounds for advice, perhaps in the multitude of opinions, we'll find our right decision. *Lord, I want to do right, I want to live rightly, I want to be right. Help me find the best answer possible for the decisions I face today. Then give me strength to follow what is right.*

Did you notice the problem was not a religious problem about the Temple, nor was it a spiritual problem with one's relationship to God? The problem was not even about obeying an obvious law of God. The problem was about the amount of work and the intensity of work. This was a problem of deceptive application. But Rehoboam made the wrong decision about a nonreligious matter and he lost 10 of the 12 tribes that followed his father Solomon—Reuben, Simeon, Dan, Naphtali, Gad, Asher, Issachar, Zebulun, Ephraim, and Manasseh (The tribe of Levi, the priests, did not have land; the Levites stayed with the southern Kingdom, where Jerusalem and the temple were.). That means every decision we make is important and every decision will ultimately impact our walk with God. *Lord, I need Your help in both spiritual and non-spiritual decisions. Keep me from harm in the decisions I make.*

Rehoboam had an arrogant attitude toward the people he led. An effective leader must first serve the people who follow him, if he expects them to continue following him. Jesus said, *"Whosoever will be leader among you, let him be your servant"* (Matt. 20:27). *Lord, convict me when I don't serve those who follow me, give me wisdom on what to do, and give me strength to do it.*

The secret of being an effective leader in the church is to follow the Lord carefully, and closely. Your followers don't want to be pulled from God, nor do they want to be led away from Scripture. If you, the leader, will sacrifice your time, talent, and treasure for God, so will your followers. If you live godly, so will they. If you pray, so will they. For they will do what you, the leader, will do. But if you lead people away from God, the young untaught Christian will follow you as they followed Rehoboam. But the elderly Christians will not follow you. *Lord, teach me to lead people as Jesus led people.*

Did you see the mistakes that Jeroboam made? First, he made worship *convenient* so his people didn't need to travel a long way to worship God. Who said more people will worship better if it's convenient or easy? *Lord, I will pay the price of worship.*

Next, Jeroboam substituted golden calves for the Ark of the Covenant. The idea for the idols could have come from Egypt, the Canaanites, the Ammonites, or any other religion. Jeroboam forgot God said, *"Thou shall not make unto me any carved image"* (Exod. 20:4). *Lord, I will not let anything get between You and me.*

Then Jeroboam introduced priests who were not Levites, the God-chosen priests. Only those who are called of God should lead, teach, and sacrifice for God's people in worship. *Lord, I will not listen to those who doubt Scripture, nor will I follow those teachers who are not Your servants. Lord, rouse up Your servants to lead Your people. Amen.*

13

THE MAN OF GOD FROM JUDAH

First Kings 13

The Lord told a man of God from Judah to go to Bethel. When he got there, Jeroboam was standing next to the altar burning incense. The Lord had commanded the man of God to speak against that altar. The man said, "O altar, O altar, the Lord says this to you: 'David's household will have a son named Josiah some day. (This inspired prophecy that would be fulfilled about 360 years later in the person of King Josiah [see 2 Kings 23:15-20].) He will butcher upon you the priests of such pagan places of worship who offer their sacrifices upon you. Josiah will burn human bones upon you.'" Then the man of God gave proof that these things would happen in the future. He said, "This is the miraculous sign that the Lord has spoken: This altar will break apart, and the ashes upon it will pour out on the ground."

When King Jeroboam heard what the man of the one true God said about the altar in Bethel, Jeroboam stretched out his hand from the altar, pointing at the man of God, saying, "Seize him!" But Jeroboam's hand became paralyzed; and he could not move it. And that altar did break into pieces. And, all of its ashes poured out on the ground, just like the sign that the Lord had given the man of God to foretell.

Then the king answered the man of the one true God, "O please pray to the Lord your God for me. Beg Him to heal my hand."

So the man of the one true God prayed to the Lord. And the king's hand was restored; it was like it was originally.

Then the king said to the man of the one true God, "Please come home with me. Refresh yourself. And, I will give you a gift." (King Jeroboam wanted to restore his own prestige, thereby creating the impression that there was no fundamental difference between himself and the prophets of God.)

But the man of the one true God said to the king, "I will not go home with you. Even if you gave me half of your household, I would not go there. I must not eat food or drink water in this place. (God wanted to demonstrate that His true prophet should not endorse this false religion [compare 1 Cor. 5:11; 2 John 1:10-11.]) Why? Because the word of the Lord has commanded me not to eat anything or drink water here. He also ordered me not to return on the same road by which I came." So, the man of God traveled on a different road, and did not return on the same road by which he had come to Bethel.

A Lying Prophet

Now there was an old prophet living in Bethel. (This old preacher may have faithfully served God in former times, but those days were now long gone!) His sons came and told him what the man of the one true God had done that day. They told their father what the man of the one true God had spoken to King Jeroboam. The father asked them, "Which road did he use when he left?" So his sons showed him which road that the man of the one true God from Judah took. Then the old prophet told his sons to put a saddle on his donkey. So they saddled the donkey for him, and the old prophet rode off. He went after the man of the one true

God. And he found the man of God sitting under the oak tree (a well-known landmark). The old prophet asked him, "Are you the man of the one true God who came from Judah?"

The man answered, "Yes, I am."

Then the old prophet said to him, "Come home and eat something."

But the man of God answered, "I cannot go back with you to your home. I cannot eat anything or drink water with you in this place. Because the word of the Lord has told me: 'You must not eat anything or drink water there. And, you must not return on the same road by which you came.'"

Then the old prophet lied to him: (The apostle John warns that we are not to believe every spirit, but to test them to discover whether they are from God or not [see 1 John 4:1]. We must always remember that the prophetic gift was sometimes mixed with differing degrees of moral lapses [see 1 Kings 22:6; Jer. 38:1].) "But I am also a prophet like you. An angel from the Lord spoke to me. (The young prophet should have known that Yahweh would not contradict Himself. It is quite possible that the motive of this old "prophet" was to curry favor with King Jeroboam, who wanted to continue the pagan policies of his apostate state-religion. If the opportunistic old prophet could discredit the man of God from Judah, then it might please King Jeroboam, and the old prophet would reap some reward because the entire city of Bethel would be indebted to him for his quick thinking. The old prophet was trying—at any cost—to remove Yahweh's pronouncement against the altar at Bethel.) He told me to bring you back to my house. He said you should eat something and drink water with me." So, the man of God returned to the old prophet's house. And, he ate food and drank some water with him there. (The public example of this "man of God" completely undermined everything that God had just said through him in Bethel previously.)

While they were sitting at the table, this word of the Lord came to the old prophet who brought the man of God back. The old prophet spoke out to the man of the one true God who came from Judah, "This is what the Lord is saying to you: Because you have not obeyed Him—you did not do precisely what the Lord your God commanded you—you have rebelled against the Lord's words. The Lord specifically told you not to eat any food or drink any water in this place. Nevertheless, you did come back here and eat and drink. Therefore, your corpse will not be buried in your family grave." (Thus, the man of God became a literal "sign" of the certain result of disobeying God.)

After the man of God finished his meal, the old prophet put a saddle on his donkey for him. And the man of God left. As he was traveling, a lion attacked him on the road and killed him. The man's body just lay there on the road. Both the donkey and the lion stood next to it. (This was completely unnatural; it could only have been arranged by the Creator Himself. The lion should have attacked and ate the donkey.) Some men were traveling down that road and saw the man's body lying there—and they saw the lion standing next to it. So they went to the town where the old prophet lived, and reported it.

The old prophet who had brought the man of the one true God back heard the news. He said, "It is the man of the one true God who rebelled against the words of the Lord. The Lord has sent a lion to kill him and tear him apart. The Lord said He was going to do this."

Then the old prophet said to his sons: "Put a saddle on my donkey." So they did. Then the old prophet went out there and found the man's body lying on the road. The donkey and the lion were still standing next to it. The lion had not eaten the body. And, the lion had not attacked the donkey. So, the old prophet put the body of the man of the one true God on top of the man's donkey, and he brought it back to the town. The old prophet wanted to grieve for the man of God and bury him. Then the old prophet buried the body in his old family grave, and they grieved for the man of God. The old prophet said, "O my brother...." (Maybe this was a weak attempt by the old prophet to make amends to a fellow "preacher.")

After the old prophet had buried the man of God, he said to his sons, "When I die, bury me in this same grave where the man of the one true God is buried. Put my bones next to his bones. The Lord has surely spoken His word against the altar at Bethel through that man of God. And, God has spoken against the pagan places of worship that exist among the towns of Samaria."

The Consequences of Jeroboam's Sin

However, King Jeroboam did not turn away from doing evil things. He continued to ordain priests for the pagan places of worship from all the Jewish people. Anyone who wanted to be a priest for their places of worship was permitted by Jeroboam to do so. This thing became the sin of the household of Jeroboam. And, that sin brought Jeroboam's family to their downfall; they were destroyed from the face of the earth.

My Time to Pray

False Altar and Lying Prophet

Behold, a man of God went from Judah to Bethel by the word of the Lord (1 Kings 13:1).

This chapter speaks to us about boldness. The man of God left Judah and went to a different new nation, Israel, the ten northern tribes. God knew all about the compromise of Jeroboam. God sent an unarmed man of God to speak against the substitute altar in the Northern Kingdom. When he spoke, the altar broke open to show God's supernatural power and His total rejection of the false altar that Jeroboam pretended was real. When Jeroboam raised his arm to say, "Seize him," he was paralyzed. Both supernatural events should have told everyone "worship God in the right way, at the right place, for the right reasons." *Lord, I believe You have rejected many pseudo-churches that don't correctly preach Your word. I will seek a church that honestly teaches Your word and serves You in that church.*

Did you notice that King Jeroboam recognized that the true God was with the young man of God? Jeroboam pleaded, "Pray to the Lord your God for me." When unsaved people get in serious trouble, they know about the true God in their heart. When Jeroboam was paralyzed, he wanted someone in touch with Jehovah to pray for him. *Lord, may unsaved people see You in my life and may they seek Your salvation.*

There will always be pseudo-preachers who claim to represent God. The old prophet may have served God when he was younger, but in this chapter he is used by the enemy, satan, to do three things. First, the old prophet made the young man of God compromise God's command. Second, the old prophet is responsible for the death of a man of God. Third, the old prophet discredited the testimony of the young man of God in the eyes of the community. The people saw him eat, and the people heard a lion had killed the young man of God. So what did the people think? They didn't believe the man of God's message was from God, that the altar was condemned by God. So what did the people do? They continued worshiping on the false altar. *Lord, I know the devil as a roaring lion walks about trying to eat me up (see 1 Pet. 5:8). Protect me when I am defenseless. Enlighten me when I am wrong. Empower me to stand against my enemy (see 1 John 4:4).*

The old prophet was a *lying prophet.* When a person claims to speak God's words, but in his heart he knows differently, the Bible calls him a *lying prophet.* No one can speak for God unless he quotes the Scriptures, or the things he says corresponds to the Word of God. *Lord, I know there are lying prophets in the world. Give me wisdom to discern who they are and courage to not let them influence my life.*

Just because a person calls himself a prophet, doesn't make him a prophet. A prophet must be called of God and his message must be in harmony with the Word of God. A prophet must draw people to God and the message of the prophet must transform their lives. *Lord, I will measure all preachers by the Word of God. When someone disagrees with Your word, I will not listen to them. Amen.*

14

AHIJAH'S PROPHECY AGAINST JEROBOAM

First Kings 14

At that time, Abijah, Jeroboam's son, became very sick. So Jeroboam said to his wife, "Please get up and go to Shiloh. (Jeroboam did *not* want his own people to know that he was seeking guidance from Yahweh instead of the idols that he sanctioned in his own country.) The prophet Ahijah (the prophet's name Ahijah was very similar to Jeroboam's son's name Abijah) is there. He is the one who told me that I would become king over these people. But you must disguise yourself, so that people will not know that you are my wife. Now, take along ten loaves of bread, some cakes, and a jar of honey and go to him. Ask him what will happen to our son, and he will tell you." So, Jeroboam's wife got up and went to Shiloh, and entered Ahijah's house.

Ahijah had gotten old, and had become blind. But the Lord had told Ahijah, "Jeroboam's son is sick. That is why Jeroboam's wife is coming to ask you about her son. When she arrives, she will pretend to be someone else. Tell her what I tell you to say."

When Ahijah heard the sound of her footsteps as she came in the door, he said, "Come in, O wife of Jeroboam. Why are you pretending to be someone else? I have some bad news for you from God. Go back and tell Jeroboam that this is what the Lord, the God of Israel, says: 'I chose you from among the people. I appointed you as the leader over My people, Israel. I tore the kingdom away from David's household and I gave it to you. But, you are not like my servant David who always obeyed my commands. He followed Me with all his heart, doing only what I see as upright. Instead, you have done more evil things than any king before you. You have quit following Me. You have made for yourself different gods and metal idols. All this makes Me very angry. Therefore, listen, I will bring disaster to the household of Jeroboam. I will kill all of the males in your household, both slaves and free men in Israel. (This was fulfilled in First Kings 15:28-29.) Yes, I will sweep out the remainder of your household as completely as fire burns up fuel. Anyone from your family who dies in the city will be eaten by dogs. And, anyone from your family who dies in the country will be eaten by the wild birds. The Lord has spoken!'"

Then Ahijah said to her, "Now, get ready to go home. When you enter your city, your boy will die. All Israel will mourn for him; they will bury him. He will be the only one of Jeroboam's family who will be buried. As far as the Lord, the God of Israel, was concerned, that boy was the only good thing present in Jeroboam's family.

"The Lord will raise up for Himself a new king over Israel. That king will destroy Jeroboam's household. And, that will happen soon. The Lord will punish Israel. They will be like the reeds moving in the water. God will pull up Israel from this good land that He gave to their ancestors. He will scatter them beyond the Euphrates River. Why? Because the Lord is angry with them for making the Asherah idols to worship. Jeroboam sinned. He caused the people of Israel to sin, too. So, the Lord will hand over the people of Israel."

Then Jeroboam's wife traveled to Tirzah. As she was entering the gate of her palace, the boy died. They buried him, and all Israel mourned for him, just as the Lord said it would occur. The Lord had spoken these things through his servant Ahijah, the prophet.

Everything else that Jeroboam did is written down in the Book of the History of the Kings of Israel. Jeroboam fought several wars, and he continued to rule as king for 22 years. Then he died, and his son Nadab became king in his place.

Rehoboam Rules Over Judah

Solomon's son, Rehoboam, was 41 years old when he became king of Judah. His mother's name was Naamah, from the land of Ammon. Rehoboam ruled in Jerusalem for 17 years. The Lord had chosen that city from all the tribes of Israel to be worshiped there.

The people of Judah did what was evil in the sight of the Lord. The people's sins made the Lord very angry at them. They made the Lord even more angry than their ancestors had done. The people also built for themselves shrines and statues of stone and Asherah poles on every high hill and under every green tree. There were also male prostitutes in the land. (Sodomites, many Canaanite fertility shrines employed temple prostitutes. This was considered normal to them. However, Moses had condemned this practice long before [see Deut. 23:17].) Doing such disgusting things, they behaved like the ethnic groups that the Lord had expelled before the people of Israel invaded Palestine.

During the fifth year that Rehoboam was king of Judah, Shishak, the king of Egypt attacked Jerusalem. (Rehoboam reigned from 940 to 919 B.C., and this invasion probably took place in 925 B.C.) He took the treasures from the Temple of the Lord and the royal palace. He took everything, even the golden shields that Solomon had made. (There is a famous inscription by Shishak that has been discovered at Karnak, which is physical proof of this Egyptian expedition at that time.) So, King Rehoboam made bronze shields to replace them. He turned them over to the officers of the guard who watched the palace gates. Whenever the king went to the Temple of the Lord, the guards carried the shields (for ceremonial purposes). After they were finished, they put the shields back in the armory.

Everything else that King Rehoboam did—all that he did—is written down in the Book of the History of the Kings of Judah. Rehoboam and Jeroboam were always having skirmishes with each other. (See First Kings 15:6 and Second Chronicles 12:15b.) Rehoboam died, and he was buried with his ancestors in Jerusalem. The name of his mother was Naamah, from Ammon. And Rehoboam's son, Abijah, became king in his place.

My Time to Pray

"Tell her..."

The Lord said to Ahijah..."Tell her what I tell you to say" (1 Kings 14:5).

When God spoke to the prophet Ahijah, He told the old blind prophet, "Tell her what I tell you to say." Isn't that the task of all God's servants today? We are not to tell others our opinions, we are not even to tell others our interpretations of the Bible. We are to say what Billy Graham the evangelist says, "The Bible says...." We should let God speak through us by telling people what God says in the Bible. *Lord, I will faithfully tell others what You say in the Bible.*

When the people didn't have access to the written Word of God, the Lord spoke through prophets. The validity of a prophet was certified when the predictions he made came true. The old prophet Ahijah predicts that Jeroboam's son will die when his mother returns to the gates of her home town. It would seem people would be convicted of their sin and repent when they saw a supernatural evidence of God's message. But the people didn't turn to God in the past, just as they don't do it today. God has spoken through the supernatural Scriptures, but the general public doesn't respond. Even when the Word of God accurately predicts things like Israel returning to the land of Palestine, the public doesn't respond to God. *Lord, I know You are omnipresent. Your existence is not limited by space or time. You exist everywhere equally at the same time, so I know You exist in the future. So I know Your predictions are true. I believe the predictions of the Bible and will act on them.*

Ahijah predicted Israel would be captured and transported beyond the Euphrates River to Babylon. *Lord, I know this prediction came true, and I know Your prediction that Israel would return to the land and have 1,000 years of peace will also come true.*

The Lord loved Jeroboam and put him on the throne of the ten northern tribes. The Lord gave him opportunity to repent, just as He gives everyone an opportunity to repent and turn to Him. *Lord, thank You for loving everyone and giving them an opportunity to repent and turn to Yourself. I know You love me, so I will seek You with my whole heart. Amen.*

15

ABIJAH BECOMES
KING AFTER REHOBOAM

First Kings 15

Abijah became king over Judah. This happened during the eighteenth
year that King Jeroboam the son of Nebat ruled Israel. And
Abijah ruled in Jerusalem for three years. His mother's name was
Maacah, the daughter of Abishalom. He did all the same sins
that his father before him had done. Abijah was not faithful to
the Lord, his God. In this way, he did not have the same kind
of heart that David, his great-grandfather had. Nevertheless, for
David's sake, the Lord, his God provided in Jerusalem a lamp—
He set up his son as king after him and stabilized Jerusalem.
David always tried to do what the Lord saw as upright. All of
David's life, he did not turn away from what God told him to
do—except in the case of Uriah the Hittite.

Now there was hostility between Rehoboam and Jeroboam all during
Abijah's lifetime. Everything else that Abijah did—all that he
did—is written down in the Book of the History of the Kings of
Judah. And, during the time that Abijah ruled, there was hostility
between Abijah and Jeroboam. And Abijah died, and they buried
him in Jerusalem. Abijah's son, Asa, became king in his place.

Asa Rules Over Judah

During the twentieth year that Jeroboam was king of Israel, Asa became the king of Judah. (Asa reigned from 910 to 869 B.C.) Asa ruled in Jerusalem for 41 years. His grandmother's name was Maacah; she was the daughter of Abishalom.

Asa did what the Lord saw as upright, just as his ancestor David had done. There were male prostitutes (Sodomites) at the places where false gods were worshiped. Asa forced them to leave the country. He also took away all the idols that his ancestors had made. In addition, his grandmother, Maacah, had made a hideous idol of Asherah. So, Asa removed her from the rank of queen mother. Asa cut down this horrible idol and burned it next to the Kidron Valley. (This was to prevent the spiritual pollution of the holy city by the ashes of this abominable idol.) The heart of Asa was faithful to the Lord all of his life. However, he did not destroy the high places where false gods were worshiped. Asa and his father had dedicated some things to God. They had donated gifts of gold, silver, and other objects. Asa brought all of these things to the Temple of the Lord.

There was hostility between Asa and Baasha, the northern king of Israel during the whole time that they were kings. Baasha, the king of Israel, attacked Judah. He wanted to stop people from leaving or coming to the country of Asa, the king of Judah. So, Baasha re-enforced the city of Ramah.

Then Asa took all the silver and gold that was left of the treasures of the Temple of the Lord and his own palace, and put it in the hands of his officers to take to Ben-Hadad, the king of Syria. Ben-Hadad was the son of Tabrimmon, the son of Hezion. Ben-Hadad was ruling in the city of Damascus. Asa sent his message: "My father and your father had a peace agreement; let's continue it. I am hereby sending you this gift of gold and silver. Go, break your treaty with Baasha, the king of Israel, so that he will leave me alone."

And, Ben-Hadad made a pact with King Asa. So, he sent his officers and army to fight against the towns of Israel. He defeated the towns of Ijon, Dan, and Abel-Beth-Maacah. And, he defeated all the area near Lake Galilee and the region of Naphtali. Baasha heard about these attacks. So, he stopped building up Ramah and stayed at Tirzah (his capital city). Then King Asa gave an order to all the people of Judah, everyone had to help. They carried away all the stones and the wood that Baasha had been using to fortify Ramah. King Asa used those things to build up Geba and Mizpah. Geba was in the territory of Benjamin.

Everything else that Asa did—all of his power, and all that he did, including the cities that he built—is written down in the Book of the History of the Kings of Judah. But, when Asa became old, he contracted a disease in his feet. Then Asa died. And, he was buried with his ancestors in Jerusalem. Then Jehoshaphat, Asa's son, became king in his place.

Nadad Rules Over Israel

And Nadab, the son of Jeroboam, became the king of Northern Israel. (Nadab reigned from 909 to 908 B.C.) This happened during the second year that Asa was the king of Judah. And, Nadab was the king over Israel for two years. Nadab did what was evil in the sight of the Lord. Jeroboam had caused the people of Israel to sin, and Nadab sinned in the same way that his father Jeroboam sinned.

Baasha Rules Over Israel

Baasha, the son of Ahijah, was from the tribe of Issachar. He made plans to kill Nadab. Nadab and all Israel were besieging the Philistine town of Gibbethon. So, Baasha killed Nadab there. This assassination occurred during Asa's third year as the king of Judah. And, Baasha became the next king of Northern Israel.

As soon as Baasha became king, he killed all of Jeroboam's family. He left no one in Jeroboam's family alive. He killed them all. This happened just as the Lord had said it would. The Lord had predicted this through his servant Ahijah from Shiloh (thus fulfilling the prophecy recorded in First Kings 14:9-14). This happened because King Jeroboam had sinned so much, and because he had caused the people of Israel to sin, too. Jeroboam had made the Lord, the God of Israel, very angry.

Everything else that Nadab did—all that he did—is written down in the Book of the History of the Kings of Israel.

There was hostility between Asa and Baasha, the king of Israel, during the whole time that they were kings.

Baasha, the son of Ahijah, became the king over Israel. This happened during Asa's third year as king of Judah. And, Baasha ruled in Tirzah for 24 years. But Baasha did what was evil in the sight of the Lord. Jeroboam had caused the people of Israel to sin, and Baasha sinned in the same way that Jeroboam had sinned.

My Time to Pray

A Chip Off the Old Block

He walked in all the sins of his father... (1 Kings 15:3).

A bijah was not a godly king, "He did the same sins that his father [Rehoboam] had done." Even though he was morally corrupt, he led Judah to a great victory over the Northern Kingdom when his army was out-manned two to one. That shows that a corrupt man can do things right politically or militarily. In this case it was not political, for he caused Judah to sin. This also shows God can use a corrupt man to do His will. *Lord, I know You have used non-Christians to accomplish Your will. Thank You for working behind the scenes to bless my life. I give myself to You. I want to be godly and useful. So use me to accomplish Your will in my life and in the life of many others.*

Did you miss the phrase David pleased the Lord *"except in the case of Uriah the Hittite"* (1 Kings 15:5)? God cleanses our sin and forgives us for what we do. But God sees the consequences of our sin. God will not erase history and treat the consequences as though they never happened. That means God forgives our sin, but we must live with its consequences.

Years ago there was a born-again believer on death row scheduled to die for murder. Even though this prisoner was a flaming witness for Christ among other prisoners and the guards. Even though my church and Christian lawyers prayed and asked for a pardon, the woman was executed. *Lord, my sins scar me because I must live with their consequences. I know You've forgiven them and I know my record is perfect in Heaven, but I still have to live with their consequences. Protect me...use me...and sovereignly overcome these circumstances.*

As we look at the kings of the Old Testament, we see the influence of the father on his son. Apples don't fall very far from the tree. The Books of First and Second Kings give many illustrations to prove that principle. Yet when there is an exception, such as good King Asa taking over after his evil father Abijah, it is noteworthy. Notice how much space is used to describe the good things that Asa did. In this we see the sovereign hand of God in history as God works in human lives. *Lord, I thank You for calling me and using me (Elmer Towns) in ministry. My father died an alcoholic, but I've never tasted alcoholic drink. I don't glory in my strength to abstain, but I give all credit to You my Lord, the One who transformed my life. This means anyone can overcome the evil influence of their parents by the power of God. "I can do all things through Christ who strengthens me" (see Phil. 4:13). Amen.*

16

ABIJAH RULES OVER JUDAH

Second Chronicles 13

Abijah became king over Judah. This happened during the eighteenth
year that King Jeroboam ruled over Israel. And Abijah ruled in
Jerusalem for three years. His mother's name was Maacah, the
daughter of Uriel. Uriel was from the town of Gibeah.

And, there was war between Abijah and Jeroboam. Abijah led an army
of 400,000 select soldiers into battle. And Jeroboam prepared to
fight him with 800,000 select soldiers. Abijah stood on Mount
Zemaraim in the mountains of Ephraim. He said, "O Jeroboam
and all Israel, listen to me. You should know this: The Lord, the
God of Israel gave this right to David with a covenant that will
last forever. But Jeroboam turned against his master. Jeroboam
was the son of Nebat, one of Solomon's officers. Solomon
was David's son. Then worthless, evil men became friends
with Jeroboam. They were against Rehoboam, Solomon's son.
Rehoboam was young and did not know what to do. So, he
could not stop them. Now you people are making plans against
the Lord's kingdom. The Lord's kingdom belongs to David's
descendants. There are many of you. And you have the golden
calves that Jeroboam made for you as gods. You have thrown out
the Lord's priests and the Levites. Our priests are Aaron's sons.
You have chosen your own priests as people in other countries
do. Anyone who comes to make himself ready to worship with

a young bull and seven male sheep can become a priest. He can become a priest of idols that are not gods. But as for us, the Lord is our God. We have not abandoned Him. The true priests who serve the Lord are Aaron's sons. And the Levites help the priests serve the Lord. They offer whole burnt offerings and sweet-smelling incense to the Lord every morning and every evening. They also put the holy bread on the table that is ceremonially clean. And, they light the lamps on the golden lampstand every evening. We obey the commands of the Lord, our God. But you have abandoned Him. Listen, the one true God is with us. He is our Ruler, and His priests are with us. Our priests will blow the trumpet to call us to war against you. Men of Israel, don't fight against the Lord, because you will not succeed. He is the God of your ancestors."

But Jeroboam had sent some troops to sneak around behind Abijah's army. So, while Jeroboam was in front of Abijah's army, Jeroboam's soldiers were behind them. The soldiers in Abijah's army turned around. Then they saw Jeroboam's army attacking them—both in front and in back. They cried out to the Lord, and the priests blew the trumpets. Then the men of Judah gave a battle cry. When they shouted, God defeated Jeroboam and the army of Israel. They ran away from Abijah and the army of Judah. So, the men of Israel ran away from the front lines of Judah. God permitted the army from Judah to defeat them. Abijah and his army killed so many of Israel's men that 500,000 of their select soldiers died. So, at that time, the people of Israel were defeated. The people of Judah won. Why? Because they depended on the Lord, the God of their ancestors.

Abijah's army chased Jeroboam's army. Abijah's army captured from Jeroboam the towns of Bethel, Jeshanah, and Ephron. They also captured the small villages near those towns. Jeroboam never became strong again while Abijah was alive. The Lord struck Jeroboam, and he died.

But Abijah became more powerful. He married 14 women, and was the father of 22 sons and 16 daughters. All the other things that Abijah did as king are written down. What he said and did are recorded in what the prophet Iddo wrote.

My Time to Pray

The One True God

Men of Israel, do not fight against the Lord, because you will not succeed (2 Chronicles 13:12).

You can fight when you know God is on your side. Abijah was out-manned two to one. Israel had 800,000 soldiers, while Judah had only half—400,000. So Abijah stood on a mountain to announce to his enemies why God was on his side. First, God made a covenant with them, not Israel. Second, Israel has a false altar not established by God, while Judah had the right place—Jerusalem—the right priests—Levites—the right sacrifices—prescribed by God, and the right articles of worship in the Temple. Because Judah was on God's side, the king announced, "Do not fight against the Lord." So when you argue or attack anyone, make sure you are right by biblical standards if you want God to help you win. *Lord, I will obey the Bible, I will fight spiritual warfare by biblical means, and I will trust Your power to give me victory.*

Who rules your life? Abijah could say, "The one true God is with us. He is our ruler." When you are on God's side, you can have confidence in battle. *Lord, I will fight Your causes by Your principles, in Your power, for Your glory. Then I will leave the results in Your hands.*

God can win *"by many or by few"* (1 Sam. 14:6). God can defeat an army twice your size. The secret is to let God fight through you. *"Greater is He who is in you, than he who is in the world"* (1 John 4:4). *Lord, You dwell in me. I yield to Your will and Your ability. Fight through me and win my battles for me.*

God controls the way all will die and the date of every person's death. Sometimes God removes a person by death when they stand against the plan of God. *Lord, I yield myself to You and I yield all circumstances to You. You take a person's life prematurely when they oppose You—only when You must. "Jeroboam never became strong again. The Lord struck Jeroboam and he died"* (2 Chron. 13:20). *Amen.*

17

ASA DEFEATS THE ETHIOPIANS

Second Chronicles 14:9–15:19

Then Zerah from Cush (the Ethiopian) came out to fight Asa's army.
Zerah had an army of a million men and 300 chariots. They
came as far north as the town of Mareshah. Asa went out to fight
Zerah. Asa's army prepared for battle in the Valley of Zephthah
at Mareshah.

Then Asa called out to the Lord, his God, saying, "O Lord Who Is
Always Present, only You can help powerless people against the
strong. Help us, O Lord our God. We depend on You. In Your
Name we fight against this huge army. O Lord, You are our God.
Don't let anyone win against You."

Then the Lord defeated the Cushites when Asa's army from Judah
attacked them. And, the Cushites ran away. Asa's army chased
them as far as the town of Gerar. So many Cushites were killed
that the army could not fight again. They were crushed by the
Lord and His army. Asa and his army carried many valuable
things away (plunder) from the enemy. They destroyed all the
towns near Gerar. The people living in these towns were afraid
of the Lord. These towns had many valuable things. So, Asa's
army took those things away. Asa's army also attacked the
camps where the herdsmen lived. And they took many sheep and
camels. Then they went back to Jerusalem.

King Asa Seeks God's Favor

Second Chronicles 15

The Spirit of God came upon Azariah, the son of Oded. Azariah went to meet Asa, and told him, "Listen to me, Asa and all you people of Judah and of Benjamin. The Lord is with you, when you are with Him. If you obey the Lord, you will find Him. But, if you abandon Him, then He will abandon you. For a long time, Israel has been without the true God. And, they were without a priest to teach them so they were without God's teachings. But when they were in trouble, they turned to the Lord again. He is the God of Israel. They looked for the Lord, and they found Him. In those days, no one could travel safely. All the people who lived in various lands had lots of problems. One nation was trying to crush another nation. And, one city wanted to destroy another city. Why? Because God inflicted upon them all kinds of trouble. Nevertheless, you people should be strong. Don't give up, because you will receive a reward for your good work."

Asa felt encouraged when he heard these words and the prophecy of Azariah, the son of Oded the prophet. So, Asa removed the disgusting idols from all the land of Judah and of Benjamin. And, he removed them from the towns that he had captured in the hills of Ephraim. He repaired the Lord's brazen altar that was in front of the porch of the Temple of the Lord. Then Asa gathered all the people of Judah and of Benjamin. He also gathered the people of the tribes of Ephraim, Manasseh, and Simeon who were living in the territory of Judah. Many people came over to Asa from the kingdom of Israel. They came because they saw that the Lord, Asa's God, was with him.

Asa and all the people gathered in Jerusalem. This happened in the third month of the fifteenth year of Asa's rule. At that time, they sacrificed 700 bulls and 7,000 sheep and goats to the Lord.

Asa's army had taken these animals and other valuable things from their enemies. Then they entered into a covenant. They promised to obey the Lord, the God of their ancestors, with all their heart and soul. Anyone who refused to obey the Lord, the God of Israel, was to be killed. It did not matter if that person was important or unimportant. It did not matter if that person was a man or a woman. Then Asa and the people made a vow to the Lord. They shouted with a loud voice. They also blew trumpets and ram's horns. All the people of Judah were happy about that vow. They took the oath with all their heart. They truly wanted to seek God, and they found Him. So, the Lord gave them peace on every side.

King Asa also removed his grandmother Maacah from being queen mother. He did this because she had made an obscene Asherah (a fertility pole). Asa cut down that idol and smashed it into pieces. Then he burned it in the Kidron Valley. However, Asa did not destroy those pagan places of worship from Judah. Nevertheless, Asa's heart was faithful all of his life. Now Asa and his father had dedicated some things that were made of silver and of gold. Asa brought these objects into the Temple of the one true God.

There was no more war until the thirty-fifth year of Asa's rule.

My Time to Pray

Look Where You Lost It

...If you seek Him [the Lord] *He will be found by you...* (2 Chronicles 15:2).

Once I lost a $20 bill. That was a lot of money to me as a teen. I was running all over the house to look for it, but couldn't find it.

My mother asked, "Where were you when you realized it was lost?" I answered, "On the back porch where I keep my bicycle." She said, "Go look thoroughly there." I did, and I found it had fallen out of my pocket when I reached for my keys. The $20 bill had caught in the spokes of the bicycle.

When you lose God, go back for Him where you lost Him. Did you stop attending church? Did you stop tithing? Did you curse in front of someone? When you lose God, go back to that place physically, and start doing what you did when you lost God. Maybe you must go back in your mind, revisit a bar and repent of drinking, or revisit a conversation and repent of a lie or cursing. *Lord, I will go back to the place where I lost You, and I will repent of my sin that drove You away.*

Sometimes you can't find a lost item with a quick cursory look. It takes getting close to the spot, or looking under something like a table, or moving things around. To find God, spend time confessing your sins, showing remorse and a contrite spirit. Maybe one quick prayer of confession won't turn around your situation. Maybe you'll have to move things around to look under the clutter of your life to find God. God is there waiting for you as you search for Him. Maybe God is not easy to find because He wants to see if you are sincere; do you mean business this time? So keep searching, God can be found. *Lord, I will search for You with all my heart. I will search for You everywhere. I will go back to search for You at the place I lost You. I will keep searching, and I will not give up.*

Notice the result, *"They found Him"* (2 Chron. 15:15). Can you imagine the joy of finding God? Think how happy you were when you found your lost keys or lost money. How much more happy were you when you found a lost child or parent? But our greatest rejoicing should be finding God. *Lord, I praise You for searching for me as I searched for You.*

King Asa was so committed to finding God that he decreed, *"Whoever would not seek the Lord God of Israel is to be put to death"* (2 Chron. 15:13). This threat shows the seriousness of the king. We as followers of God should realize how serious the Lord's challenge is to us. If those we witness to about Christ won't seek Him, eventually they will be put to death in hell. *Lord, I will be serious in seeking You, and I will be serious in telling others to seek You, knowing the consequences if they don't find You.*

Revival spread under Asa, he repaired the brazen altar for sacrifices, repaired the Temple. Seven hundred bulls and seven thousand sheep were sacrificed. He smashed idols, destroyed pagan places of worship. He put his grandmother out of office and smashed her obscene Asherah. Yet there was one thing he missed, *"The high places were not removed"* (2 Chron. 15:17). These were probably a grove of trees on the high hills where idols were worshiped. Every time an Israelite saw the trees, they remembered the place where they previously worshiped. Were the trees a constant temptation to pull the Israelites back to idol worship? *Lord, I will smash any idol in my heart. I will get rid of anything between You and me, including my friends or relatives (Asa's grandmother). Lord, I will cleanse my life of sin, wrong attitudes, and things that tempt me to sin.*

It's important when we have a great victory for God that we renew our allegiance to Him. Asa had just destroyed a much larger army, the Ethiopians. As Asa was returning home, the prophet met him to tell Asa what he had to do to keep the blessing of God in his personal life and the life of the nation. Asa had enough common sense to do what the prophet said. *Lord, thank You for many victories in my life. Because You've been good to me, I commit myself to completely doing Your will. Cleanse me of any and every sin I know is wrong. If I have ignorant sins in my life, show them to me. I will confess them to You and rid myself of them. I want to be clean for Your continued use in my life. Amen.*

18

ASA RELIES ON MAN, NOT GOD

Second Chronicles 16

In the thirty-sixth year of King Asa (dating from the time of the split between the two kingdoms, rather than from the last year of Asa's reign), Baasha, the king of Israel, attacked Judah. He wanted to stop people from leaving or coming to the country of Asa the king of Judah. So, Baasha reinforced the city of Ramah. Then Asa took silver and gold from the treasures of the Temple of the Lord and his own palace, and sent it to Ben-Hadad, the king of Syria. Ben-Hadad was ruling in the city of Damascus. Asa sent this message: "My father and your father had a peace agreement; let's continue the same thing. I am hereby sending you this gift of silver and gold. Go, break your treaty with Baasha, the king of Israel, so that he will leave me alone."

And, Ben-Hadad heeded King Asa. So, he sent his officers and army to fight against the towns of Israel. They defeated the towns of Ijon, and Dan, and Abel-Main. And, he defeated all the storage cities of Naphtali. Baasha heard about these attacks. So, he stopped building up Ramah. Then King Asa took all the people of Judah and they carried away all the stones and the wood that Baasha had been using to fortify Ramah. King Asa used those things to build up Geba and Mizpah.

At that time, Hanani the seer came to Asa, the king of Judah. Hanani said to him, "You depended on the king of Syria to help you, and you did not depend on the Lord to help you. So, God permitted you to defeat them. The Lord has searched the entire earth for people who have given themselves completely to Him. He wants to make them strong. Asa, you did a foolish thing. From now on, you will have wars."

Asa was angry with Hanani the seer, because of what he had said. Asa was so angry that he put Hanani in prison. At that time, Asa was cruel to some of the people.

King Asa Dies

Look at the things that Asa did as king—from the beginning to the end—they are written down, in the Book of the Kings of Judah and Israel. In the thirty-ninth year of his rule, Asa contracted a disease in his feet. His disease was very bad, but he did not ask for help from the Lord. He asked for help only from the doctors. Then Asa died with his ancestors in the forty-first year of his rule. The people buried Asa in the tomb that he had dug for himself in Jerusalem. They laid him in a casket, filled it with spices and different kinds of mixed perfumes. Then, they made a large fire to honor Asa.

My Time to Pray

Total Commitment

The eyes of the Lord search the whole earth in order to strengthen those whose hearts are fully committed to him. What a fool you have been! From now on you will be at war (2 Chronicles 16:9 NLT).

Did you see the heart of the Lord in that Scripture? The Lord is "searching the whole earth" for a person He can use. Will God choose to use you, or will God bypass you to search the whole earth? For what is God searching? "For people whose hearts are fully committed to Him." Do you measure up to that standard? D.L. Moody said over 100 years ago, "The world has yet to see what God can do with a person who is totally committed to Him." *Lord, I want to be that person. I want to do more for You than I've ever done. I want to do more for You than anyone in my generation.*

Asa did many wonderful things for God, but remember, *"Asa did not completely remove the high places from Israel"* (2 Chron. 15:17 TLB). Is Asa a picture of us? We love God and get rid of most of the sin in our lives, but not "completely." *Lord, I will search my heart for unbelief and disobedience. I will repent of every rebellious thing I find in my life. Then You Lord—Your eyes are perfect—search me thoroughly. Show me any resistance I have to Your will. I will remove it.*

When God spoke through the prophet Hanani, Asa got angry and put him in prison. How could good King Asa be so blind? This incident tells me that good people who follow God make mistakes because they are blinded to truth. *Lord, shine some light over here today. Jesus is the Light of the world, shine Your truth on my sin and blindness. I will repent and follow You. Amen.*

19

BAASHA RULES OVER ISRAEL

First Kings 16

Then the word of the Lord came to Jehu the son of Hanani (Hanani was also a prophet [see 2 Chron. 16:7-10]) against King Baasha. The message said: "You were nothing but dust. Then I raised you up, and I allowed you to be a leader over My people Israel. Instead, you have followed the ways of Jeroboam. You have caused My people Israel to sin. And, their sins have made Me very angry. Listen, Baasha, I will completely destroy you and your family. I will cause your family to be like the family of Jeroboam, the son of Nebat. Anyone belonging to your family who dies in the city will be eaten by dogs. And, any of your family who dies in the fields will be eaten by wild birds."

Everything else that Baasha did—all that he did, and his power—is written down in the Book of the History of the Kings of Israel. So Baasha died with his forefathers. And, he was buried in Tirzah. His son Elah became king in his place.

The Lord spoke His word to Baasha through the prophet Jehu, the son of Hanani. The message was addressed to Baasha and to his family. It was against every evil thing that Baasha had done in the sight of the Lord. Baasha's deeds were very upsetting to the Lord; Baasha's regime was just like the household of Jeroboam.

Also, God was very angry because Baasha had murdered Jeroboam.

Elah Rules Over Israel

Elah, the son of Baasha, became the king over Israel. This happened during Asa's twenty-sixth year as king of Judah. And, Elah ruled in Tirzah for two years.

Zimri, one of Elah's officers, was in charge of half of Elah's chariots. But Zimri plotted against Elah. Elah was in Tirzah, getting drunk in the house of Arza. Arza was the man in charge of the palace in Tirzah. So, Zimri went into Arza's house and assassinated Elah. This was during Asa's twenty-seventh year as king of Judah. Then Zimri became the king of Israel in Elah's place.

As soon as Zimri became king, Zimri killed all of Baasha's family. He did not permit any male of Baasha's family or any of his friends to live. So Zimri destroyed all of Baasha's family, just like the Lord predicted to Baasha that it would happen. The Lord predicted this against Baasha through the prophet Jehu. This occurred because of all the sins of Baasha and the sins of his son Elah. They sinned, and they caused the people of Israel to sin. They also made the Lord, the God of Israel angry because of their worthless idols. Everything else that Elah did—all that he did—is written down in the Book of the History of the Kings of Israel.

Zimri Rules Over Israel

So, Zimri became the king of the northern tribes of Israel. This happened during Asa's twenty-seventh year as king of Judah. Zimri ruled in Tirzah for seven days. The army of Israel was camped near Gibbethon, a Philistine town. The soldiers in the camp heard that Zimri had made secret plans against the king. And they heard that Zimri had assassinated the king. So, in the camp, on that day, the army made Omri the new king over all Israel. Omri was the general over the army of Israel. So, Omri and all the supporting Israelites left Gibbethon and attacked Tirzah. When Zimri saw that the city would be captured, he went into the palace and set it on fire. He burned up the palace, and he died. So, Zimri died because he had sinned in doing evil in the sight of the Lord. Zimri was living the same way that Jeroboam lived, causing the people of Israel to sin. Everything else that Zimri did—the whole conspiracy against Elah—is written down in the Book of the History of the Kings of Israel.

Omri Rules Over Israel

The people of Israel were divided into two groups. Half of the people were supporting Tibni to be king. Tibni was the son of Ginath. The other half of the people were following Omri. But Omri's followers were stronger than the followers of Tibni, the son of Ginath. So Tibni died, and Omri became the king.

Omri became the new king over Israel, during the thirty-first year that Asa was king of Judah. And, Omri ruled for 12 years. (The first four years were contested by Tibni, but Omri was the unopposed ruler of Israel for his final eight years.) He ruled in the city of Tirzah for six of those years. Omri purchased the hill of Samaria from Shemer. He paid about 150 pounds of silver for it. Omri built his capital city Samaria on that hill after the name of its previous owner, Shemer.

But Omri did what was evil in the sight of the Lord. He did more evil than all the kings who were before him. Jeroboam, the son of Nebat, had caused the people of Israel to sin. And, Omri sinned in the same way that Jeroboam had sinned. So, the Israelites made the Lord, the God of Israel, very angry. God was angry because they worshiped worthless idols.

Everything else Omri did—all of the power that he possessed—is written down in the Book of the History of the Kings of Israel. So Omri died, and he was buried in Samaria. His son Ahab became king in his place.

Ahab Rules Over Israel

Later, Ahab the son of Omri became the king over Israel. This happened during Asa's thirty-eighth year as king of Judah. Ahab, the son of Omri, ruled over Israel in the city of Samaria for 22 years (from 874 to 853 B.C.). Ahab, the son of Omri, did many things that were evil in the sight of the Lord. Ahab did more evil than anyone who lived before him. To Ahab, it was a small thing to sin in the same ways that Jeroboam the son of Nebat had sinned. However, Ahab did something even worse—he married Jezebel (Jezebel was determined to introduce her native Tyrian, pagan, fertility worship into every sector of her adopted country, Israel) the daughter of Ethbaal. Ethbaal was king of the Sidonians. Then Ahab began to serve Baal and worship him. Ahab also built a shrine and altar for Baal in Samaria. Moreover, Ahab made an idol for worshiping Asherah. Ahab did so many things to make the Lord, the God of Israel, angry—more than any other king before Ahab.

During the time of Ahab, Hiel from Bethel rebuilt the city of Jericho. It cost Hiel the life of Abiram, his oldest son, when he began work on the city. And, it cost the life of Segub, his youngest son, to build the city gates. Through Joshua, the son of Nun, the Lord had predicted that this would happen. (See Joshua 6:26, this incident occurred about 500 years after the inspired prediction in the Book of Joshua.)

My Time to Pray

God's Anger

Ahab did more to provoke the Lord God of Israel to anger than all the Kings of Israel who were before him (1 Kings 16:33).

A person must be totally evil to do more than anyone before him to make God angry at him. Ahab didn't just compromise true worship, he allowed all forms of previous idol worship to continue. Ahab built a temple to Baal. Then he reintroduced the false religion from Phoenicia, the home of his wife Jezebel. Tyrian fertility worship was absent of anything good and corrupted the worshiper to a deeper level of lasciviousness. *Lord, help me turn away from false religion and false worship. I pray against evil religions so You will stop the spread of their influence. I pray that You will destroy false religions.*

Ahab was ruled by his wife Jezebel, as we will see in later chapters. He could have been a good man and helped his people, but Ahab did much to destroy true worship. Later, Elijah will complain to God that he was the *"only one left who didn't bow the knee to Baal"* (1 Kings 19:10,14). Yet God told Elijah there were still 7,000 who had never bowed to Baal (see 1 Kings 19:18). *Lord, help me look beyond my discouragement to see Your work in the world. Forgive me when I whine and complain. Give me victory over my emotions and temper me.*

Ahab completed building the city of Samaria that his father Omni began building. Archaeological discoveries show that Ahab's "ivory house" (see 1 Kings 22:39; Amos 3:15) was actually faced with white stone to give it the appearance of ivory. It did have some ivory inlays. The building was more similar to the Phoenicians than to his native land of Israel. Too bad Ahab chose to be like other nations, rather than like the people of God. *Lord, help me be influenced by the people who are influenced by You. Lord protect me from the influence of the world that would pull me away from You.*

Again God is true, and His prophecies will come to pass. God had predicted the person who tried to rebuild Jericho would be "cursed." *"Cursed be the man before the Lord who rises up and builds this city, Jericho: he shall lay its foundation with his first son born, and with his youngest he shall set up its gates"* (Josh. 6:26). *Lord, Your word is still true. You do what You predict You will do. I believe Your word and will obey it. Amen.*

20

JEHOSHAPHAT RULES OVER JUDAH

Second Chronicles 17

Then Jehoshaphat (reigned from 872 to 848 B.C., he co-ruled with his
father from 872 to 869 B.C. [see 2 Chron. 20:31]), then Asa's
son became king in his place. Jehoshaphat made Judah strong, so
that they could fight against Israel. He stationed troops in all the
strong, walled towns of Judah. And, he put garrisons in the land
of Judah and in the towns of Ephraim, which his father Asa had
captured.

The Lord was with Jehoshaphat, because, at the beginning, he lived as
his ancestor David did. Jehoshaphat did not ask for help from the
Baal idols. He asked for help from the God that his father had
followed. Jehoshaphat obeyed God's commands, and did not live
as the people of Israel were doing. The Lord made Jehoshaphat a
strong king over Judah. All the people of Judah brought gifts to
Jehoshaphat, so he gained much wealth and honor. He wanted
very much to obey the Lord. He also removed the places for
worshiping false gods and the Asherah idols from Judah.

Jehoshaphat sent his officials to teach in the towns of Judah, during the
third year of his rule. These officials were: Ben-Hail, Obadiah,
Zechariah, Nethanel, and Micaiah. Jehoshaphat sent these Levites
with them: Shemaiah, Nethaniah, Zebadiah, Asahel, Shemiramoth,
Jehonathan, Adonijah, Tobijah, and Tob-Adonijah. He also sent

the priests Elishama and Jehoram. These leaders taught the people in Judah the Book of the Teachings (Torah) of the Lord, going throughout all the towns of Judah to teach all the people.

The nations that surrounded Judah were afraid of the Lord. So, they did not start a war against Jehoshaphat. Some of the Philistines brought gifts and silver to Jehoshaphat as payments of money. Some Arabs brought him flocks. They brought him 7,700 male sheep, and 7,700 male goats.

Jehoshaphat became more and more powerful, so that he built fortresses and storage towns in Judah. He kept supplies in the towns of Judah, but kept his trained soldiers in Jerusalem. These soldiers were listed by families.

From the family heads of Judah, these were the commanders of groups of 1,000 men: Adnah was the commander of 300,000 soldiers. And next to him was Jehohanan, the commander of 280,000 soldiers. And next to him was Amasiah, the commander of 200,000 soldiers. Amasiah, the son of Zichri, had volunteered to serve the Lord.

Now these were the commanders from the families of Benjamin: Eliada had 200,000 soldiers who could use shields and bows and arrows. Eliada was a brave soldier. And next to him, Jehozabad had 180,000 men prepared for war. All these soldiers served King Jehoshaphat. The king also put more men in the strong, walled towns throughout all of Judah.

My Time to Pray

Lights in the Darkness

And his heart took delight in the ways of the Lord; moreover he removed the high places and wooden images from Judah (2 Chronicles 17:6).

Asa and Jehoshaphat—father and son—are bright lights on the dark horizon of idolatry, immorality, and compromise. Jehoshaphat demonstrated a delight in the Lord, so much so, that he sent teachers throughout Judah to teach the Torah, the law of God. It does little good to remove idols and their altars if the people don't know the Lord and know how to properly worship Him. *Lord, teach me Yourself so I can know You better. Teach me how to worship so I can please You.*

In times of danger, Jehoshaphat prayed to the Lord. *"Jehoshaphat feared and set himself to seek the Lord and proclaimed a fast throughout all Judah. So Judah gathered together to ask help from the Lord"* (2 Chron. 20:3-4). We should learn from Jehoshaphat, we should pray and fast when we face danger. Whether that danger is physical, financial, spiritual, or from any other source. *Lord, I will fast when my prayers don't get through to You. I will fast to take my prayers to a higher level. I will fast to seek Your presence in my life and search to seek Your protection.*

Strength of nations comes from spiritual strength of individual character. Jehoshaphat became more and more powerful because he strengthened himself in the Lord. *Lord, this is a great lesson for my nation. I pray for national revival where people would seek Your will in their life. God bless America, but most of all, God save America. Amen.*

21

YAHWEH TAKES CARE OF ELIJAH

First Kings 17

Now Elijah was a prophet from the town of Tishbeh. However, he came
from those who were living temporarily in the region of Gilead.
Elijah said to Ahab, "I stand in the presence of the Lord, the God
of Israel. As surely as the Lord lives, there will be no rain or dew
during the next three years—unless I command it." (Drought was
one of the severe punishments from God mentioned in the Law
of Moses.)

Then the Lord spoke His word to Elijah: "Go away from this place.
Turn east and hide yourself next to Cherith Brook. It is east
of the Jordan River. You can drink from the brook, and I have
commanded the ravens to feed you there." So, Elijah did what
the Lord told him to do. He went to Cherith Brook, east of the
Jordan River, and lived there. The ravens brought Elijah bread
and meat every morning and every evening. And, he drank water
from the brook. After a long time—because there was no rain in
the land—the brook dried up.

Elijah and the Widow

Then the word of the Lord came to Elijah: "Get up, go to Zarephath
in Sidon. (This was a Phoenician town in the land of Canaan.
Today, it is probably to be identified with "Surafend," which is

about 13 miles north of Tyre.) Live there. I have commanded a widow there to supply you with food."

So, Elijah got up and went to Zarephath. When he arrived at the town gate, there was a widow gathering sticks of wood to make a fire. Elijah called out to her, "Would you please being me a little water in a cup, so that I could have a drink?" As she was going to get his water, Elijah also called out, "And, please bring me a piece of bread, too."

The woman answered, "As surely as the Lord your God lives—I tell you the truth—I have no bread. I have only a handful of flour in a jar. And, I have only a little cooking oil in a jug. I came here to gather some wood. I was going to take it home and cook our last meal. My son and I were planning to eat it, after that, we'll starve to death."

Elijah said to her, "Don't be afraid. Go home and cook your food, just as you have said. But first, make a little loaf of bread from the flour you have and bring it to me. Afterward, cook something for yourself and your son. This is what the Lord, the God of Israel, says: 'That jar of flour will never become empty. And, the jug will always have oil in it. This will continue until the day when the Lord sends rain upon the land.'"

So the woman went home, and did what Elijah told her to do. The woman and Elijah—and her household—had enough food for many days. The jar of flour was never empty, and the jug always had oil in it. This happened just as the Lord said it would happen by the hand of Elijah.

Sometime later, the son of the woman who owned that house became sick. He got worse and worse. Finally, he stopped breathing. So the woman said to Elijah, "You are a man of the one true God. What do we have in common? Did you come here to remind me of my sin? Did you come here to kill my son?"

Elijah said to her, "Give me your son." So, Elijah took the boy from her arms and he carried him upstairs. Elijah laid the boy on the bed in the room where he was staying. Then Elijah prayed to the Lord, saying, "O Lord Who Is Always Present, my God, this widow has been letting me stay in her home. Why have You brought this tragedy to her? Why have You caused her son to die?" Then Elijah lay down on top of the boy three times. Elijah called out to the Lord: "O Lord Who Is Always Present, my God, please let this boy live again."

And the Lord did answer Elijah's prayer. The boy began breathing again. He was alive. Then Elijah carried the boy downstairs in the house, and gave the boy back to his mother and said, "Look, your son is alive."

The woman said to Elijah, "Now I know that you really are a man of God. I know that the Lord truly speaks through you."

My Time to Pray

Prayer Answered

The effective, fervent prayer of a righteous man avails much. Elijah was a man with a nature like ours, and he prayed earnestly that it would not rain; and it did not rain on the land for three years and six months. And he prayed again, and the heaven gave rain, and the earth produced its fruit (James 5:16-18).

The *Old* Testament says Elijah told King Ahab, *"There will be no rain or dew..."* (1 Kings 17:1), yet the *New* Testament adds, *"He prayed earnestly that it would not rain"* (James 5:17). Both actions took place. Elijah prayed in *private* to fulfill God's will, no rain. Elijah spoke boldly in *public* based on what God told him and how he prayed. We should learn to "say" what we want from God when we are sure it is God's will. *"If you have faith as a grain of mustard seed, you will say to this mountain, 'Move from here to there,' and it will move"* (Matt. 17:20). *Lord, give me faith to pray confidently and **privately** based on the promises You made in Scripture. Then I will say in **public** how You will answer.*

In First Kings 17:1, Elijah says there will be no rain for three years. Yet in James 5:17 it didn't rain for three and a half years. There is no problem with chronology here. God sends a famine to punish His people, it had not rained for half a year when Elijah prayed. There is a spiritual lesson of faith here. When you are in a drought, you don't pray for the heavens to dry up as it had already done for six months. Why? Because the cycle of rain suggests it may start raining any day. The fact Elijah prayed to shut up Heaven longer demonstrates his faith. Elijah was praying what God wanted him to ask. *Lord, help me look only to You when I pray, and not keep my eye on the weather forecast. I will pray according to Your Word, not according to circumstances.*

When everyone was suffering from a famine, God providentially supplied the needs of His servant. Elijah had water to drink from a mountain stream, and the ravens brought him food in the morning and evening. *Lord, I will not look to the stock market, nor to jobs to provide for my needs. I look to You. Yet, I'll not be lazy and refuse to work, teach me faith's balance—to trust You to supply my needs as I work daily at the jobs You give me.*

Sometimes when things are bad, they will not get better; things will get worse. God led Elijah to a creek in the mountains, then the creek dried up. Next God led Elijah to a widow in Zarephath. She didn't have anything but a little meal, then she planned to die. The word *Zarephath* means "crucible." God took Elijah from a hard place in the mountains and put him in the fire, the crucible. *Lord, I'll not complain when things are bad, because they can get worse. I'll trust You in both hard days and in days when things go from bad to worse. Trust is an attitude that's not dependent on circumstances, so I will always trust You in spite of the circumstances.*

The widow was from Phoenicia (today's Lebanon) and apparently had head knowledge of *Jehovah,* the God of Israel. Yet she trusted in Jehovah perhaps because there was no one else to trust for food. She had head knowledge, not heart commitment. Is that you, with only a *profession* of salvation without *possession* of salvation? After her son was resuscitated, she became a believer. *"Now I know"* (1 Kings 17:24). *Lord, I believe in You, not because of the story of the widow's son being raised from the dead, but because Your Son—Jesus Christ—was raised from the dead and lives in my heart. Amen.*

22

ELIJAH CONFRONTS KING AHAB

First Kings 18

Three long years had passed, and there was still no rain. Then the Lord spoke His word to Elijah, saying, "Go, show yourself to Ahab. I am about to send rain." So Elijah went to meet Ahab.

By this time, there was almost no food left in Samaria. So, King Ahab summoned Obadiah, who was in charge of the king's palace. Obadiah was a true follower of the Lord. Previously, Jezebel was killing all of the Lord's prophets, so Obadiah took 100 of them and hid them in two caves. He put 50 in one cave and 50 in another cave. And he brought them food and water.

King Ahab said to Obadiah, "Let's go look at every spring and brook in the land. Maybe we can find enough grass to keep our horses and mules alive. Then we will not have to kill our animals." So, each one chose a part of the country to search. Ahab went in one direction separately. Obadiah went in another direction.

While Obadiah was walking along, Elijah met him. Obadiah knew who Elijah was. So, he bowed face-down on the ground before Elijah, saying, "Elijah? Is it really you, my master?"

Elijah answered him, "Yes. Go, tell your master the king that I am here."

Then Obadiah said, "If I tell Ahab that, then he will kill me. I have done nothing wrong that I should be killed. As surely as the Lord, your

God, lives; the king has looked everywhere for you. He has sent
people to every country to look for you. If the ruler said you were
not there, that was not enough. Ahab then forced that ruler to
swear that you could not be found in his country. Now, you want
me to go to my master and tell him: 'Elijah is here?' The Spirit
of the Lord may carry you to some other place after I leave. If I
go to tell King Ahab that you are here, then he will come. If he
doesn't find you, then he will kill me. I have followed the Lord
since I was a boy. Haven't you heard what I did? When Jezebel
was killing the Lord's prophets, I hid 100 of them. I put 50
prophets in one cave and 50 prophets in another cave. I brought
them food and water. Now, you want me to go and tell the king
that you are here? He will kill me."

Elijah answered, "I serve the Lord of the armies of Heaven. As surely as
the Lord lives, I will show myself before Ahab today."

So, Obadiah went to Ahab and told him where Elijah was. Then Ahab
went to meet Elijah.

When Ahab saw Elijah, Ahab said to him, "Is it you, the biggest
troublemaker in Israel?"

Elijah answered, "I am not the one who has caused trouble for Israel. It
is you and your father's dynasty that have caused all this trouble.
You have abandoned the commands of the Lord. You have
followed the Baals. Now, tell all Israel (probably referring only to
the main leaders of the northern kingdom of Israel) to meet me
at Mount Carmel. (The whole ridge is 12 miles long, but at its
north-northwest extremity is a bold peak of 600 feet overlooking
the Mediterranean Sea. Toward the east, there is a panoramic
view of the entire Valley of Armageddon. So, this spot was the
perfect outdoor "pulpit" for one of God's greatest prophets. Near
the top, there is a flat place that is large enough to accommodate
a large crowd.) Gather the 450 prophets of Baal there. (This

shows the great extent to which the Baal fertility cult had permeated Israel's religion.) And, bring the 400 prophets of Asherah, too. They are supported from the rich supply of food from Jezebel's table."

God Prevails Over Baal

So, Ahab summoned all the Israelites, and Ahab gathered those false prophets to Mount Carmel. Elijah stood in front of all the people and said, "How long will you people try to serve both Baal and the Lord? If the Lord is the one true God, follow Him. But if Baal is the true god, follow him."

The people said nothing.

Elijah said to them, "I am the only prophet of the Lord here. But there are 450 prophets of Baal. So, bring us two bulls. And, let the prophets of Baal choose one bull for them. Let them kill it and butcher it. Then, let them put the meat on the wood. However, they must not set fire to it. Then I will do the same thing with the other bull—I'll lay it on the wood, but I won't set fire to it, either. Then you prophets of Baal should pray to your god Baal. And I, I will pray to the Lord. The one who answers will set fire to the wood supernaturally—He is the one true God."

All the people agreed that this was a good idea.

Then Elijah said to the false prophets of Baal, "There are so many of you. So, you men go first. Choose a bull and prepare it. Pray to your god, but do not start the fire."

So, they took the bull that someone gave them and prepared it. Then they prayed to Baal from morning until noon. They cried out: "O Baal, answer us." But there was no sound. No one answered. They danced around the altar that they had built.

At noon, Elijah began to mock them. He said, "Pray louder! If Baal really
is a god, maybe he is preoccupied with thinking about something
else. Or, maybe he is busy...or he is gone away on a trip?
Perhaps he's asleep? You might have to wake him up."

So, the false prophets prayed even louder. They even cut themselves
with swords and spears until their blood flowed out on them.
This was the way they usually worshiped. (This sort of thing was
forbidden by the Law of Moses [see Lev. 19:28; Deut. 14:1].)
The middle of the day passed. The prophets of Baal were acting
like wild men. They continued doing this until it was time for
offering the evening sacrifice (3 P.M.). But no sound came from
Baal. Baal did not answer. Baal paid *no* attention.

Then Elijah spoke to all the people, "Come here to me." So they all
gathered around him. And Elijah rebuilt the altar of the Lord
because it had been torn down. And Elijah took 12 stones—the
12 stones represented the 12 tribes of the 12 sons of Jacob.
Jacob was the man to whom the Lord said: "Your name will
be 'Israel.'" Then Elijah used these stones to rebuild the altar
in honor of the Lord. Then he dug a small ditch around it big
enough to hold almost three gallons of seed. Elijah arranged the
wood on the altar, butchered his bull, and laid the pieces of meat
on the wood. Then Elijah said, "Fill four big jars with water. Pour
the water on top of the meat and on the wood." They did it.

Then Elijah said, "Do it again." And they did it again.

Then he said, "Do it a third time." And they did it the third time. So, the
water ran off the altar and filled up the ditch.

It was now time for the evening sacrifice. So the true prophet Elijah
went near the altar. He prayed: "O Lord Who Is Always Present,
You are the God of Abraham, Isaac, and Israel. I ask You today
to prove that *You* are the true God in the nation of Israel.
And, prove that I am Your servant. Show these people that You

commanded me to do all these things. O Lord Who Is Always Present, answer me. Answer my prayer. Show these people that *You*, O Lord Who Is Always Present, are the one true God! Then the people will know that You are bringing them back to You again." (This Hebrew perfect tense is to be taken as a prophetic perfect tense, which means that the future will certainly be fulfilled—the action is as good as done.)

Suddenly, the fire of the Lord came down and burned up the meat sacrifice, the wood, the stones, and the soil around the altar. It also dried up all the water in the ditch. When all the people witnessed this, they fell face down to the ground. They cried out, "The Lord, *He* is the one true God. The Lord, *He* is the one true God."

Then Elijah told them, "Seize the prophets of Baal. Do not let any of them run away." So the people captured all those prophets. Then Elijah led them down to Kishon Brook, where he executed all the false prophets (according to the punishment prescribed by the Law of Moses for false prophets [see Deut. 13:13-18; 17:2-5]).

The End of the Drought

Then Elijah said to Ahab, "Now, go, eat and drink. I hear the sound of a heavy rain." So, King Ahab went to eat and drink. At the same time, Elijah climbed to the top of Mount Carmel. There Elijah stretched out on the ground with his head between his knees.

Then Elijah said to his servant, "Please go up and look toward the Mediterranean Sea."

The servant went up and looked. He said, "I don't see anything."

Elijah told him to go back and look again. This happened seven times. On the seventh time, the servant said, "Look, I see a tiny cloud the size of a man's fist. It's coming up from the sea."

Elijah told the servant, "Go tell King Ahab to get his chariot ready and go down *now*. If Ahab doesn't leave now, the rain will stop him."

After a short time, the sky became black with dark clouds, and the wind began to blow. Then a heavy rain began to fall immediately, Ahab got in his chariot and started back to Jezreel (about 10 miles away). The Lord gave His power to Elijah so that he tightened his clothes around him and ran ahead of King Ahab all the way to Jezreel.

My Time to Pray

And it came to pass after many days that the word of the Lord came to Elijah, in the third year, saying, "Go, present yourself to Ahab, and I will send rain on the earth" (1 Kings 18:1).

Notice how God uses time. He allowed Israel to suffer a famine for three and a half years (see James 5:17). God usually touches us in the pocketbook to get our attention. So God moved Elijah to "shut up Heaven" to bring conviction of sin on the nation. Will God send a recession or depression on the United States for its sin? If so, God doesn't answer to remove His punishment until His people repent deeply and completely. It was so bad in Israel that the king went out personally to search for water (see 1 Kings 18:5-6). If the king had searched for the Lord, he might have found water much sooner. *Lord, when You punish me, I will search for You quickly and seriously. I will repent and pray sincerely for You to pour Your Holy Spirit on Your people.*

God has patience, He will wait for His people to seek His presence. Yes God loves, and it's difficult for a God of love to punish His people.

But also, God is holy, and a holy God can't look on the sin of His people. Israel was guilty of the worst sin of all—idolatry. So God waited while the people suffered. Time is always on God's side. I get time on my side when I get on God's side. *Lord, I yield to Your will and I will wait patiently for You to work in my life. Lord, hold back Your hand of punishment on my nation. I will fast and pray for national revival.*

The people were looking for water, but the Lord sent fire. What does that say? Sometimes we pray deeply about the thing that hurts us more. But God is concerned about His primary concern—worship. We pray about the crushing need of money or the pain of sickness. Or alienation from friends or people. But God wants a relationship with us, *"The Father seeks worship"* (John 4:23 ELT). So Elijah prayed and God sent fire. Then the people worshiped. *Lord, don't send me the things I request that are selfish and ill-requested. Lord, send me Your will. Lord, send me the things that will be used of You and will glorify Your name.*

Fire was a symbol of God's judgment. God judged Sodom and Gomorrah with *"fire from the Lord"* (Gen. 19:24). When God appeared to Moses, it was in the flames of a burning bush (see Exod. 3:2). He will finally judge the world in fire (see 2 Pet. 3:7). God was telling Israel that He would judge their sins. *Lord, I repent of my sin, I don't want Your punishment in my life. Cleanse me by the blood of Christ.*

Again, look at how God used time. Apparently the prophets of Baal began at 9 A.M. and prayed until 3 P.M. Six hours! But Baal didn't answer. Elijah was waiting calmly and patiently for the Baal-prayer-intercessors to do their thing. Elijah wasn't worried; he knew there was no real person named Baal. He knew Baal wouldn't answer. Elijah waited, just like God waits. God allows us to try our false religion and our human ways. God waits for us to come to Him in His prescribed way. So finally at 3 P.M., Elijah began to approach God in the right way. *Lord, I will come to You in the right way, with the right motives of my heart. I will come to You sincerely as You prescribed in Scripture.*

It takes patience to reverse God's punishment. It hadn't rained for three and a half years. So Elijah put his head between his knees to pray—complete humility and sincerity. Then he prayed seven times. No one quick "word of prayer" would turn around God's judgment. Finally the answer came "a cloud about the size of a man's fist." *Lord, give me patience to pray sincerely and continually. Help me to "pray without ceasing" (1 Thess. 5:17). When I see Your answer coming in a small way, help me to keep on praying. When I see Your answer coming slowly, help me keep on praying.*

It seems severe for Elijah to execute the false prophets. We don't do that in the world today. Yet that is the way God dealt with heresy and apostasy in the dispensation of the Law because God was dealing with His people, the Jews (see Deut. 13:13-18;17:2-5). God was dealing primarily with the nation of Israel and He wanted to keep it pure. Today in the dispensation of Grace, God is dealing with Gentiles in all nations. God doesn't execute a person for heresy today, but they will pay the same price in hell. *Lord, help me see the world through Your eyes. Help me see heresy through Your eyes. Because You hate heresy, I want to be as doctrinally pure as possible.*

Ahab was blind to what God was doing. Ahab accused Elijah, "Are you he who is troubling Israel?" Ahab was mistakenly attributing the lack of rain to Elijah, as he failed to see the judgment of God on the nations of Israel because of their sin. God sent the judgment; Elijah was just the instrument God used when Elijah prayed to shut up Heaven. Isn't it true the world blames Christians for what God is doing in their lives? *Lord, I will live godly to be a good testimony to the world. When the world criticizes me, may I be blameless.*

There was a spiritual battle between Elijah and the prophets of Baal, but it really was between God and satan. The issue: who was the real God. There was no issue in Heaven; all angels knew the Lord was God and that satan was a rebel against God. Satan wants to take God's place, but he cannot, nor will he ever do it. *Lord, I know You are the God of creation, You own all the universe. Come be Lord of my life and rule everything I have.*

If Baal were truly a god, he should have had an advantage. There were 850 to 1, advantage Baal. There was the government of Israel and its power versus a lone prophet, advantage Baal. But Elijah represented the omniscient Lord God, versus Baal, advantage Elijah. *Lord, teach me that one plus God is a majority. Give me courage to stand for You, as did Elijah.*

Where were the 100 prophets of the true Lord hidden by Obadiah? Elijah stood alone. It would have been nice if some of the 100 stood with Elijah. But there are believers who are timid and there are believers who are courageous. Which one are you? *Lord, I will stand for You, no matter what other believers do. Even if no one stands with me, I will stand alone.*

Notice the emptiness of Baal worship. Elijah—knowing he was right—mocked the Baal worshipers: "Cry aloud" and "perhaps he is talking," and "he is on a journey," and "he is sleeping." (Contrast that to the Lord who never sleeps, see Ps. 121:3-4.) Then the prophets of Baal jumped in excitement, but nothing happened. Finally, they submitted to self-torture; they slashed themselves. (Were they thinking spilt blood got their god's attention?) *Lord, I know there is nothing in false religion, and prayers to false gods are not answered. You, Lord, are the only God.*

Remember, God has a history of responding in fire. When Elijah prayed, "The fire of the Lord fell." God had visited the Temple dedication in fire (see 2 Chron. 7:1). Also, fire fell on the believers at Pentecost. While we don't have actual fire falling on us today, we do seek purifying fire when we sin, and evangelistic fire when we win souls, and worshiping fire when we praise and exalt His name in adoration—just as God did for Solomon when dedicating the Temple. *Lord, send fire to cleanse me when I sin, send soul-winning fire when the gospel is preached to the unsaved, and send worshiping fire when we praise You. Amen.*

23

Elijah Runs Away to Mount Horeb

First Kings 19

King Ahab told Jezebel everything that Elijah had done, how Elijah had killed all the prophets with a sword. So Jezebel sent a messenger to Elijah, saying, "By this time tomorrow, I will kill you. I will kill you, just as you killed those prophets. If I don't succeed, may the gods punish me terribly."

When Elijah heard this, he was afraid. (He realized how weak Ahab was as king, that Ahab was not going to take the Israelite government away from his pagan wife. Elijah became very discouraged and fell into a deep depression. Elijah felt that he needed to get out of a hopeless situation in Israel.) So, he and his servant ran away to save their lives. When they came to Beer-Sheba in Judah (95 miles from Jezreel), Elijah left his servant there. (Elijah wanted to be alone with God.) Then Elijah walked for a whole day into the desert. (Elijah wanted to be out of Jezebel's reach.) He sat down under a broom tree and asked God, "Let me die." (Completely exhausted, his depression finally reached its lowest point.) Elijah prayed: "It is too much! Now, O Lord Who Is Always Present, take my life, because I am no better than my ancestors." Then Elijah lay down under the broom tree and slept.

Suddenly, an angel came to him and touched him. The angel said, "Get up and eat." Near his head, Elijah saw a loaf baked over coals and a jar of water. So he ate and drank. Then he went back to sleep.

Later, the Lord's angel came to him a second time. The angel touched him and said, "Get up and eat. If you don't, then the journey will be too hard for you." So Elijah got up and ate and drank. The food made him strong enough to walk for 40 days and nights. He walked to Mount Sinai (the names Horeb and Sinai are used interchangeably because Horeb is a range of mountains, and Sinai is a peak), the mountain of the one true God.

The Lord Speaks to Elijah

There Elijah went into a cave and stayed all night. And, the Lord spoke His word to him: "Elijah! Why are you here?"

Elijah answered, "O Lord Who Is Always Present, the God of the armies of Heaven, I have always served You the best I could. But the people of Israel have broken their covenant with You. They have torn down Your altars. They have killed Your prophets with swords. I am the only true prophet left. And now, they are trying to kill me, too."

Then the Lord said to Elijah, "Go, stand in front of Me on the mountain. Behold, I will pass by You."

Then a very strong wind blew. It caused the mountains to break apart. It tore up large rocks in the presence of the Lord. But the Lord was not in the wind. After the wind, there was an earthquake. But the Lord was not in the earthquake. After the earthquake there was a fire. But the Lord was not in the fire. After the fire, there was a still, small voice.

When Elijah heard this, he covered his face with his coat. He went out and stood at the entrance to the cave. Then, a Voice said to him, "Elijah, why are you here?"

Elijah answered, "O Lord Who Is Always Present, the God of the armies of Heaven, I have always served You the best I could. But the people of Israel have broken their covenant with You. They have torn down Your altars. They have killed Your prophets with swords. I am the only true prophet left. And now, they are trying to kill me, too."

The Lord said to him, "Go back on the road south of Damascus. Enter that city, and consecrate (pour olive oil on) Hazael (Hazael reigned from 841 to 798 B.C.) to make him king over Syria. Then pour oil on Jehu, the grandson of Nimshi, to make him king over Israel. Later, pour oil on Elisha, the son of Shaphat, from Abel-Meholah. He will be a prophet in your place. Jehu will kill anyone who escapes from Hazael's sword. And, Elisha will doom anyone who escapes from Jehu's sword. But I have reserved 7,000 people living in Israel. (These people needed Elijah's leadership.) Those 7,000 have never bowed down in front of Baal. Their mouths have never kissed his idol."

Elisha Serves Elijah

So, Elijah left there and found Elisha, the son of Shaphat. Elisha was plowing a field with a team of oxen. There were 11 teams of oxen ahead of him (indicating Shaphat was a rich man). Elisha was plowing with the twelfth team of oxen. Elijah came up to Elisha, took off his coat, and put it on Elisha. (Elijah's power was being transferred to the new prophet, Elisha.) Then Elisha left his oxen and ran to follow Elijah. Elisha said, "Please let me kiss my father and my mother goodbye. Then I will go with you."

Elijah answered, "Go on. Return. I won't stop you." So, Elisha went back to his oxen and his workers. He took his pair of oxen and killed them. He used the wooden yoke for the fire. Then he cooked the meat and gave it to the people, and they ate it. Then Elisha went and followed Elijah and became his helper.

My Time to Pray

Staying Strong

What are you doing here, Elijah? (1 Kings 19:9 NLT)

Everyone gets tired, that was Elijah's problem. When we get tired we are vulnerable to satan's temptation and attacks. Perhaps because we don't have a reserve of physical strength to resist the evil one. Elijah traveled 95 miles, probably walking two days and nights. Physically exhausted, he prayed, "Let me die." Physical exhaustion can lead to emotional depression. When we reach the lowest point, we give up, some even pray to die. *Lord, help me realize I need food and rest to be physically strong so I can remain spiritually strong. I will look after the needs of my body.*

Have you noticed how God doesn't answer some of our foolish prayers we make to Him? Elijah asked God to die. There is no record that God said, "No," although God may have audibly told Elijah, "No." God had something better for Elijah. So remember, when God tells you, "No," He may have something better for you. I can hear God in Heaven saying, "How about a chariot and whirlwind? How about coming home without dying?" When God tells you, "No," He may have something much better than death. *Lord, I want Your best for my life.*

Everyone fails. Elijah felt he had failed because he was looking at things from human eyes, not the Lord's perspective. Elijah wanted the contest on Mount Carmel to prove to the Israelites beyond the shadow of a doubt that the Lord who answered by fire was the true God. When Jezebel sent word that she would kill him, it made Elijah realize that he couldn't turn around the nation's government. Ahab was not the power, it was Jezebel. Since Elijah knew he couldn't do anything greater than what he did on Mount Carmel, all was lost. He had not turned the nation around. So he sat down to mope and pray, "God kill me." *Lord, keep me from discouragement and despondency. Help me look at everything in life through Your eyes, not through my eyes. Keep me from doubt and fear.*

Have you noticed how God usually asks a question, rather than making a divine pronouncement that we are evil or backsliding? God asked Adam, "Where are you?" God knew where Adam was, God wanted Adam to realize his desperate spiritual condition. So God asked Elijah, "Why are you here?" God knew the fear and uncertainty of Elijah's heart. God wanted Elijah to examine his motives to see his problem as God saw it. *Lord, help me look at my problems and weaknesses. Lord, help me see my weak spiritual condition and do something about it. Lord, thank You for questioning me to give me a chance to repent.*

Have you ever pitied yourself? Elijah thought he was the only one who served God. So he ran away and hid in a cave. Have you ever thought that people were out to get you, so you were paranoid? Elijah said "they" were trying to kill him, when only Jezebel was the one with murder in her heart. *Lord, I confess to my sin of feeling sorry for myself. I look at my problem rather than looking to You and searching for Your solutions to my predicament.*

Did you see how God dealt with Elijah? God didn't shout, nor did God do another extraordinary miracle like He did at Mount Carmel. This time God spoke in the quiet stillness of a cave. God spoke softly. Sometimes when we're running from God, He will shout or trip us up. Has God done that to you? Sometimes when we're discouraged over our failures, God comes with a soft voice to speak quietly to our heart. *Lord, I will listen for Your whisper. Come to me in the darkness of my lonely night and speak to me in quietness. Lord, when I'm seeking answers from You... speak.*

One of the best ways to break up discouragement or hopelessness is with work. When we've got something to do, we have purpose in life. We have self-worth and meaning. God gave three tasks to His discouraged prophet. First, anoint Hazael as King of Syria. Second, anoint Jehu king over Israel, and third, anoint Elisha to take his place. *Lord, thank You for all the commands in the Bible to serve You. It's a privilege to serve the Lord God. You give me hope and encouragement with work. May I never get so low that I won't serve You. Amen.*

24

Syria and Israel at War

First Kings 20

Now Ben-Hadad (not a name, but a title, like president of the United States, this particular one was probably Ben-Hadad I [circa 909 to 885 B.C.]) was the king of Syria. He gathered together all of his army. There were 32 rulers with their horses and chariots. They went with him and surrounded Samaria and attacked it. The king sent messengers into the city to Ahab, the king of Israel, "Ben-Hadad says, 'Your silver and gold now belong to me. You must also surrender the best of your wives and your children.'"

Ahab, the king of Israel, answered, "O my master and king, I agree to what you say. I—and everything I have—belong to you."

Then the messengers came to Ahab again, "Ben-Hadad says: 'I sent a message to demand that you must give your silver and gold, your wives, and your children to me. About this time tomorrow, I am going to send my officials to you. They will search everywhere in your palace and the homes of your officials. My men will take away anything they want.'"

So, Ahab, king of Israel, called a meeting of all the elders of his country. He said, "See how Ben-Hadad is trying to ruin us? First, he demanded that I give him my wives, my children, my silver, and my gold. I agreed to that."

But the elders and all the people said to Ahab, "Pay no attention to Ben-Hadad. Don't do anything he says."

So, Ahab said to Ben-Hadad's messengers, "Say this to your master, the king: 'I will do everything that you said at first. But I cannot obey your second command.'" So, Ben-Hadad's men carried Ahab's answer back to Ben-Hadad.

Then Ben-Hadad sent another message to Ahab: "I will demolish Samaria. There won't even be enough of it left for each of my men to get a handful of dust. May the gods punish me terribly, if I don't do this."

Ahab, the king of Israel, answered, "Say this to Ben-Hadad: 'The man who puts *on* his armor should not brag too soon. The one who has the right to brag is the man who lives long enough to take *off* his armor.'"

Now Ben-Hadad was drinking alcohol in his hut along with the other rulers. They heard the response from Ahab. Then Ben-Hadad ordered his men: "Prepare to attack the city." So, they moved into position for battle.

And, a prophet approached Ahab, the king of Israel. The prophet said, "The Lord says to you: 'Do you see that huge army? I am handing it over to you today. Then you will know that I am the Lord.'"

Ahab said, "How will God do it?"

The prophet answered, "The Lord says: 'The young officers of the district governors will defeat them.'"

Then the king asked, "Who will join the battle?"

The prophet answered, "You."

So, Ahab gathered the young officers of the district governors (inexperienced assistants). There were 232 of them. Then Ahab called together the whole army of Israel. There was a total of 7,000 of them.

Ben-Hadad and his 32 allied rulers were getting drunk in their tents. It was noon when Ahab's troops began the attack. The young officers of the district governors attacked first.

Ben-Hadad's scouts told him that some soldiers were coming out of the city of Samaria. So Ben-Hadad said, "They may be coming out to fight, or they might be coming out to ask us for terms of peace. In either case, capture them alive."

The young officers of the district governors marched out of the city with the army of Israel right behind them. Then each Israelite soldier killed every man whom they encountered. The Syrians ran away, and Israel chased them. But Ben-Hadad, the king of Syria, escaped on a horse with some of his horsemen. Ahab, the king of Israel, went out and captured the Syrian horses and chariots. So, King Ahab inflicted heavy losses upon the Syrian army.

Then the prophet (Micaiah, the son of Imlah) went to Ahab, the king of Israel, and said to him, "The king of Syria will attack you again next spring. So, you should go home now and make your army stronger. Get ready to defend yourself."

Meanwhile, the officers of Ben-Hadad, the king of Syria, advised him: "The gods of Israel are gods of the mountains. Therefore, the Israelites were stronger than us. However, if we fight them on flat land (where the chariots of the Syrians would be effective) then we will certainly beat them. This is what you should do: Remove each of the 32 political rulers from being in command of their armies. Instead, put military commanders in their places. Raise yourself another army like the one that deserted you. Gather just as many horses and chariots as you had before. Let us fight the

Israelites on flat land. This time, we will have the advantage."
Ben-Hadad was convinced, and did what they advised.

The next spring, Ben-Hadad gathered the Syrian army. He went up to
Aphek (a high, level plain) to fight against Israel.

The Israelites also prepared for war. They marched out to meet the
Syrians and camped opposite them. The Israelites looked like
two small flocks of goats. But the Syrians completely covered the
countryside.

A man of the one true God approached the king of Israel with this
message: "The Lord says: 'The people of Syria say that I, the
Lord, am a god of the mountains. They think I am not a god
of the valleys. Therefore, I will hand this vast army over to you.
Then you and your people will know that I am the Lord.'"

For one week, the two armies were camped across from each other. On
the seventh day, they started the fighting. The Israelites killed
100,000 Syrian soldiers in one day. The rest of the Syrians ran
away to the city of Aphek. There a city wall fell on 27,000 of
them. And, Ben-Hadad escaped to a stronghold and hid within
an inner chamber. His officers said to him, "Now listen, we have
heard that the kings of the nation of Israel are merciful. Please
let us put on rough cloth (sackcloth) on our bodies, and let us
wear ropes around our necks (a sign of surrender, their lives were
completely at the disposal of King Ahab). Then let's go to the
king of Israel. Perhaps he will let you live?"

So, the officers dressed up in rough cloth, and wore ropes around
their necks. Then they went to the king of Israel and said, "Your
servant Ben-Hadad says: 'Please spare my life.'"

Ahab answered, "Is he still alive? (Ahab thought that Ben-Hadad had
been slain during the battle.) He's my brother."

Now Ben-Hadad's men picked up on this word, "brother." They were quick to realize that Ahab might not kill Ben-Hadad. So, they quickly agreed, "Yes, Ben-Hadad is your brother."

Ahab said, "Go get him; bring him to me." When Ben-Hadad came out to him, Ahab invited him to join Ahab in the chariot.

Ben-Hadad said to him, "O Ahab, I will restore to you the towns which my father took away from your father. And, you will be permitted to put in your own shops in Damascus, like my father once set up in the city of Samaria."

Ahab answered, "If you agree to this pact, I will let you go free." So the two kings made a peace treaty. Then Ahab let Ben-Hadad go free.

A Prophet Condemns King Ahab

By the word of the Lord, one of the prophets told another prophet, "Please hit me." But the man refused to hit him.

So the first prophet said to the second prophet, "Because you did not obey the Lord's command, a lion will kill you as soon as you leave me." When the second prophet left him, a lion found him and killed him.

Then the first prophet went to another man and said, "Hit me, please." So the man hit him and wounded him. Then the first prophet wrapped his face in bandages, so that no one could recognize who he was. Then he went and waited beside the road for the king of Israel to pass. As Ahab, the king, passed by, the prophet called out to him and said, "I went out into the thick of the battle to fight. And, look, a man turned aside and brought a captured, enemy soldier to me and said, 'Guard this man. If he escapes, then you must give your life in his place. Or else, you will have to pay a fine of 75 pounds of silver.' However, I became busy doing other things. And, the man escaped."

The King of Israel answered, "You have said what the punishment was going to be. You must pay the penalty."

Then the prophet quickly took away the covering from his face. When the king of Israel recognized him, he knew that he was one of the prophets.

Then the prophet said to the king, "This is what the Lord says: 'You set free the man whom I said should die. Therefore, your life will be exchanged for his life. And, the lives of your people will be exchanged for the lives of his people.'"

Then Ahab, the king of Israel, went back to his palace in the city of Samaria. He was very angry and upset.

My Time to Pray

Victory With God

Let not the one who puts on his armor boast like the one who takes it off (1 Kings 20:11).

There's a basic lesson about boasting here. Don't boast about a victory until you win the battle. Ben-Hadad had a much larger army, but didn't win the battle. With a much smaller army, Israel won the battle, or should we say: God gave Israel the victory. So when we're in spiritual warfare, never boast. It's God who gave the victory. *Lord, You are my strength and wisdom. I know I win battles in Your strength and with Your guidance. Thank You for Your presence in my life. I do not boast in myself, I glory in Your protection.*

Many times an athletic team will yell, "We're number one" or a team will boast in their ability. They do it to lift their expectation, or to give them an edge in competition. They even do it to get their adrenaline pumping. But the child of God doesn't need internal stimuli to get ready for battle. He has the inner Holy Spirit to guide and prepare him. He has the indwelling Holy Spirit to protect him. *Lord, I ask in prayer for You to be with me in spiritual warfare. Equip me for every conflict I must face. Guide me, protect me, and keep me in battle.*

Remember, God is omnipresent in space and time. He is equally present in all places at all times. Therefore, God stands now at the place and time of your next battle. He knows the outcome, so put your trust in God to fight with you, in you, and through you. *Lord, You know what will happen in my next battle, and You know what will be the outcome. I put my trust in You, and trust the outcome to You.*

When running a race, we should never stop before we reach the finish line, and when we are fighting a battle, we should never quit before final victory. Ahab didn't win total victory because he didn't execute Ben-Hadad. Big mistake! The nation would suffer because of Ahab's disobedience. Sometimes both we and others suffer because we do a sloppy job or a half-hearted job. *Lord, convict me when I don't do the best I can possibly do, and Holy Spirit guide me to do the best in all that I do.*

There's another lesson about using people for political purpose, as opposed to letting people serve because they are gifted and trained to do the job. Ahab used 232 young officers to win a decisive victory over Syria. Syria did the same thing but it *didn't* work for Syria. *Lord, I will spend my life doing what You gifted me to do, and serving where I am trained to serve. I want to be as effective as possible for Your glory. Amen.*

25

THE VINEYARD OF NABOTH

First Kings 21

Now Naboth lived in a vineyard in Jezreel, next to the palace of Ahab, the king of Samaria. One day, Ahab said to Naboth, "Let me have your vineyard, since it is next to my palace, I want to turn it into my vegetable garden. I will give you a better vineyard for it. Or, if you prefer, I will pay you what it is worth."

But Naboth answered Ahab, "No. The Lord would never permit me to sell the land to you (the Promised Land belonged to God, and He had granted a perpetual lease to each Israelite family as permanent inheritance [see Lev. 25:23-28; Num. 36:7]). It has been in my family for generations."

Ahab went home angry and very upset. He didn't like what Naboth of Jezreel had said to him: "I will not give up the land inheritance of my forefathers to you." Then Ahab lay down on his bed, and turned away his face, and refused to eat.

His wife Jezebel asked him, "Why are you so upset? Why are you refusing to eat?"

Ahab answered her, "…because I talked to Naboth of Jezreel. I asked him to sell me his vineyard. Or, if he chose, I wanted him to let me find another vineyard for him…but he refused." Then Jezebel, his wife, said to him, "Is this the way that you rule as king over

Israel? Get up. Cheer up. Eat something. I will get Naboth's vineyard for you."

So, using Ahab's name, Jezebel wrote some letters. And she stamped (making it an official document when the signet ring was pressed against the document) them with the official seal of King Ahab. Then she sent the letters to the elders and the important men who lived in Naboth's town with him. This is what she wrote in the letters: "Call all the people together. Announce a special day when people must fast. (She wanted the people to think that this disaster could only be prevented if the culprit could be found and removed.) And give Naboth a seat of honor among them. Put two men (the Law of Moses required two witnesses in capital offenses [see Num. 35:30; Deut. 17:6; 19:15]), troublemakers, across from him. Let them testify against Naboth, saying, 'You have cursed God and the king.' Then they must take Naboth out of town and kill him by throwing stones at him."

So, the men of Naboth's town—the elders and the important men who lived in his town—did these things. They followed the exact instructions that Queen Jezebel had sent to them in the letters. They called the people together. They declared a special day for fasting. And, they put Naboth in the seat of honor, in a prominent place among the people. Then, two men (the troublemakers) came and sat across from Naboth. And, in front of the people, the troublemakers accused Naboth: "Naboth has cursed God and the king." So the townspeople brought Naboth out of that town, and they threw rocks at Naboth until he was dead. Then the leaders of the town sent a message to Queen Jezebel. It said: "Naboth has been stoned. He's dead."

When Jezebel heard that Naboth had been stoned to death, she informed Ahab, "Naboth of Israel is no longer alive. Get up. Take possession of Naboth's vineyard. He wouldn't sell it to you for money, but he's dead now." As soon as Ahab heard that Naboth was dead, he left to go down to Naboth's vineyard in Jezreel to take it for himself. (It was now considered "forfeited" to the crown.)

But, the word of the Lord came to Elijah, the prophet from Tishbeh. The Lord said: "Get up and go down to meet Ahab, the king of Israel; he is in Samaria at Naboth's vineyard; he has gone down there to take possession of it. Tell Ahab: 'This is what the Lord says: "You have committed murder and stolen land. So, I tell you this: 'The dogs that licked up Naboth's blood will lick up your blood in the same vicinity.'" (Ahab was later killed in battle at Ramoth-Gilead [see 1 Kings 22:29-37], and his body was brought to Samaria where the dogs did lick the blood that flowed out of his chariot [see 1 Kings 22:38].)

When Ahab saw Elijah, Ahab said to him, "So...you have found me, O my enemy."

Elijah answered, "Yes, I have found you because you have always chosen to do whatever the Lord says is wrong. So the Lord says to you: 'Listen, I am about to bring destruction upon you. I will utterly sweep your descendants away. I will cut off every male of yours— slave or free—in your household in Israel. I will cause your dynasty to become like the dynasty of King Jeroboam, the son of Nebat. And, it will be like the dynasty of King Baasha, the son of Ahijah. (Both of these family lines were completely destroyed.) I will do this to you because you have made Me angry. You have caused the people of Israel to sin.'

"And, regarding Jezebel, the Lord also has this to say: 'The dogs will eat the body of Jezebel at the wall of Jezreel.' (See the literal fulfillment of this in Second Kings 9:10;34-37.)

"Ahab, regarding those associated with you, the dogs will eat anyone who dies inside the city. And, wild birds will eat anyone who dies in the countryside."

There certainly was no one else like Ahab—he was so committed to doing anything that the Lord said was wrong. His wife Jezebel urged him on to do evil. Ahab's sins were so abominable—he worshiped idols. This was the same thing the Amorite people did. So the Lord took their land away from them, and gave it to the people of Israel.

When Ahab heard these words from Elijah, he tore his own clothes. (This was a cultural, outward sign of feelings of deep remorse, fearing the consequences of sin. Ahab was sincere, but it did not last long.) Then he started wearing sackcloth. He even wore sackcloth when he laid down. Ahab would not eat. And, Ahab was always dejected.

Then the word of the Lord came to Elijah of Tishbeh: "Have you noticed how penitent Ahab is now? Therefore, I will not cause this punishment to come upon him during his lifetime. I will wait until his son becomes king. Then I will bring all this trouble upon Ahab's family."

My Time to Pray

Godly Counsel Only

I will do this to you because you have made me angry. You have caused the people of Israel to sin (1 Kings 21:22).

Be leery when someone promises to get you something that is illegal, especially when they promise to get you what you couldn't get for yourself. Naboth said "no" to the king because God, the greater King, had told His people their land was a gift from Him. Their spiritual inheritance was tied to the land, so it was easy for Naboth to say no to King Ahab. *Lord, I will not try to enter doors where You said "no entrance." Teach me to joyfully accept the "STOP" signs of life.*

King Ahab probably knew enough of Israel's inheritance policy to realize why Naboth had told him no. Ahab didn't accept no cheerfully. He went to bed and turned his head to the wall, then pouted. *Is that you? Do you pout when you can't get your way?* If so, you're acting childish. Adjusting to the closed doors of life is a sign of your growing maturity. Learn to adjust to health doors, and vocation doors, and even family doors. Sometimes you'll face money doors, or physical limitation doors. Success is doing the best you can do within the obvious limitations of life. *Lord, teach me happiness within the limitations I find in life. And may I live for You successfully within the barriers I face.*

Be careful of counsel from people who are not spiritual, or when they don't have a biblical orientation to life. Jezebel probably didn't understand Israel's land-inheritance. And even if she knew about it, she didn't care. God's priorities were nowhere on her radar screen. She was raised in the palace of her father the king and she operated by the power of the monarchy, "Take what you want!" So, Jezebel continued a "power plot" to get the land for her husband. *Lord, I will analyze the counsel of non-Christians by Your principles found in Scripture. I want to act right by the laws of the land and I want to live right by the laws of the Bible.*

Even though Jezebel was the greater sinner in this situation, God judged Ahab. Why? Because Ahab knew better and should have done the right thing. Sometimes God judges Christians more than a non-Christian, even when the children of the world do a much worse thing. Why? Because the sin of the Christian is done knowingly against the standards of God. Their sin is against God Himself. So God said the dogs would "lick the blood" of Ahab. *Lord, I fear You and will obey You. Forgive me when I've sinned in the past. I repent and want Your blessing on my life.*

Remember, even if God punished the believer more severely than the unbeliever, the unsaved will not get away with their sin. There are natural consequences in this life for breaking the laws of nature. There is a future spiritual judgment at the Great White Judgment Throne. *Lord, I don't gloat when the unsaved are judged for their sin. I pray for those I know, that they will get saved and accept the forgiveness of sins by the blood of Christ* (see 1 John 1:7). *Amen.*

26

THE PROPHET MICAIAH
PREDICTS AHAB'S DEFEAT

First Kings 22:1-43,46,51-53

For three years, there was no war between Israel and Syria. During the third year, Jehoshaphat, the king of Judah, went down to visit Ahab, the king of Israel. (Ahab and Jezebel's daughter—Athaliah—was given as a bride to Jehoshaphat's son, Jehoram. Israel and Judah had one thing in common—the menacing enemies of the Syrians.) At this same time, Ahab the king of Israel asked his officers, "Do you remember that the king of Syria took Ramoth-Gilead from us? Why have we done nothing to get it back from him?" So, Ahab asked King Jehoshaphat, "Will you go with me? Will you fight against the army of Syria at Ramoth-Gilead?"

Jehoshaphat answered the king of Israel, "I will go with you." (Literally, "As I, so you.") My soldiers and my horses are ready to join with your army." Jehoshaphat said to the king of Israel, "But first, we should ask the Lord to guide us."

So, Ahab the king of Israel called the prophets together. There were about 400 men. Ahab asked them, "Should I go to war against the army of Syria at Ramoth-Gilead? Or, should I wait?"

The false prophets answered, "Go up, because the Lord will deliver it into the hand of the king."

But Jehoshaphat asked, "Isn't there a prophet of the Lord still here? (King Jehoshaphat knew that those hireling prophets of Ahab were tainted with Baal worship.) Let's ask him what we should do."

Ahab the king of Israel answered Jehoshaphat, "There is still one man. We could ask the Lord through him, but I hate him. When he prophesies, he never says anything good about me. He always says something bad. He is Micaiah, the son of Imlah."

Jehoshaphat said, "King Ahab, you shouldn't say that."

So, Ahab the king of Israel told one of his officers: "Summon Micaiah, the son of Imlah, immediately."

Ahab the king of Israel and Jehoshaphat the king of Judah were wearing their royal robes. They were sitting on their thrones (kings had portable thrones that they took with them on their trips) at the open area. This was near the entrance to the gate of Samaria. All the false prophets were standing before them, speaking so-called divine "messages." One of the false prophets was Zedekiah, the son of Chenaanah. He had made for himself some iron horns. He said to Ahab, "This is what the Lord says: 'You will use these horns to gore Syria until you finish them off.'"

And, all the other false prophets said the same thing, "Attack Ramoth-Gilead and win. The Lord will give you the victory over the Syrians."

Meanwhile, the messenger who had gone to summon Micaiah said to Micaiah, "Please listen, all the other prophets are saying the king will succeed. You should agree with them. Give the king a favorable answer."

But Micaiah answered, "As surely as the Lord lives, I will tell him only what the Lord tells me." Then Micaiah came to King Ahab. The king asked him, "Micaiah, should we attack Ramoth-Gilead, or should we wait?"

Micaiah answered, "Attack and win. The Lord will deliver it into the king's hand." (This answer was spoken sarcastically, because Micaiah did not say, "Thus Yahweh says," which was the usual preface of a true prophet's prophecy.)

But King Ahab said to Micaiah, "Tell me the truth in the Name of Yahweh. How many times have I insisted that you do this?"

So Micaiah answered, "I have seen all Israel scattered on the hills (in full retreat) like sheep without a shepherd. The Lord said, 'They have no leaders. Each of them should go home in peace.'"

Then Ahab the king of Israel said to Jehoshaphat, "I told you. This prophet never says anything good about me. He only says bad things about me."

But Micaiah continued to speak: "Listen to the word of the Lord: I saw the Lord sitting on His throne. His entire, heavenly army was standing near Him on His right side and on His left. The Lord said, 'Who will deceive Ahab so that he attacks Ramoth-Gilead and gets killed?'

"The spirits did not agree about what they should do. Then one spirit came and stood in the presence of the Lord. He said, 'I will trick him.'

"The Lord asked him, 'How would you trick Ahab?'

"The spirit answered, 'I would go out to Ahab's prophets, and I would cause all of them to tell lies.'

"Then the Lord said, 'You will succeed in deceiving Ahab. Go out and do it.'" (This command was giving permission to the lying spirit. Ahab wanted to believe his own lies. So, God allowed Ahab to do it.)

Micaiah said, "Ahab, listen, this has now happened. The Lord has caused all of these prophets of yours to lie to you. The Lord has decided that a disaster will happen to you."

Then Zedekiah, the son of Chenaanah, approached Micaiah and hit him in the face. (Micaiah was probably bound at the time.) Zedekiah said, "Do you really believe the Spirit of the Lord has left me and is now speaking through you?"

Micaiah answered, "Listen, you will find out on that day when you go to hide in the innermost room. The king will certainly be searching for you, Zedekiah, to kill you for delivering a false prophecy about Ahab."

Then Ahab the king of Israel ordered: "Take Micaiah and send him back to Amon, the governor of the city of Samaria, and over to Joash, the king's son. Tell them that I said to keep Micaiah in prison. Give him only a little bread and water until I come home safely."

Micaiah answered, "Ahab, if you return safe from the battle, then the Lord has not spoken through me." And Micaiah added, "Remember all of my words, all you people."

King Ahab Is Killed in Battle

So, Ahab the king of Israel and Jehoshaphat the king of Judah went up to Ramoth-Gilead. Ahab the king of Israel said to Jehoshaphat, "I will go into battle, but I will change my appearance, so that no one would recognize me. But you go ahead and wear your royal clothes." So, Ahab the king of Israel disguised himself and went into battle.

The king of Syria had 32 chariot commanders. He ordered them: "Don't fight with anybody except the king of Israel. It doesn't matter if they are important or unimportant." When these chariot commanders saw Jehoshaphat, they thought that he was surely the king of Israel. So they turned to attack him. But Jehoshaphat began shouting his battle cry. Then the chariot commanders realized that he was not Ahab the king of Israel. So they stopped chasing him. But a soldier shot an arrow without aiming at anyone in particular. And, he hit Ahab, the king of Israel. The arrow hit him where two pieces of his armor joined. King Ahab yelled to his chariot driver, "Turn this chariot around. I am wounded. Get me out of the fighting." The battle continued all that day. King Ahab was in his chariot, leaning against it to hold himself up facing the Syrians. The blood from his wound flowed out and covered the floorboard of the chariot. That evening, Ahab died. Near sunset, the order went out through the army of Israel: "Each man must retreat to his own land and town."

So, that was the way that King Ahab died. His body was taken to Samaria, and they buried him in Samaria. The men cleaned out Ahab's chariot at a pool of Samaria, where prostitutes bathed. And, the dogs licked up King Ahab's blood from the chariot. These things happened just as the Lord had said they would. (According to Elijah's prophecy found in First Kings 21:19.)

Everything else that Ahab did is written down in the Book of the History of the Kings of Israel. That book also tells about the palace that Ahab built and decorated with ivory. (Archaeologists have found this complex.) And it tells about all the other cities that he built. So Ahab died. And, his son Ahaziah became king in his place.

PRAYING WITH THE KINGS

Jehoshaphat Rules Over Judah

Jehoshaphat, the son of Asa, was the king of Judah. During Ahab's
fourth year as king over Israel, Jehoshaphat at 35 years old
became king. And, he ruled in Jerusalem for 25 years. His
mother Azubah was the daughter of Shilhi. Jehoshaphat was a
good man, like his father Asa was before him. He did what the
Lord said was upright. But, Jehoshaphat did not destroy the
high places where false gods were worshiped. So, the people
continued offering sacrifices and burning incense in those
locations.

Now there were male prostitutes (Sodomites) in the places where false
gods were worshiped. Jehoshaphat's father, Asa, had not forced
them out, but Jehoshaphat forced the rest of them to leave.

Ahaziah Rules Over Israel

Ahaziah, the son of Ahab, became the king of Israel in Samaria, during
Jehoshaphat's seventeenth year as king over Judah. Ahaziah ruled
Israel for two years and did what was evil in the sight of the
Lord, he did the same things his father Ahab, his mother Jezebel,
and Jeroboam, the son of Nebat had done. All of these rulers
led the people of Israel into more and more sin. So, Ahaziah
worshiped and served Baal. Therefore, Ahaziah made the Lord,
the God of Israel, angry. In these ways, Ahaziah did what his
father Ahab had always done.

My Time to Pray

The Lord Says

*But Micaiah answered, 'As surely as the Lord lives, I will
tell him only what the Lord tells me' (1 Kings 22:14).*

"Iwill tell him only what the Lord tells me" (1 Kings 22:14). When can we know we are absolutely, positively right? Sometimes we think we are right, but don't know all the facts. To be partially right is to be fully wrong. Sometimes we let our attitudes or desires influence the things we say. We think we are speaking truthfully, but we are actually speaking our opinions. But, when we speak the Scripture, we are speaking truth. The Bible is truth (see John 17:17). *Lord, I will learn Your Scriptures as best I can and live by their principles. I will speak Your Word to be sure I am speaking accurately. I will hide Your Word in my heart to let it influence my attitudes, desires, and thinking.*

There were 400 false prophets who agreed, but they were all wrong. Why do false prophets continue to give false messages? Are they saying what people want to hear? Are they doing it for money? Perhaps they are naïve, thinking they only have a job to do so they say what was taught to them by their teachers. Maybe they are just spiritually blinded. *Lord, there are false prophets in my world, just as false prophets deceived King Ahab. I will judge them by the Word of God. Not every preacher who claims to be a Christian actually speaks the truth.*

The prediction of Elijah came true. Elijah said the dogs would "lick Ahab's blood," and they did. It took a long time, but God's clock and ours run on different schedules. When people think they get away with sin, they really don't. Judgment eventually catches up with them, just as surely as Ahab's judgment day came. *Lord, help me see things from Your perspective of time. While You wait patiently to judge sin, I'm impatient. Lord, open my eyes to see as You see.*

Did you know that God delights to work in small, unseen ways? Ahab thought he was clever to disguise himself as he went into battle. Maybe he heard the scouting results that Syria would focus on him and not Jehoshaphat. But God knew where he was. When the Syrians chased Jehoshaphat instead of him, Ahab probably thought his disguise was working. But God knew. A bowman pulled an arrow without aiming at anyone, but God knew exactly where Ahab was. And the arrow didn't just hit him; it went between an opening where the armor joined together. God knew where Ahab was, and God knew within inches where to hit him. Let's not say the archer was a good shot, let's say God made an accurate shot. *Lord, You guide the little details in my life. You are the God of minutia. I will never ignore little things again. Amen.*

27

JEHOSHAPHAT APPOINTS JUDGES

Second Chronicles 19

Jehoshaphat, the king of Judah, returned in safety to his house in
Jerusalem. But Jehu, the son of Hanani the seer (a prophet) went
out to meet Jehoshaphat and said, "Why would you help an evil
man and love those who hate the Lord? Because of this, the Lord
is angry with you. Nevertheless, there are some good things in
you. You removed the Asherah idols from the land, and you did
set your heart to seek the one true God."

Jehoshaphat lived in Jerusalem; and he went out again among the
people, from Beer-Sheba to the hill-country of Ephraim, and
turned them back to the Lord, the God of their ancestors. He
appointed judges in the land, in each of the strong, walled towns
of Judah. Jehoshaphat told them, "Be careful in what you do,
because you are not judging for human being but for the Lord.
He will be with you whenever you make a decision. Now, may
the reverence for the Lord be upon you. Be careful in what you
do, because the Lord, our God, wants people to be fair. He wants
all people to be treated the same way. And, He does not want
judges to accept a bribe to change their judgments."

And, in Jerusalem, Jehoshaphat appointed to be judges some of the
Levites, the priests, and the leaders of Israelite families. They
were to decide cases on the basis of the Lord's law. And, they

were to settle criminal and civil cases. They lived in Jerusalem. Jehoshaphat gave them strict orders, "You must always serve the Lord faithfully and wholeheartedly. You must revere Him. You will have cases about homicides or cases concerning the teachings, the commands, the rules, or some other law. These cases will come up from among your people living in the towns. In all these cases, you must warn the people not to sin against the Lord. If you don't, the Lord will be angry with you and your people. But if you warn them, then you won't be guilty.

"Amariah is the high priest over you in all matters concerning the Lord. And Zebediah, the son of Ishmael, the governor of the people of Judah, will be over you in all the king's matters. And the Levites will serve you as officers. Have courage! May the Lord be with those who do what is right!"

My Time to Pray

God the Judge

Now may the reverence for the Lord be upon You (2 Chronicles 19:7).

Are you a reverent person? That depends on what the word *reverent* means. First, it reflects an attitude. When you reverence God, you think of Him and act the way He wants you to act. That can mean a quiet spirit in God's presence because You are more concerned about Him, than yourself. But when you shout *Hallelujah* or *Praise the Lord*, you reverently think about the One you are praising. *Lord, teach me reverence to You in the right way at all times.*

Did you notice that God would be with the judges when they made a right decision in the right way? You too can claim God's presence when you make the right decisions in the right way. *Lord, I want Your presence for every decision I make. Guide me to always make right decisions in the right way.*

Jehoshaphat told the judges God would be angry with them if they didn't tell the people not to sin. God holds us to that same standard today. We must stand up for God and His laws; and if we don't, the Lord will be angry with us. *Lord, I will faithfully uphold Your standards against sin. I will not break Your laws, and will also teach others not to sin. Amen.*

28

JEHOSHAPHAT DEFEATS THE MOABITES AND THE AMMONITES

Second Chronicles 20

Later, soldiers came to start a war with Jehoshaphat. They were the Moabites, the Ammonites, and some Meunites. Some men came and told Jehoshaphat: "A huge army is coming up against you from Edom. They are coming from the other side of the Dead Sea. They are in Hazazon-Tamar already." Hazazon-Tamar is also called En-Gedi. Jehoshaphat was afraid, so he decided to ask the Lord. He set his face to seek Yahweh. He announced that no one in Judah should eat any meals (he proclaimed a fast) accompanied with a time of prayer to God. The people of Judah came together to ask the Lord for help. They came from every town in Judah to pray to the Lord.

The congregation of Judah and Jerusalem met in the new courtyard in the Temple of the Lord. Then Jehoshaphat stood up before them and prayed, "O Lord Who Is Always Present, the God of our ancestors, You are the God in Heaven. You rule over all the kingdoms of the nations. You have power and strength. No one can stand against You. O God, You forced out the people who lived in this land when Your people Israel moved in. And, You gave this land permanently to the descendants of Your friend Abraham. They lived in this land and built a sanctuary for Your

Name. They said, 'Trouble may come to us. It might be war, punishment, sickness, or famine. If it comes, we will stand in Your presence and in the presence of this Temple. Your Name is in this Temple. We will cry out to You when we are in trouble. Then You will hear and save us.'

"But now, look, there are men from Ammon, Moab, and Edom. You would not allow the Israelites to enter their lands when the Israelites came from Egypt. So, the Israelites turned away and did not destroy them. But look how they repay us for not destroying them. They have come to force us out of Your land. And, You gave us this land as our own. O our God, punish those people. We have no power against this huge army that is attacking us. We don't know what to do. So, we look to You for help."

All the men of Judah stood in the presence of the Lord, and their wives, and their little ones were with them. Then the Spirit of the Lord came upon Jahaziel, Zechariah's son. Zechariah was Benaiah's son. Benaiah was Jeiel's son, and Jeiel was Mattaniah's son. Jahaziel was a Levite and a descendant of Asaph. He stood up in the meeting, and said: "Pay attention, King Jehoshaphat. Listen, all you people living in Judah and Jerusalem! The Lord says this to you: 'Don't be afraid or discouraged because of this vast army. The battle is not yours; it belongs to God. Go down tomorrow and fight those people. Listen, they will be coming up through the Pass of Ziz. You will find them at the end of the ravine that leads to the Desert of Jeruel. You won't need to fight in this battle. Just stand firm in your positions. You will watch the Lord save you.' O Judah and Jerusalem, don't be afraid. Don't be discouraged. The Lord Who Is Always Present is with you. So, go out against those people tomorrow."

Then Jehoshaphat bowed face-down on the ground, and all the people of Judah and Jerusalem bowed down in the presence of the Lord. They worshiped Him. Then some Levites from the Kohathite clans stood up to give praise to the Lord Who Is Always Present. They praised the God of Israel with loud voices. (Their anthem was sung as if the victory were already won.)

Jehoshaphat's army went out into the Desert of Tekoa early in the morning. As they were starting out, Jehoshaphat stood and said, "Listen to me, you people of Judah and Jerusalem. Have faith in the Lord, your God. Then you will stand firm. Believe in the true prophets of the Lord. Then you will succeed."

Jehoshaphat listened to the people's advice, then appointed some men to be singers to the Lord. They were to praise the Lord for His holy splendor. They marched in front of the army, and sang:

"Give thanks to the One Who Is Always Present.
His constant love continues forever."

As they began to sing and praise God, the Lord set ambushes for the people of Ammon, Moab, and Edom, who came to attack Judah. And, they were defeated. The men of Ammon and Moab started to attack the men from Edom. They killed them, completely destroying the Edomites. After they had killed the men from Edom, they started attacking each other.

The men from Judah came to a place where they could see the desert. (It would have taken them about six hours to march from Jerusalem to this spot.) They looked at the enemy's huge army, but they saw only corpses lying on the ground. No one had escaped. Jehoshaphat and his army went to take valuable things from the corpses (plunder the spoils). They found equipment, much clothes, and other valuable things. There was more than they could carry away. There was so much that it took three days to gather it all. On the fourth day, Jehoshaphat and his army gathered in the Valley of Beracah. There they praised the Lord. This is why that place has been called the Valley of Beracah (the Valley of Blessing) to this day.

Then Jehoshaphat led all the men from Judah and Jerusalem back to Jerusalem. They were happy. The Lord caused them to rejoice, because their enemies were defeated. They entered Jerusalem with lyres, with harps, and with trumpets. And, they went to the Temple of the Lord.

All the kingdoms of the lands around them heard how the Lord had fought against the enemies of Judah. So, the dread of God was upon them. So, Jehoshaphat's kingdom was quiet again. His God gave him peace from all the countries around him.

Jehoshaphat the king of Judah made a treaty with Ahaziah the king of Israel. It was wrong for him to do this. Jehoshaphat agreed with Ahaziah to build trading ships. They built them at the port of Ezion-Geber. Then Eliezer, the son of Dodavahu, prophesied against Jehoshaphat. Eliezer was from the town of Mereshah. He said, "Jehoshaphat, because you have allied yourself with Ahaziah, the Lord will destroy what you have made." The ships were wrecked. So, Jehoshaphat and Ahaziah were not able to send them out to trade.

The End of Jehoshaphat's Rule

Jehoshaphat was 35 years old when he became king. And, he ruled in Jerusalem for 25 years. His mother was Azubar, the daughter of Shilhi. Jehoshaphat was a good man, like his father—Asa—was before him. He did what the Lord said was upright. But, Jehoshaphat did not destroy the high places where false gods were worshiped. So, the people had not trusted the God of their ancestors. The other things that Jehoshaphat did as king—from the beginning to the end—are written down in the writings of Jehu, the son of Hanani. These writings are recorded in the Book of the Kings of Israel.

My Time to Pray

Time to Fast

Jehoshaphat was afraid, so he decided to ask the Lord. He set his face to seek Yahweh. He announced that no one in Judah should eat any meals accompanied with a time of prayer to God (2 Chronicles 20:3).

Do you see the phrase, "Jehoshaphat was afraid"? Have you ever been afraid, really afraid, when you heard serious trouble was coming? If so, then next time do what Jehoshaphat did—fast. Go without eating. Follow the *Yom Kippur* fast (the Day of Atonement fast is observed by orthodox Jews to this day). Since the Jews measure a day from sundown to sundown, begin by not eating the evening meal, then skip breakfast and lunch. But abstaining from food doesn't impress God. Spend meal times in prayer, beside the other normal times each day you pray. *Lord, when troubles scare me, I will fast and pray. I will place my troubles into Your hand. I will trust You to deliver me in my hour of deepest need.*

Next time you pray, use the words of Jehoshaphat. *"O Lord Who Is Always Present, the God of our ancestors, You are the God in Heaven. You rule over all the kingdoms of the nations. You have power and strength. No one can stand against You. O God, You forced out the people who lived in this land when Your people Israel moved in. And, You gave this land permanently to the descendants of Your friend Abraham. They lived in this land and built a sanctuary for Your name. They said, 'Trouble may come to us. It might be war, punishment, sickness, or famine. If it comes, we will stand in Your presence and in the presence of this Temple. Your Name is this Temple. We will cry out to You when we are in trouble. Then You will hear and save us.' But now, look, there are men from Ammon, Moab, and Edom. You would not allow the Israelites to enter their lands when the Israelites came from Egypt. So, the Israelites turned away and did not destroy them. But look how they repay us for not destroying them. They have come to force us out of Your land. And, You gave us this land as our own. O our God, punish those people. We have no power against this huge army that is attacking us.*

We don't know what to do. So, we look to You for help." Lord, I now pray these words.

Sometimes the threats that scare us the most never happen. When this huge army came around the south end of the Dead Sea, they never got to shoot one arrow against Israel. God intervened. Think back over your life, the things you feared the most, never happened. *Lord, help me look at my troubles through Your eyes. You know all about my coming trouble and what will happen. Teach me to trust You in threatening dangers.*

In World War II, the phrase, "Praise the Lord and pass the ammunition" was the application of a spiritual principle. It meant we should pray before trouble comes and put all our trust in God as we fight. But then like Jehoshaphat, we must go out with complete military preparedness, prepared to fight to the death. Yes, prayer and preparation is God's principle. *Lord, I will pray as though the whole battle depends on You. But, I'll also prepare as though the whole battle depends on me. Amen.*

29

Elijah Predicts
Death of King Ahaziah

Second Kings 1

After Ahab died, the country of Moab revolted against Israel's domination. (The Moabites had been soundly conquered as far back as King David's time [see 2 Sam. 8:2], according to the Moabite Stone [discovered in 1869].)

King Ahaziah fell through the wooden lattice in his upstairs room in the city of Samaria, and was badly injured. So, Ahaziah sent messengers, saying to them, "Go, ask for a revelation from Baal-Zebub (one of the many names used for the false god, Baal—"lord of the flies," unclean insects. Later rabbis made an additional change in the spelling so that the meaning of the name was "the god of the dunghill") the god of Ekron, if I will recover from my injuries."

But the Angel of the Lord told Elijah, the man from Tishbeh: "Get up, go up to meet the messengers of the king of Samaria. Tell them: 'Why are you going to seek an answer from Baal-Zebub, the god of Ekron? Is it because you think there is no God in Israel?' Therefore, this is what the Lord says: 'You will not get up from the bed that you are lying on. You will certainly die.'" Then Elijah left.

So, the messengers went back to Ahaziah. He asked them, "Why have you come back here?"

They said, "A man came up to meet us. He said, 'Go back to the king who sent you and tell him what the Lord says: "Why do you send men to ask questions of Baal-Zebub, the god of Ekron? Is it because you think there is no God in Israel? (This was a public insult of Yahweh.) This is why you will not get up from your bed. You will certainly die."'"

Ahaziah asked them, "The man who came up to meet you and told you these words, what did he look like?"

They answered, "He had a fur coat and a leather belt tied around his waist."

Ahaziah said, "That was Elijah from Tishbeh!"

Then Ahaziah sent a captain with his 50 men to Elijah. The captain went up to arrest Elijah. (These ungodly men were trying to enforce the orders of an apostate, reprobate king upon a true prophet of God.) They saw Elijah sitting on top of a mountain. The captain said to Elijah, "O man of the one true God, the king says: 'Come down.'"

Elijah answered to the captain of the 50 men, "Since I am a man of God, let fire come down from the sky (since God was being insulted, Elijah the prophet had the hand of God fall directly upon these blasphemers) and consume you and your 50 men." Then fire came down from the sky, and burned up the captain and his 50 men.

Again, Ahaziah sent another captain and 50 men to Elijah. The captain said to him, "O man of the one true God, this is what the king says: 'Come down immediately.'"

Elijah answered, "Since I am a man of the one true God, let fire come down from the sky and consume you and your 50 men." Then the fire of God came down from the sky, and burned up the captain and his 50 men.

For the third time, Ahaziah sent a captain with his 50 men. But the third captain came and fell down on his knees in front of Elijah, begging Elijah, "O man of the one true God, I ask you. Please let my life and the lives of my men be precious to you. Fire did come down from the sky twice before. It burned up the first two captains of 50, along with all of their men. But now, please let me live."

The Angel of the Lord said to Elijah, "Go down with him. Don't be afraid of him." So, Elijah got up and went down with him to see the king.

And, Elijah told Ahaziah, "This is what the Lord says: 'You have sent messengers to ask a question of Baal-Zebub, the god of Ekron. Is it because you think there is no God in Israel to ask for His word? Therefore, you will get not get up from your bed that you are lying on, because you will certainly die.'" So Ahaziah died, just as the Lord spoke through Elijah.

Joram became the king in Ahaziah's place. This happened during the second year that Jehoram, the son of Jehoshaphat, was king of Judah. Joram ruled because Ahaziah had no son to take his place. (Joram was Ahaziah's brother [see 2 Kings 3:1].) The other things that Ahaziah did are written down in the Book of the History of the Kings of Israel.

My Time to Pray

He Knows Your Heart

Is it because you think there is no God in Israel? (2 Kings 1:3)

It is important what you think about God, for He knows what you think about Him. You don't even have to tell another, or speak it audibly. God knows the thoughts of your heart, but more importantly, he holds you responsible for your thoughts as well as your actions. But just maybe God is more concerned about your thoughts because He knows thoughts load the gun that murders another. *Lord, You know my thoughts, forgive me for every rebellious thought, and for every impure thought, and for every revengeful thought. Lord, teach me to discipline my mind to keep sinful thoughts out of my mind. Help me learn to think my thoughts after You.*

The Ten Commandments teach that God "is a jealous God," so we should be careful of doing anything to make Him jealous. If we worship an idol, God becomes jealous and will judge us. But look at Ahaziah, he wasn't worshiping Baal, he just went to ask a question. Is that worthy of death? Yes, because Ahaziah recognized the legitimacy of an idol. We think people back then were dumb for worshiping a carved piece of stone or wood. But people have idols today, but not those carved out of stone or wood. An idol is anything that is more important than God, or anything that takes the place of God, or is treated like God. Do you have anything like that in your life? *Lord, if I'm spiritually blinded to anything like an idol in my life, please reveal it to me. I will repent and put it out of my life. I will worship You alone. I will follow and serve You alone.*

Was this a "sin unto death" (see 1 John 5:15-17)? A sin unto death is when God prematurely takes the life of a person. This is not just the sin of unsaved people. Christians can be taken home for a sin that is continual, purposeful, and committed against God or the things of God. Someone got drunk at the Lord's table in Corinth and died prematurely (see 1 Cor. 11:30). Also, probably Ananias and Sapphira committed the sin unto death (see Acts 5:1-11). *Lord, I fear You. I will not knowingly sin, and I will not repeatedly sin, and surely, I will not sin against holy things. Amen.*

30

ELIJAH TAKEN UP TO HEAVEN

Second Kings 2

It was almost time for the Lord to take Elijah to Heaven. (God was going to take him by a whirlwind into Heaven.) Elijah and Elisha set out from Gilgal when Elijah said to Elisha, "Please stay here. The Lord has told me to go to Bethel."

But Elisha said, "As surely as the Lord lives, and as you live, I will not leave you." So, both of them went down to Bethel. A group of the prophets at Bethel (Elijah had established schools for the prophets at Gilgal, Bethel, and Jericho—he was saying goodbye to each of them) came to Elisha. They said to him, "Do you know that the Lord will take your master away from you?"

Elisha said, "Yes, I know, but don't talk about it."

Elijah said to Elisha, "Please stay here, because the Lord has told me to go to Jericho."

Elisha said, "As surely as the Lord lives, and as you live, I will not leave you." So they went to Jericho.

A group of the prophets at Jericho approached Elisha. They said, "Do you know that the Lord will take your master away from you today?"

Elisha answered, "Yes, I know, but don't talk about it."

And Elijah said to Elisha, "Please stay here. The Lord has told me to go to the Jordan River."

Elisha answered, "As surely as the Lord lives, and as you live, I will not leave you!" So the two of them went on.

Fifty men from the school of the prophets came and stood far away from Elijah and Elisha. Both of them were next to the Jordan River. Elijah took off his robe and rolled it up and hit the water with it. The water divided to the right and to the left. Then Elijah and Elisha crossed over on dry ground.

As they were crossing over, Elijah said to Elisha, "What can I do for you before I am taken from you?" (Elijah knew that Elisha would be his successor [see 1 Kings 19:16;19-21].)

Elisha said, "Leave me a double share of your spirit."

Then Elijah said, "You have asked for a difficult thing. (But nothing is too difficult for God [see Gen. 18:14; Luke 1:37].) However, if you see me when I am taken from you, your wish will be granted. But, if you do not see me, your wish will not be granted."

Elijah and Elisha were still walking and talking. Suddenly, a fiery chariot and horses of fire appeared. They separated Elijah from Elisha. Then Elijah went up to Heaven in a whirlwind. (Like Enoch [see Gen. 5:24], Elijah was transported to Heaven without experiencing death.) As Elisha was watching this, he shouted, "My father! (He called Elijah his spiritual father.) My father! The chariots of Israel and their horsemen!" Elisha did not see him anymore. Elisha took his own clothes and tore them in two (to show sadness).

He picked up Elijah's robe that had fallen down from him. (Symbolized that Elisha was the divinely appointed successor to Elijah. This prophetic mantle was an outer sign that the spirit of Elijah now rested upon Elisha.) Then Elisha returned and stood on the bank of the Jordan River. And, Elisha hit the water with Elijah's robe that had fallen down from Elijah. He said, "Where now is the Lord, the God of Elijah?" When Elisha hit the water, it divided to the right and to the left. Then Elisha crossed over. (God was showing Elisha that His divine power would be with Elisha just as it had been operative with Elijah previously.)

A group of the prophets at Jericho were waiting on the other side of the Jordan River. They said, "Now the spirit of Elijah is upon Elisha." And they went to meet Elisha, and bowed themselves to the ground in front of him. They said, "Look, there are 50 strong men with us. Please let them go and look for your master. May the Spirit of the Lord has taken up Elijah and set him down somewhere else. He may be on some mountain or in some valley."

Elisha answered, "No. Don't send them."

But they begged Elisha until he didn't refuse them anymore. Then he said, "Send them." So, they sent 50 men to look for three days, but they could not find Elijah. Then they came back to Elisha at Jericho where he was staying. He said to them, "I told you not to go, didn't I?"

Elisha Heals the Water

The men of the city said to Elisha, "Look, my master, this city is a nice place to live. You can see that. But the water is bad. That is why the land cannot grow crops."

Elisha said, "Bring me a new bowl, and put salt in it." So they brought it to him. Then Elisha went out to the spring (source) of water and threw the salt in it. He said, "This is what the Lord says: 'I have healed this water. From now on, it won't cause death. And it won't prevent the land from growing crops.'" The water was healed. It happened just as Elisha said.

Elisha Is Mocked

From there, Elisha went up to Bethel. On the way, some teen boys came out of the city and made fun of (mocked) Elisha. They said to him, "Go up, baldy! Go up, baldy!" (They were mocking Elijah's entrance into Heaven.) Elisha turned around and looked at them. He put a curse on them in the Name of the Lord. Then two female bears came out of the woods and tore 42 of the boys to pieces. Then Elisha left and went on to Mount Carmel. From there, he went back to Samaria, the capital city of Israel.

My Time to Pray

A Double Portion, Please

Give me a double portion of your spirit (2 Kings 2:9).

Of all the things a student can ask of his teacher, to ask to do twice what the master has done is both presumptuous and risky. To have twice as much as the master teacher suggests you must work twice as hard as the master. And in this case it involved spirituality, so the student had to be willing to do twice as much for God. It suggested the pupil would go through twice the study, twice the suffering, and twice the sacrifice. When you say you want to do twice as much as another person, are you willing to pay the price? *Lord, I am willing. Because You did so much for me, how can I do less than my best for You?*

Did you see how many times old Elijah tried to dissuade young Elisha from following him? Three times the old prophet told his young student to wait behind, but the young Elisha had faith to go all the way with his teacher. *Lord, give me persistence to go all the way for You, and with You.*

Both men knew God was going to do something big that day. I'm not sure they knew what would happen, but they both knew Elijah was going home. There's a principle for you: when something big is happening at your church, or anywhere, be there. If God shows up, you want to see Him, experience Him, and be changed by what God does.

On Easter Sunday evening, Jesus appeared to ten disciples in the upper room. Thomas was missing; Judas had hanged himself. Thomas missed the first appearance of Jesus to the disciples; and as a result he doubted. When Jesus shows up, be there. *Lord, I want to experience Your presence when You manifest Yourself among Your people. Since I don't know what will happen, I'll always be in church because You command it (see Heb. 10:25) and You promise to be there (see Matt. 18:20).*

When Elisha returned to the Jordan River, he asked, "Where now is the Lord God of Elijah?" The answer is that God is present everywhere at all times. He can do what He wills, but He works through His servants like Elijah and Elisha. So the question is now, "Where are the Elijah's of the Lord God?" *Lord, I want to have the faith of Elisha—give me a double portion. I will pay the price.*

There will always be doubters. There were 50 men who wanted to go search for Elijah. Perhaps they thought Elijah hadn't gone to Heaven, but was hiding in the mountains. *Lord, I know that doubt is never eradicated, just as sin is never eradicated. Don't let doubt control my thinking; I will resist its temptation to doubt Your word. Lord, increase my faith. Amen.*

31

MOAB REBELS AGAINST ISRAEL

Second Kings 3

Joram, the son of Ahab, became the king over Israel at Samaria. He began to rule in Jehoshaphat's eighteenth year as king of Judah. Joram ruled for 12 years, and he did what was evil in the sight of the Lord. However, he was not like his father and his mother. He did remove the stone pillars that his father had set up for Baal. But he continued to do the same sins that Jeroboam the son of Nebat had done. Jeroboam had caused the people of Israel to sin, and Joram did not stop doing these same sins.

Mesha (Mesha's name is mentioned in a secular account called the Moabite Stone, which was discovered in 1869—the Moabite Stone contains a confirmatory, parallel account of Second Kings 3, but from a Moabite perspective), the king of Moab, raised sheep. Each year, Mesha had to pay 100,000 lambs and the wool of 100,000 male sheep to the king of Israel. But when Ahab died (853 B.C.), the king of Moab turned against the king of Israel. (The Moabites had been soundly conquered as far back as King David's time [see 2 Sam. 8:2].) So, King Joram gathered all Israel, and went out from Samaria. He sent messengers to Jehoshaphat, the king of Judah, saying, "The king of Moab has revolted against me. Will you go with me against Moab in battle?"

Jehoshaphat said, "I will go up with you. (In the preceding year, Jehoshaphat had been attacked by the Moabites. So, Jehoshaphat was glad to participate with the hope of conquering or weakening his enemies.) I am ready to join you. My soldiers and my horses are ready to join your army."

Jehoshaphat asked, "Which way should we go up to attack?"

Joram answered, "Through the Desert of Edom." (Going around the long way, by the southern end of the Dead Sea.)

So, the king of Israel went with the king of Judah and the king of Edom (a deputy king, Edom was a vassal state of Judah). They marched for seven days (a difficult journey of about 100 miles). There was no more water for the army or for their animals that were with them. (They expected a water supply in a stream called "Wady es-Ahsy" at the boundary line between Edom and Moab to be there when they arrived, but an extended drought had dried it up completely. With no water to continue, they were in a desperate situation.)

The king of Israel said, "How terrible this is. Has the Lord summoned us three kings together so that the Moabites can defeat us?"

Elisha Is Consulted

But Jehoshaphat asked, "Is there a prophet of the Lord here? We could ask the Lord through a prophet."

An officer of the king of Israel answered, "Elisha, the son of Shaphat, is here. He once was Elijah's servant."

Jehoshaphat said, "He speaks the Lord's truth." So, the king of Israel and Jehoshaphat and the king of Edom went down to see Elisha. (Instead of demanding that the prophet come to them, they humbled themselves and went to Elisha.)

Elisha spoke to the king of Israel, saying, "I have nothing to do with you. Go to the prophets of your father and to the prophets of your mother." (The false prophets of Baal and Asherah served by Jezebel, who was still alive.)

The king of Israel said to Elisha, "No, the Lord has called us three kings together to let the Moabites defeat us."

Elisha said, "I serve the Lord of the armies of Heaven. As surely as He lives, I would not even look at you or notice you, if Jehoshaphat, the king of Judah, were not here. I respect him. Now, bring me someone who plays the harp."

While the harp was being played, the hand of Yahweh came upon him. Then Elisha said, "The Lord says: 'Dig holes or ditches that could hold water in the valley.' The Lord says that you won't see wind or rain. (Elisha was predicting that God would cause a huge cloudburst to occur in the highlands of Edom where the wady originated. And, by the following morning [see 2 Kings 3:20], the whole area to the south would be completely flooded.) The streambed will be filled with water, then you, your cattle, and other animals will drink water. This is an easy thing for the Lord to do. He will also let you defeat Moab. You will destroy every strong, walled city and every important town. You will cut down every good tree. You will stop up all springs of water. You will ruin every good field by dumping rocks on them."

The next morning, about the time the sacrifice was offered, there was water! It came from the direction of Edom and filled the valley with water.

All the Moabites had heard that the three kings had come up to fight against them. They mustered everyone old enough to put on armor. And, the Moabites waited at the border (on the north side of the wady). But when the Moabites got up early in the morning, the sun was shining on the water. They saw the water across from them. It looked as red as blood. (The sediments of red soil from that region may have contributed to the reddish illusion.)

The Moabites said, "This is blood! (The Moabites thought that they were seeing pools of blood that glistened in the early morning sunlight.) Surely the three kings have fought and killed each other! Come on, O Moabites, let us take what is valuable from the corpses!"

The Moabites Are Defeated

The Moabites came to the camp of the Israelites. But the Israelites came out and fought them until the Moabites ran away. The Israelites went on into the land of Moab to fight the Moabites. They tore down the cities. They scattered rocks onto every good field and filled it. They stopped up all the springs of water. And, they cut down all the good trees. Kir-Hareseth (located about 9 miles from the southern tip of the Dead Sea) was the only city with its stones still left in place. But the men with slings surrounded Kir-Hareseth and harassed it, too.

The king of Moab saw that the war was too much for him. So, he took along 700 men with swords to break through to the king of Edom (he was a recent, former ally to the Moabites [see 2 Chron. 20:22]). But they could not break through. Then the king of Moab took his oldest son, who would have become king after him. And, he offered his son as a whole burnt offering on the wall (to appease his god, Chemosh, and seek his help in defeating the invaders to his country). So, there was great anger against Israel. (Apparently, the Moabites were so incited to a frenzied state of war because of the ultimate sacrifice of Mesha's own son that they defeated the Jews and the Edomites later.) The armies of Israel and Judah left and went back to their own land. (The allied armies may have displeased Yahweh through their own acceptance of the idea of the transference of "wrath" from the Moabites to them in the offering of Moab's son as a ransom. And, God was displeased with Jehoshaphat for making an unholy alliance with idolatrous Israel [see 2 Chron. 19:1-3]. Some major sin here might be unrecorded.)

My Time to Pray

Dig Holes!

This is but a light thing in the sight of the Lord (2 Kings 3:18).

The armies of Judah and Israel were marching across a desert, and there was no water. The stream where they expected to find water was dried up. They had marched ten days and had no water. The situation was desperate. To supply water for two armies would take a massive miracle, yet it was going to be a "light" thing to the Lord. Isn't that often our case? We panic and think the miracle we need is too big for God to do. At least too big at that time in that place. *Lord, give me faith to see my problem through Your eyes.*

"Dig holes!" I'm sure the army thought that was a foolish command. Each soldier must have known it would take a deep well to reach water—a well deeper than they could dig in one day. And tired, thirsty men couldn't dig wells that deep. But God knew what He was going to do. He was going to rain up in the mountains, and when the rain ran down they needed holes to capture the water. Next time you think God's command to "dig holes" is foolish, try to see things from God's perspective. *Lord, give me Your eyes to see my problems. Lord, give me faith to obey Your commands. Lord, give me courage to "dig holes." And help me do it quickly before the water passes me by.*

We must learn the promise of God, *"I will even make…a river in the desert"* (Isa. 43:19). God was going to do a "light" miracle. What is a light miracle? It's when God doesn't have to override the laws of nature, He doesn't even do something miraculous. A "light" miracle is when God uses the natural laws of nature—rain the mountains—that they won't see or hear. *Lord, give me faith to believe Your work in my life. Sometimes I don't need a miracle, I just need to understand how You work Your plan through the normal laws of nature.*

Have you ever been in a desert, a place that's hot and dry? A place where you think you will die of thirst? We all go through dry seasons where everything seems to turn to dry, hot sand. When that happens, remember, God maketh *"rivers in the desert"* (Isa. 43:19). *Lord, run some water by me. I'm thirsty and I need refreshment. I need Your water. Oh, that's good. Amen.*

32

Elisha Helps a Widow

Second Kings 4

The wife of one of the prophets cried out to Elisha, saying, "Your servant, my husband, is dead! You know that he revered the Lord. But now, the creditor is coming to take away my two boys. He will make them his slaves."

Elisha answered her, "How can I help you? Tell me, what of value do you have in your house?"

The woman said, "I don't have anything there except a jar of oil."

Then Elisha said, "Go outside and borrow some empty jars from all of your neighbors. Don't ask for just a few. Then you must go into your house and shut the door behind you and your sons. Then, pour a little bit of the oil into all the jars. Set the full ones to one side."

She left Elisha and shut the door; only she and her sons were in the house. As they brought the jars near to her, she poured out a tiny bit of the oil. When the jars were all full, she said to one of her sons, "Bring me another jar."

But he said, "There are no more jars." Then the oil stopped flowing.

She went and told Elisha, the man of the one true God. Elisha said, "Go, sell that oil and pay whatever you owe the creditor. You and your sons can live on what is left."

Elisha Restores the Son of the Woman From Shunem

One day, Elisha was passing by the town of Shunem where a rich woman lived. She begged Elisha to stay and eat something. So, every time Elisha traveled through Shunem, he stopped there to eat. The woman said to her husband, "I now know that Elisha is a holy man of God. He passes by our house often. Please let us prepare a small room above the porch. And, let us put a bed in that room for Elisha. We could also put a table, a chair, and a lamp stand there. Then, whenever he comes by, he can stay there."

One day, Elisha came there and went to this room to lay down. He said to his servant Gehazi, "Call the woman from Shunem. Now say to her: 'Listen, you have gone to all this trouble for us. What can I do for you? Do you want me to speak to the king or the general of the army for you?'"

The woman answered, "I live among my own people."

Elisha said, "But what can I do for her?"

Gehazi answered, "Well, she has no son, and her husband is old."

Then Elisha said, "Call her." So he called her, and she stood in the doorway. Then Elisha said, "About this time next year, after nine months of pregnancy, you will hold a son in your arms."

The woman said, "No, my master, O man of the one true God. Don't lie to me." (His prophecy seemed too good to be true.)

The woman did become pregnant, and the next year she gave birth to a son, just as Elisha had told her.

The child grew older. One day he went out to his father, who was with the men harvesting grain. The boy said to his father, "O my head! My head!"

The father said to his servant, "Carry him to his mother." The servant picked him up and took him to his mother. The boy lay on his mother's lap until noon. Then he died. She went up and lay the boy on Elisha's bed. Then she shut the door and went outside.

She called to her husband and said, "Please send me one of the male servants and one of the donkeys. Then I can go quickly to the man of the one true God and come back."

The woman's husband said, "Why do you want to go to Elisha today? It is not the New Moon Festival or the Sabbath Day."

She said, "It will be all right."

Then she saddled the donkey and said to her male servant, "Lead on. Don't slow down for me unless I tell you." (The trip from the Plain of Esdraelon to the top of Mount Carmel would have taken about five hours.) So, she traveled to Elisha, the man of the one true God, at Mount Carmel.

The man of the one true God saw her coming at a distance. So, he said to his servant Gehazi, "Look, there's the woman from Shunem. Please run to meet her now. Ask her: 'Are you all right? Is your husband all right? Is the little boy all right?'"

She answered Gehazi, "Everything is all right." (The woman was vague to Gehazi; she wanted to disclose her loss only to the prophet's ears.)

Then she came to Elisha, the man of the one true God, at the mountain. She caught hold of his feet. Gehazi came near to pull her away (to protect his master's dignity from disrespect). But the man of the one true God said to Gehazi, "Let her alone. She's very upset and the Lord has not told me about it. He has hidden it from me."

She said, "O my master, I didn't tell you that I wanted a son. Didn't I say: 'Don't fool me.'"

Then Elisha said to Gehazi, "Get ready. Take my walking stick in your hand and go quickly! If you meet anyone, don't greet him. If anyone greets you, don't answer him. Lay my walking stick on the face of the boy."

But the child's mother said, "As surely as the Lord lives and as you live, I won't leave you." So, Elisha got up and followed her.

Gehazi had gone on ahead. He laid the walking stick on the boy's face. But the child did not talk; there was no response. Then Gehazi went back to meet Elisha. He told Elisha, "The boy did not wake up."

Elisha came into the house, and behold, the child was lying on Elisha's bed. He was dead. When Elisha entered the room, he shut the door. Only he and the child were in the room. Then Elisha prayed to the Lord. Elisha got up on the bed and lay on top of the child, stretching himself out on top of the little boy. Elisha put his mouth on the child's mouth, and his eyes on the child's eyes, and his hands on the child's hands. Then the boy's skin became warm. Then Elisha got off and walked around the room. And, he went back and stretched himself on the child again. Then the boy sneezed seven times. And, the boy opened his eyes.

Elisha called Gehazi and said, "Call the woman from Shunem." And he did. When she came to Elisha, he said, "Pick up your son." She went and fell at Elisha's feet, and bowed face-down on the floor. Then she picked up her son and left the room.

The Poisonous Stew

Elisha came to Gilgal again. There was a time of hunger (a famine in the land). A group of prophets was sitting in front of him. He said to his servant, "Put the large pot on the fire. Boil some stew for these men."

One of them went into the field to gather plants. He found a wild vine. (Probably, it was the Colocynthis or the Ecbalium elaterium, a species of cucumber that is poisonous.) He picked gourds from the vine and filled his shawl with it. Then he came in and sliced the gourd and put it into the pot of stew. But they did not know what kind of gourd it was. Then they poured out the stew for the men to eat. But when they began to eat the stew, they cried out, "O man of the one true God! There is death in the pot!" They could not eat the stew.

Elisha told them to bring him some flour. Then he threw it into the pot. (Elisha's faith was in God, not in the flour.) He said, "Pour it out for the people to eat." And there was nothing harmful in the pot anymore.

Elisha Multiplies Bread

A man from Baal-Shalishah came to Elisha. He brought 20 loaves of barley bread from the first harvest to Elisha, the man of the one true God. (It is remarkable that this man brought these first-fruit, agricultural gifts to the prophet Elisha instead of to a priest as the Law of Moses specified. This is direct evidence that the godly men of Israel regarded the state religion introduced by Jeroboam as apostate. The true religion was then to be found only in the schools of the prophets.) He also brought ripened grain in his sack. Then Elisha said, "Give it to the people to eat."

Elisha's servant said, "How can I feed 100 men with so little?"

But Elisha said, "Give the bread and grain to the people to eat. This is what the Lord says: 'They will eat, and they will have food left over.'" Then Elisha's servant served them the food. And, the people ate and had food left over, just as the Lord had said.

My Time to Pray

Multiplication

Borrow not a few (2 Kings 4:3).

According to your faith, be it unto you (Matthew 9:29).

This story of "oil" is a wonderful illustration of faith. The woman's husband was dead, and she was about to lose her children to slavery. She was at the end of her wits. All she had was a little oil. Elisha was going to show her how God would multiply her oil into much. She was told to borrow pots and fill them with her oil. "Little is much, when God is in it." God used what she already had to solve her problem. Maybe that's what you need to hear today. God will use what you've already got to solve today's problem. *Lord, help me see with Your eyes the things I've already got that could solve my problems.*

When the woman filled the last pot she borrowed, the oil stopped flowing. When there were no other places to pour it, the flow stopped. Have you ever stopped God's flow of oil because you didn't provide more pots? Some churches have lost their evangelistic flow of oil because leadership didn't supply a bigger auditorium to hold more people, or they didn't begin another church service, or they didn't plant another new church. Maybe God was doing something in your life, but your lack of faith didn't provide "pots" for more oil from God. *Lord, give me faith to provide things I must provide, so You can continue the flow of oil in my life.*

Oil is a symbol of the Holy Spirit. Oil was burned in the Tabernacle to provide light, spiritual insights. Oil is cleansing to wash germs from a wound, symbolic of the Holy Spirit cleansing sin from our lives. Oil is a symbol of life, vitality, and lubrication. When you ask for God to anoint you with oil (as Elijah did Elisha in First Kings 19:16), you will receive the Holy Spirit. God will give you as much of the Holy Spirit as you will prepare to receive. *Lord, I repent of every known sin, so I can receive more of the Holy Spirit. Lord, I will learn as much as possible, so I can be used by the Holy Spirit to a greater degree. Lord, because I want more of You, I will prepare myself to receive more.*

There are many lessons in the story of Elisha raising the son from the dead. Perhaps *persistence* is a good principle to see. The mother was persistent. She would not be denied, she insisted on seeing Elisha. When Gehazi laid the walking stick on the boy, it didn't heal the boy. When Elisha lay on the boy and prayed, the dead skin became warm—a partial miracle. But Elisha didn't stop when God only began to answer his prayer. Elisha stretched himself again over the boy and the Lord worked further. The boy then opened his eyes and sneezed. When you begin praying, don't stop interceding with a partial answer. *Lord, I will continue praying, because I enjoy fellowship with You. I will continue praying because an answer depends on Your mercy, not my persistence. I will continue praying because I believe You exist and You hear me when I diligently seek You (see Heb. 11:6). Amen.*

33

Naaman Cured of Leprosy

Second Kings 5

Naaman was the general over the army of the king of Syria. To his
master, Naaman was a great man. He had much honor because
the Lord had used him to give victory to Syria. Naaman was a
strong warrior. However, Naaman had leprosy.

The Syrians used to go out to raid the Israelites. In so doing, they
captured a little girl from the land of Israel. She became a servant
girl to Naaman's wife. She said to her owner, "I wish that my
master would meet the prophet who lives in Samaria. Then he
would heal the skin disease of Naaman."

So, Naaman went to the king of Syria, and Naaman told him what the
Israelite girl had said.

The king of Syria said, "Go enter the land of Israel. I will send a letter to
the king of Israel." So, Naaman left on the trip. And, for gifts, he
took with them about 750 pounds of silver. He also took along
with him about 150 pounds of gold as a gift, and 10 sets of
clothes. Naaman brought the official letter to the king of Israel
(Joram). It read: "Listen, I am hereby sending my servant Naaman
to you, so that you can heal him of his skin disease."

After the king of Israel read the letter, he ripped his clothes. He said, "I
am not the one true God. I cannot give life or take it away. Why

does this man send someone with such a bad skin disease for me to heal? You can see that the king of Syria is trying to pick a fight with me."

Elisha, the man of the one true God, heard that the king of Israel had ripped his clothes. So, Elisha sent a message to the king, saying: "Why have you become so upset? Please let Naaman come to me. Then the king of Syria will know there is a true prophet in Israel."

So Naaman, along with his horses and chariot, went to Elisha's house. And, Naaman stood outside his door.

Elisha sent out a messenger to Naaman. The messenger said, "Go and wash in the Jordan River seven times. (The prophet wanted Naaman to learn that the power comes from Yahweh, but only if Naaman obeyed the word of God's prophet. The number seven is a symbol of completeness.) Then your skin will be restored, and you will be cured."

Naaman became angry and left. He thought to himself: "Look, I thought that Elisha would surely come outside and stand here, and that he would call upon the Name of the Lord, his God. Then, he would wave his hand over the leprous spot and cure the skin disease. Abana and Pharpar are the rivers of Damascus in my home country. They are better rivers than all the waters of Israel. Why couldn't I wash in those rivers and be cured?" So, Naaman turned and went away angry.

But Naaman's servants came and talked to him, reasoning: "My father, if that prophet had told you to do some great thing, wouldn't you have done it? Of course, you would. Therefore, it makes sense just to do it. It's simple. The only thing he told you was: 'Wash in the Jordan, and you will be cured.'" So, Naaman went down and dipped himself in the Jordan River seven times. He did exactly as Elisha, the man of the one true God, had said. Then Naaman's skin was restored; it became like the skin of a little boy. And, Naaman was cured.

Then Naaman and his entire group went back to the man of the one true God. He came and stood in the presence of Elisha and said, "Listen, now I know there is no God in all the earth except in Israel. Please accept a gift from me now."

But Elisha said, "I serve the Lord. As surely as the Lord lives, I will not accept anything." Naaman urged him to take the gift, but Elisha refused.

Then Naaman said, "Since you won't take the gift, please give me some dirt from the land of Israel. (He desired to use special earth to build an altar upon which he would continually offer sacrifices to the true God, Yahweh.) Give me as much as two of my mules can carry. From now on, I will not offer any whole burnt offerings or sacrifice to any other gods. I will worship only the Lord. May the Lord pardon me for doing this one thing: my master, the king, goes into the temple of his god Rimmon to worship. When he goes there, he will lean on my arm. Then I must bow down in that temple, too. May the Lord forgive me whenever I do that."

And Elisha said to him, "Go in peace."

Then Naaman left Elisha, and traveled a short distance.

Gehazi Was Greedy and Deceitful

Gehazi was the servant of Elisha, the man of the one true God. Gehazi thought: "Behold, my master has not accepted what Naaman the Syrian brought. As surely as the Lord lives, I will run after him. I'll obtain something from him." So, Gehazi went after Naaman.

When Naaman saw someone running after him, Naaman got off the chariot to meet Gehazi. He said, "Is everything all right?"

Gehazi said, "Everything is all right. My master has sent me, and said, 'Listen now, two young men just came to me. They are from the school of the prophets in the hill-country of Ephraim. Please give them 75 pounds of silver and two changes of clothes.'"

Naaman said, "Please take 150 pounds." And he urged Gehazi to take it. He tied 150 pounds of silver into two bags with two changes of clothes. Then he gave them to two of Naaman's servants. They carried them ahead of Gehazi. When they came to the hill, Gehazi took these things from Naaman's servants, and put them in the house. He let Naaman's servants go, and they left.

Then Gehazi went in and stood in the presence of his master. Elisha said to him, "Where have you been, Gehazi?"

Gehazi said, "I didn't go anywhere."

But Elisha said to him, "My spirit was with you. I knew when the man turned around from his chariot to meet you. It is not the proper time to receive money, clothes, olives, or grapes. It is not a time to receive sheep, oxen, male servants, or female servants.

"Naaman's leprosy will come on you and your children forever." When Gehazi left Elisha, he had the disease. He was as white as snow.

My Time to Pray

Deceit's Consequences

Be not deceived, God is not mocked, whatsoever a man soweth, that shall he also reap (Galatians 6:7).

The obvious application is that God punishes us with the thing we use to deceive others. The lies we tell become a tangled knot used to hang us. When Gehazi deceived Naaman and Elisha, he didn't deceive

God. God knew what he did, and God judged him with the leprosy that had just been cleansed from Naaman. *Lord, my heart is deceitful, give me wisdom to know myself. Forgive me for my unbelief when I don't realize You know all I think and do.*

God uses people when they faithfully witness for Him, no matter where they are, no matter the conditions. Here was a little Jewish girl who had been kidnapped and taken to a heathen culture and forced into servitude in the home of a military man. Yet her faithfulness led to Naaman's recovery and ultimate faith in the Lord. *Lord, teach me to give a faithful testimony for You in all conditions, no matter my circumstances.*

Did you see in the story how obedience led to blessing? When Naaman received his instructions to go dip in the Jordan River, he initially rejected the direction. He wanted to dip in the rivers back in his home of Syria. Also notice that Naaman wasn't partially healed with only one or two dips. It took complete obedience to realize the blessing of God. The same principle applies today. *Lord, I will obey You completely and instantly. When I don't act graciously, forgive me for my unbelief and rebellion.*

The potential of greed lurks within all of us if we don't recognize its presence and put it to death. We are told, *"They who are Christ's have crucified the flesh with its affections and lust"* (Gal. 5:24). And isn't greed nothing but lust for things or money? If it squeezes you, like the pressure of a python, it can kill. *Lord, by the blood of Christ I ask for forgiveness of sin. By the power of the cross, give me victory over greed so I can crucify its lust in my life. Amen.*

34

An Iron Ax Head Floats

Second Kings 6

The sons of the prophets said to Elisha, "Look, the place where we meet with you (the classroom) is too small. Please let us go to the Jordan River (where plenty of timber was available). So, each man could bring a log back, and let us build a shelter."

Elisha said, "Go."

One of them said, "Please come with us."

Elisha said, "I will go."

So, he went with them to the Jordan River, where they cut down some trees. As one man was cutting down a tree, the iron head of his ax flew off the handle into the water. He yelled, "O no, I borrowed that ax! (He had no money to buy another ax to replace the borrowed one, and could be sold into slavery over such a trivial debt. Compare Amos 2:6.)

Elisha, the man of the one true God, asked, "Where did it fall?" The man showed Elisha the place. Then Elisha broke off a stick and threw it into the water, and it made the iron ax head float. Elisha said, "Pick up the ax head." Then the man reached out and grabbed it.

Enemy Troops Blinded

King Ben-Hadad of Syria sponsored guerrilla warfare (bands of Syrian soldiers conducting troublesome raids into Israelite territory) against Israel. He had a staff meeting with his officers, and said, "I will set up my camp in such-and-such a place."

But Elisha, the man of the one true God, sent a message to the king of Israel, "Be careful, don't camp in that place; the Syrians are going down there."

The king of Israel checked the spot about which Elisha had warned him several times. So, the king added outposts for those places, and he protected himself there.

The king of Syria was very troubled about this. He summoned his officers, and said to them, "Tell me who of us is working for the king of Israel" (because the Israelites were anticipating every tactical move of the Syrian marauders).

But one of his officers said, "No, my master and king! It is Elisha, the prophet who is in Israel. He tells the king of Israel what you say in your bedroom."

The king said, "Go and locate him. Then I will send men and catch him."

The servants came back and reported: "He is in the village of Dothan." Then the king sent horses, chariots, and a large army to Dothan. They arrived at night and surrounded the village.

The servant of Elisha, the man of the one true God, got up early. When he went out, he saw a Syrian detachment with horses and chariots all around the village. The servant said to Elisha, "O no, my master, what can we do?"

Elisha said, "Do not be afraid, the army that fights for us is bigger than those who are with them." Then Elisha prayed: "O Lord, Who Is Always Present, please open my servant's eye. Let him see."

So, the Lord opened the eyes of the young man. And, he saw that the mountain was full of horses and chariots of fire all around Elisha.

As the Syrians came down toward Elisha, he prayed to the Lord, and said, "Please confuse these non-Jews." So, the Lord caused the Syrian detachment to be fooled, just as Elisha had asked. Elisha said to them, "This is not the right road. This is not the right city. Elisha doesn't even live here in this village. Follow me, and I will take you to the man you are looking for." Then Elisha led them to the city of Samaria. (The Syrians really wanted the king of Israel, not Elisha. Elisha was merely an obstacle in the way of defeating the king of Israel.)

After they entered Samaria, Elisha said, "O Lord, Who Is Always Present, open the eyes of these Syrian men, so that they can see." So, the Lord opened their eyes. And, the Syrian detachment saw that they were inside the city of Samaria.

The king of Israel saw the Syrian detachment and said to Elisha, "My father, should I kill them? May I kill them?"

Elisha answered, "No, you must not kill them! Kill only those people whom you captured with your sword and your bow. Instead, give them food and water. And, let them eat and drink. Then let them go home to their master." (Thus demonstrating Yahweh's mercy and kindness, as well as Israel's desire for peace.)

So, Joram prepared a big banquet for the Syrian detachment. They ate and drank. Then the king of Israel sent them away. They went home to their master. The marauders of Syria did not go into the land of Israel for quite awhile.

Famine Results From the Siege of Samaria

Later (a few years later, after the Syrians had forgotten the kind
treatment that they had received from the Israelites), Ben-
Hadad, the king of Syria, gathered all of his army and went up
to surround and besiege the city of Samaria. This was a time
of terrible hunger in Samaria. (The Syrians were attempting to
starve them to surrender.) It was so bad that a donkey's head
(the worst and cheapest part of this unclean animal) was sold for
about 2 pounds of silver. Half of a pint of dove's dung was sold
for about 2 ounces of silver. The king of Israel was passing by
on top of the wall. A woman yelled out to him: "Help me, O my
master and king."

The king said, "If the Lord won't help you, how can I help you? Can
I get food from the threshing floor or from the wine press?
No, they are empty." Then the king said to her, "What is your
trouble?"

She answered, "This woman said to me: 'Give up your son, so that we
can eat him today. Then we will eat my son tomorrow.' So, we
boiled my son and ate him. Then, the next day, I said to her,
'Give up your son, so that we can eat him.' But she has hidden
her son!"

When the king heard the woman's words, he ripped his clothes. As the
king was passing by on top of the wall, the people saw that he
was wearing sackcloth (an outward sign to show his "contrition").
He said, "The head of Elisha, the son of Shaphat, will be
removed from his body today. May God punish me terribly if this
doesn't happen."

The king sent a messenger to Elisha who was sitting in his house. The
elders were sitting with him. But before the messenger arrived,
Elisha spoke to them, saying, "This son of a murderer is sending

men to take off my head. Listen, when the messenger arrives, shut the door. Push against it and don't let him in. The sound of his master's feet is behind him." (Elisha wanted them to detain the executioner long enough until King Joram himself arrived.)

While Elisha was still talking with the elders, the king came down to him. (The king was intending to enforce his rash order in person.) The king said, "Listen, all this trouble has come from the Lord. Why should I wait for the Lord any longer?"

My Time to Pray

God of Creation

Nothing is impossible with God (Luke 1:37).

Did you notice that God is concerned with things like an ax head being lost in a river? First the "preacher" told his leader Elisha; and because of the faith of Elisha, God returned the ax head to the "preacher." The Lord is concerned about all the things in our lives, and we can pray about them. *Lord, help me see Your hand in the small and large things of my life. Thank You for guiding me in the things I lose and find* (see Rom. 8:28).

God can overrule the laws of nature, in this case the law of density. Remember, laws are the power by which God runs His universe, because laws are an extension of His person and His power. So when you believe in a God like this, miracles are possible. C.S. Lewis said, "A miracle is the interruption of the laws of nature for a divine purpose." In this case, the Lord made the ax head float to "save" the preacher who borrowed it. *Lord, I know You run the universe by Your power through Your laws. But You Lord are not mechanistic; You can override Your laws for Your purpose and glory. Thank You for Your personal care of me to work all things to Your glory.*

The "preacher" was not only embarrassed because he had borrowed the ax, it probably represented a price he didn't have. He could possibly be thrown into slavery if he couldn't pay for the ax head. No wonder the preacher was alarmed when he lost the ax head in the water. God did a miracle to "save" the preacher's life. Do you think God has done a "miracle" for you—that you did not see—to "save" your life on an occasion? *Lord, thank You for protecting my life even when I didn't know it.*

God loves symbols, so Elisha threw a stick into the water, perhaps because a stick could float. Then the floating ax head could be retrieved. Notice what God *didn't* do. God didn't lead the "preacher" to dive into the water to find the ax head. God didn't give the "preacher" money to pay for the ax head. The ax head didn't float on the air to the preacher, it floated on water so it could be retrieved. God did the miracle that was understandable. *God, thank You for doing things in my life that I can understand and relate to.*

The servant of Elisha expected the worst when he saw that Dothan was surrounded by the Syrian army. He was a realist or a pessimist, seeing only danger. He didn't look at things from God's perspective. This is another way of saying the servant didn't have faith in God that the Lord works all things together for His purpose. Is that you? Do you panic in the face of danger? *Lord, give me faith to see Your hand working in my life. I confess I get discouraged when things go against me. Forgive me. Help me look beyond trouble to the end result that You are planning. Help me work aggressively to be victorious in all things.*

The servant was "blinded" to see God's protection. God has angels everywhere to protect His children, but we don't always see them, as the servant was ignorant to God's plan. We are promised that we *"unwittingly entertain angels"* (Heb. 13:2). They are, *"Sent forth to minister for those who will inherit salvation"* (Heb. 1:14). *Lord, I believe You have angels that protect me. Thank You for the abundant times You've protected me, that I didn't know I had been in danger. Then for those scary times I remember, I praise You for Your protecting hand.*

Did you see the double reverse blinding in the story? First, Elisha's servant was blinded to the protection of God's army. Second, the Syrian army was blinded so they didn't know Elisha was talking to them, and leading them into the capital city of Samaria. It was then Elisha prayed for the Syrian soldiers, *"Lord, open the eyes of these men that they may see"* (2 Kings 6:20). In both cases, God was the source of illumination. *Lord, open my eyes that I may see all the things You have for me. Amen.*

35

Open Windows of Heaven

Second Kings 7

Elisha said, "Listen to the word from the Lord, 'About this time tomorrow, 7 quarts of fine flour will be sold for two-fifths of an ounce (a shekel) of silver, and 13 quarts of barley will be sold for two-fifths of an ounce of silver. This will happen at the gate of Samaria!'"

Then the officer who was close to the king answered Elisha, the man of the one true God, saying, "Look, even if the Lord opened windows of Heaven, that could not happen."

Elisha said, "Because you have said that, you will see it with your own eyes. However, you will not eat any of it!"

The Syrian Army Leaves Quickly

There were four men with leprosy at the entrance to the city gate. They said to each other, "Why are we sitting here...until we die? A state of hunger exists inside the city. So, if we go into the city, we will die there. But, if we stay here, we will die. So now, let us go to the Syrian camp. If they spare us, we will live. But, if they kill us, then we die."

So, the lepers got up at twilight and went to the edge of the Syrian camp. But, when they arrived, no one was there. The Lord had caused the Syrian army to hear the sound of chariots, horses, and a large army. They had said to each other, "The king of Israel has hired the Hittites and the Egyptian princes to attack us." So, they ran away in the twilight. They left their tents, horses, and donkeys. They left the camp standing and ran for their lives.

The men with leprosy came to the edge of the camp, and went into one of the tents. They ate and drank. They carried silver, gold, and clothes out of the camp and hid them. Then they came back and entered another tent. They carried valuable things away from this tent, and went and hid those things, too.

Then they said to each other, "We are doing the wrong thing. Today we have good news, but we are remaining silent. If we wait until the sun comes up, we will be punished. Let us go now and tell the people in the king's palace."

So, they went and called to the gatekeepers of the city, saying, "We went to the Syrian camp—but, listen, no one is there. We didn't hear anyone. But, the horses and donkeys were still tied up, and the tents were still standing." Then the gatekeepers shouted out and told the people in the king's palace.

So, the king got up during the night and said to his officers, "Now, let me tell you what the Syrians are up to. They know that we are starving. They have left the camp to hide in the fields. They are thinking: 'After the Israelites come out of the city, we will capture them alive. Then we will enter the city.'"

One of King Joram's officers answered, "Please let some of our men take five horses that are still left in the city. These are doomed like all the Israelites who are left. They are also about to die. Let us send them out to see what has happened."

So, the men took two chariots with horses. The king sent them after the Syrian army. He told them, "Go out and see what has happened." The men followed the Syrian army as far as the Jordan River (about 40 miles). The road was full of clothes and equipment. The Syrians had thrown these things away as they had run away. So, the messengers came back and told this news to the king.

Then the people went out and took valuable things from the Syrian camp.

So, it did occur that 7 quarts of fine flour were sold for two-fifths of an ounce (a shekel) of silver. And, 13 quarts of barley were sold for two-fifths of an ounce of silver. It happened just as the Lord had said (fulfilling Elisha's prediction of Second Kings 7:1).

The king appointed the officer who was close to him to be in charge over the gate. But the people trampled the officer at the gate, and he died. This happened just as the man of the one true God had told the king (see 2 Kings 7:2).

My Time to Pray

Share Good News

This is not right. This is wonderful news, and we are not sharing it with anyone! (2 Kings 7:9 TLB)

There are some people on earth who are so desperate and frustrated, that they would just as soon die. That was the condition of the lepers. They were going to die prematurely because of their leprosy. If they went into the city where people were starving, they would die. If they sat at the gate and did nothing, they would die of starvation. If they went out to the Syrian camp, they could be killed. They went to the only place where they knew there was food, they went to the Syrians. Have you ever noticed that God doesn't do anything for you until you are desperate, then He answers your prayers? *Lord, I'm desperate for spiritual food, I'm starving spiritually on the husk of this world's food. Feed me with the food of abundance I find in Your presence.*

Sometimes the dangers that most scare us are not really threats at all. We are afraid, even terrified, of a future event. But when the event arrives, it isn't as bad as we expected. Sometimes a terrifying future event turns out to be good or wonderful. Just as the four lepers found food and riches in the place where they expected a probable death. *Lord, help me look at future terror through Your eyes. Give me faith to see Your hand in the future. Remind me that You are already in the future and You will work all things for Your plan.*

God loves to take lepers with no hope and give them an abundance of blessing. We once were in the leprosy of sin, but God saved us and washed us of our sin in the blood of Christ. Then He gives us spiritual abundance in Christ. Sometimes when we suffer in the poverty of this world, God wants to feed us with His grace. If all you want is happiness in money, you may be starving in the sin city of Samaria. But if you surrender everything to Christ, you will find life more abundantly. *Lord, I don't want money, but I want the joy that money gives. Give me that joy, even if I live in poverty on this earth. Teach me satisfaction that comes from Your presence.*

That's another lesson in this story. God may have already defeated the enemy that scares you to death. Also, God may have already routed your enemy and sent him fleeing, but you're still in bondage. Why? Because you still think your enemy is bigger than you see. So you stay bound in bondage in the city of Samaria, starving to death. *Lord, teach me the lesson, "Greater is He who is in you, than he who is in the world"* (1 John 4:4). *Amen.*

36

THE SHUNEMITE WOMAN RETURNS

Second Kings 8

Elisha had talked to the woman whose son he had brought back to life. He said, "Get up and go with your family. Stay any place you can. This is because the Lord has called for a famine. And, this one will last for seven years in this land." (It was to be twice as long as the drought called for in the time of Elijah [see 1 Kings 17:1ff; James 5:17].) So, the woman got up and did just as the man of the one true God said. She left with her family, and stayed in the land of the Philistines for seven years.

At the end of the seven years, the woman came back from the land of the Philistines, and went to appeal to the king for her house and fields to be restored to her. The king was talking with Gehazi. (This incident probably happened well before the time that he was cursed with leprosy [see 2 Kings 5:27].) Gehazi was the servant of the man of the one true God. The king had said to Gehazi, "Please tell me all the great things that Elisha has done." Now as Gehazi was telling the king how Elisha had brought a corpse back to life, the woman whose son Elisha had brought back to life, came to appeal to the king for her house and her fields.

Gehazi said, "O my master and king, this is the woman. And, this is her son whom Elisha brought back to life." (Her arrival was not a coincidence; it was the providence of God, compare Romans 8:28.)

The king asked the woman about it, and she told him that it was true. Then the king chose an officer to help her. He ordered: "Give the woman everything that belongs to her. Give her all the money that was made from her land, from the day she left the country until now."

Hazael Murders King Ben-Hadad

Elisha went to Damascus, the capital city of Syria. Now Ben-Hadad, the king of Syria, was sick. Someone told him, "The man of the one true God has come here to Damascus."

Then the king said to Hazael, "Take a gift in your hand and go meet the man of the one true God. Ask the Lord through him: "Will I get well from my sickness or not?"

So, Hazael went to meet Elisha and took a gift with him. It was 40 camels loaded with every good thing in Damascus. He came and stood in front of Elisha. Hazael said, "Your son Ben-Hadad, the king of Syria, has sent me to you. He wants to know whether he will get well from his sickness or not?"

Then Elisha said to Hazael, "Go and tell Ben-Hadad, 'You will surely get well.' Then Elisha added this comment to Hazael: But the Lord has told me that he will really die—by your hand.'" Elisha stared at Hazael until Hazael felt ashamed. (The penetrating look of Elisha convinced Hazael that Hazael's plot was known to the prophet.) Then Elisha, the man of the one true God, wept.

Hazael asked, "Why are you crying, master?"

Elisha answered, "Because I know what harm you will do to the Israelites. You will set their strong, walled cities on fire. You will kill their young men with the sword. You will hurl their tiny babies to the ground. And, you will rip open their pregnant women."

Hazael said, "I, your servant, am only a dog. How could I do such things?"

Elisha answered, "The Lord has shown me that you will be king over Syria."

Then Hazael left Elisha and went to see his master. Ben-Hadad said to Hazael, "What did Elisha say to you?"

Hazael answered, "He told me that you will surely get well."

But the next day, Hazael took a blanket and dipped it in water. Then he put it over Ben-Hadad's face (to smother him) and he died. (Neither God nor Elisha instructed Hazael to assassinate Ben-Hadad, but they knew what he would do.) So Hazael became the king in Ben-Hadad's place.

Jehoram Rules Over Judah

Jehoram, the son of Jehoshaphat, became the king of Judah. This was during Joram's fifth year as king of Israel. Joram was the son of Ahab. Jehoram was 32 years old when he became king of Judah. He ruled eight years in Jerusalem. But Jehoram followed the ways of the kings of Israel, just like the household of Ahab had done. It was because Ahab and Jezebel's daughter was Jehoram's wife. Jehoram did what was evil in the sight of the Lord. Yet, for the sake of David, His servant, the Lord was not willing to destroy Judah. The Lord had promised David that his descendants would always have a kingdom.

In Jehoram's time, the nation of Edom broke away from Judah's rule. The people of Edom chose their own king. So, Jehoram and all his chariots went to Zair. At night, the Edomites surrounded Jehoram and his chariot commanders. Jehoram got up and attacked the Edomites, but his army ran away to their tents. (King Jehoram and his chariots were able to break through the lines of the Edomites so that Jehoram escaped with his life.) So, the Edomites broke away from the rule of Judah. And they are still separate today (at the time the Book of Second Kings was written).

About the same time, Libnah (a small Canaanite state) also broke away from Judah's rule.

The other deeds of Jehoram and all the things that he did are written down in the Book of the History of the Kings of Judah. Jehoram died, and was buried with his ancestors in the City of David. Jehoram's son, Ahaziah, ruled in his place.

Ahaziah Rules Over Judah

Ahaziah, the son of Jehoram, became the king of Judah during Joram's twelfth year as the king of Israel. Ahaziah was 22 years old when he became the king of Judah. He ruled for one year in Jerusalem. His mother's name was Athaliah. She was a granddaughter of Omri, the king of Israel, the daughter of Ahab and Jezebel. Ahaziah followed the ways of Ahab's household. He did what was evil in the sight of the Lord, just as Ahab's household had always done. He did this because he was a son-in-law in Ahab's household.

Ahaziah went with Joram, the son of Ahab, to Ramoth-Gilead. (These two Jewish kings were attempting to recover Ramoth-Gilead. Fourteen years earlier [see 1 Kings 22:3-36], King Ahab and King Jehoshaphat had attempted to do the same thing, but they failed to accomplish it.) There they fought against Hazael, the king of Syria. But the Syrians wounded Joram. So, King

Joram returned to Jezreel to heal from his injuries. He had been wounded by the Syrians at Ramoth-Gilead. This was when he fought Hazael, the king of Syria.

And Ahaziah, the son of Jehoram, the king of Judah, went down to see Joram, the son of Ahab, at Jezreel because Joram had been wounded.

My Time to Pray

Time to Weep

"For My thoughts are not your thoughts, nor are your ways My ways," says the Lord (Isaiah 55:8).

God uses evil people to punish good people when good people rebel against God and do evil. Often the believer will complain in prayer to God, "Why does the evil person prosper?" Perhaps God is getting ready to use the evil person to punish the good person who has turned against God. In this chapter, God sees the kingdom of Syria is transferred from Ben-Hadad to Hazael. God will punish the ten northern tribes of Israel with Hazael. But this action is not without emotions. Elisha, the man close to God, weeps because he knows the evil things this evil man will do. *Lord, I know You use evil men to punish Your rebellious children. Don't punish me. I repent of my rebellion. I look to You for grace.*

Evil kings are allowed to rule in God's great plan. We may not understand why God would use an evil person, but God's ways are not our ways, and God's thoughts are not our thoughts (see Isa. 55:8-9). An evil king can have no authority, except God allows him to rule (see Rom. 13:1). God raised up Nebuchadnezzar to punish His rebellious nation in 586 B.C. *Lord, when I see evil in my rulers, help me always do right in the right way. Amen.*

37

JEHU IS PRIVATELY ANOINTED KING OF ISRAEL

Second Kings 9

The prophet Elisha summoned a man from the school of the prophets. Elisha said to him, "Tighten your clothes around you. Take this small container of olive oil in your hand, and go to Ramoth-Gilead. When you arrive there, you will see Jehu, the son of Jehoshaphat. Jehoshaphat was the son of Nimshi. Go in and cause Jehu to get up from among his friends. Take him into a private room. Take this container of olive oil and pour it on Jehu's head. Say this: 'This is what the Lord says: I have anointed you as king over Israel.' Then, you must open the door and run away. Do not delay."

So the young man, the servant of the prophet Elisha, went to Ramoth-Gilead. When he arrived, he saw the captains of the army sitting together. He said, "Captain, I have a message for you."

Jehu asked, "Which one of us is it for?"

The young man said, "For you, O captain."

Jehu got up and went into the house. Then the young prophet poured the olive oil on Jehu's head. He said to Jehu, "This is what the Lord, the God of Israel, says: 'I have anointed you as king over the Lord's people—over Israel. But you must destroy the dynasty

of Ahab, your master. I will punish Jezebel for the murders of My
servants, the prophets, and for all of the servants of the Lord who
were murdered by her hand. So, all of Ahab's household will die.
I will cut off every male in Ahab's family in Israel—whether he
is a slave or a free person. I will cause Ahab's dynasty to become
like the dynasty of Jeroboam, the son of Nebat. They will be
like the dynasty of Baasha, the son of Ahijah. The dogs will eat
Jezebel on a certain property (the land that formerly belonged to
Naboth and his sons [see 1 Kings 21:1-3,15]) at Jezreel. And, no
one will bury her.'"

Then the young prophet opened the door and ran away.

Jehu went out to his master's captains. One of them said to Jehu, "Is
everything all right? Why did this crazy man come to you?"

Jehu answered them, "Oh, it was nothing. You know that sort of fellow
and how he talks."

They answered, "That's not true. Tell us now."

Jehu said, "These are the exact words that that young prophet told me:
'This is what the Lord says: "I have anointed *you* to be king over
Israel."'"

Then each of the captains hurried to remove his outer robe, and
spread them out for Jehu to go up on the stairs. (As a substitute
for a throne.) Then they blew the trumpet (signifying that a
"coronation" was in progress [see 2 Sam. 15:10; 1 Kings 1:39;
2 Kings 11:14]). They said, "Jehu is king!"

Jehu Kills Joram and Ahaziah

So, Jehu, the son of Jehoshaphat, made plans against Joram. Now, Joram
and all Israel had been defending Ramoth-Gilead from Hazael,
the king of Syria. But King Joram had to return to Jezreel to

heal from the injuries that the Syrians had given to him when he fought against Hazael, the king of Syria.

Jehu said, "If you agree with this, don't let anyone leave the city. They might tell the news in Jezreel."

Then Jehu got into his chariot and set out for Jezreel. Joram was resting there. And the king of Judah, Ahaziah, had gone down to visit Joram.

Now, the lookout man was standing on the watchtower in Jezreel. He saw Jehu's troops coming. He said, "I see some soldiers."

Joram said, "Pick a horseman and send him to meet them. Tell him to ask, 'Do you bring good news?'"

So, the horsemen rode out to meet Jehu. The horseman said, "This is what the king says: 'Do you bring good news?'"

Jehu said, "That's none of your business. Come along behind me."

The watchman reported, "The messenger reached them. But he is not coming back!"

So, Joram sent out a second horseman. This rider came to Jehu's group and said, "This is what the king says: 'Do you bring good news?'"

Jehu answered, "That's none of your business. Come along behind me."

The watchman reported, "Look, the messenger reached them, but he is not coming back. There is a man driving a chariot, and he is driving like Jehu, the grandson of Nimshi. He drives like a crazy man."

Joram said, "Get my chariot ready." Then the servant got Joram's chariot ready. Both Joram and the king of Israel, and Ahaziah, the king of Judah, went out. Each king went in his own chariot to meet Jehu. And, they met him at the former property of Naboth of Jezreel.

When Joram saw Jehu, he said, "Is everything all right, Jehu?"

Jehu answered, "There will never be any peace as long as your
    mother Jezebel worships so many idols and practices so much
    witchcraft."

Immediately, Joram turned the horses to run away. He yelled to Ahaziah,
    "It's a trick, Ahaziah."

Then Jehu drew back his bow and shot Joram between his shoulders.
    The arrows went through Joram's heart, and he fell down in his
    chariot.

Then Jehu ordered Bidkar, his chariot officer: "Pick up Joram's body and
    throw it onto the field of Naboth of Jezreel. Do you remember
    when you and I rode together with Ahab, Joram's father? The
    Lord spoke this prophecy against King Ahab: 'Yesterday I saw the
    blood of Naboth and the blood of his sons,' says the Lord. 'So,
    I will punish Ahab in this field,' says the Lord." Then Jehu said,
    "Therefore, take Joram's body and toss it onto that field, just as
    the Lord has said."

When Ahaziah, the king of Judah, saw all this, he ran away in the
    direction of Beth-Haggan. But Jehu chased him, shouting, "Shoot
    Ahaziah, too." Ahaziah was wounded in his chariot on the way
    up to Gur near Ibleam. Ahaziah got as far as Megiddo, but he
    died there. The servants of Ahaziah carried his body in a chariot
    to Jerusalem. They buried him with his ancestors in his tomb
    in Jerusalem. Ahaziah had become king over Judah in Joram's
    eleventh year as king of Israel. Joram was the son of Ahab.

Jezebel Is Killed

When Jehu came to Jezebel, Jezebel heard about what happened. So,
    she painted her eyes and fixed her hair. Then she looked out of

the upstairs window. Jehu entered the city gate, and Jezebel said, "Have you come in peace, O Zimri you who have killed your master?" (Jezebel sarcastically calls Jehu "Zimri" because Zimri was the assassin of Baasha and his entire household [see 1 Kings 16:8-20].)

Jehu looked up at the window and said, "Who is on my side? Who?" Two or three eunuchs looked out of the window at Jehu. Jehu said to them, "Throw her down." So, they threw Jezebel down, and the horses trampled her body. Some of her blood spattered on the wall and on the horses.

Then Jehu went into the house. He ate and drank. After that, Jehu said, "Now let's see about this cursed woman. Bury her, because she was a king's daughter."

The men went to bury Jezebel, but they could not find her body. They could only find her skull, the feet, and the palms of her hands. So, they went back and told Jehu. Then Jehu said, "The Lord did say this through His servant Elijah from Tishbeh: 'The dogs will eat the flesh of Jezebel on the property at Jezreel. And, her corpse will be like manure on the surface of the field on the property at Jezreel. Then people cannot say: "This is Jezebel's *grave*.""

My Time to Pray

God's Plan in Motion

The whole house of Ahab shall perish (2 Kings 9:8).

When Jehu was anointed by the unnamed prophet, he was asked by one of the other captains what happened. Jehu answered, "It was nothing." Yet the oil dripping from his head told the story. They demanded the truth. The fact that the other officers rallied to support Jehu showed his popularity with them was greater than their loyalty to the king. The anointing of Jehu in inauguration into the office of king was quickly approved when they shouted, "Jehu is king." God's plan was set in motion. *Lord, help me see Your plan in my life, just as You have a plan in politics.*

Our character is reflected in our actions. Jehu was an activist. He immediately acted on his anointing. He went to kill both Joram and Ahaziah, followed quickly by killing Jezebel. What can we say of Jehu, *"He is driving like Jehu...he drives like a crazy man"* (2 Kings 9:20). *Lord, my inner character is reflected in my actions. Where my actions don't reflect my faith in You, change me to be like You.*

The Lord had predicted the elimination of Ahab's line (see 1 Kings 21:17-24) and carried it out years later by the hand of Jehu. Just as dogs originally licked the blood of Ahab (see 1 Kings 22:38), so again dogs ate the flesh of Jezebel on Naboth's property (see 2 Kings 9:35-37). *Lord, Your prophecies always come true. Forgive me when I don't believe Your predictions. I will take comfort in Your sovereignty, that You rule in the affairs of men.*

There was a great sermon preached by R.G. Lee, "Payday Someday."[1] God doesn't always judge sin immediately, when a person sins. Sometimes it looks like the sinner has gotten away with their sin. But there will be a day when God judges all sin—payday someday. *Lord, I know You will judge sin, so I will live holy. Amen.*

Endnote

1. I heard this sermon in Columbia, South Carolina, in 1951, and at Thomas Road Baptist Church in 1978, and at Liberty University in 1982.

38

Ahab's Descendants Are Killed

Ahab had 70 descendants in Samaria. Jehu wrote letters and sent them to Samaria and to the officials of Jezreel, the elders. He also sent them to the guardians of the sons of Ahab. Jehu said: "Now then, as soon as this letter gets to you, here's what you must do. You have your master's sons with you, and you have chariots, horses, and a city with strong walls. You also have weapons. So, choose the best and most worthy person among your master's sons. Make him king. (Jehu is challenging anyone to defend the descendants of Ahab. Jehu knows that he is stronger than anyone.) Then fight for your master's household."

But they were very scared. They thought: *Listen, the two kings* (Joram and Ahaziah [see 2 Kings 9:21-28]) *could not stop Jehu. So, how could we stop him?* The palace manager, the city governor, the elders, and the guardians sent a message to Jehu, saying, "We are your servants. We will do everything that you tell us to do. We won't make any man king. Do whatever you think is best."

Then Jehu wrote a second letter, saying: "If you are on my side, and you will obey me, cut off the heads of your master's sons. And, come to me at Jezreel tomorrow about this time." (Jehu was demanding absolute loyalty to himself.)

There were 70 sons of the king's family. They were with the leading men of the city who were raising them. When the leaders received this letter, they took the king's sons and killed all 70 of them. They put their heads in baskets, and sent them to Jehu at Jezreel. The messenger came to Jehu and reported to Jehu: "They have brought the heads of the sons of the king."

Then Jehu said, "Put the heads in two piles at the city gate until morning." (The purpose was to strike terror into the hearts of the people, so that they would not resist his takeover.)

In the morning, Jehu went out and stood in front of the people and said to them all, "You are innocent. Look, I made plans against my master, and I killed him. But who killed all these? You should know therefore that nothing that the Lord says will fail to come true. Everything that the Lord said about Ahab's household would come true. The Lord has spoken through His servant Elijah. And, the Lord has done what He said."

And Jehu killed everyone of Ahab's household in Jezreel who was still alive. He also killed all of Ahab's leaders, his close friends, and his priests. No one who had helped Ahab survived.

Ahaziah's Descendants Are Killed

Then Jehu got up and traveled to Samaria. He went on the road to Beth-Eked of the Shepherds. There Jehu met some relatives of Ahaziah, the king of Judah. Jehu asked them, "Who are you?"

They answered, "We are relatives of Ahaziah. We have come down to visit the families of the king and the king's mother (Jezebel)."

Then Jehu said, "Take them alive." So, Jehu's soldiers captured Ahaziah's relatives alive. But, later they killed them at the well near Beth-Eked. There were 42 relatives. Jehu did not leave anyone alive.

After Jehu left there, he met Jehonadab, the son of Rechab. (The Rechabites lived in tents and worshiped Yahweh. They were Kenites who accompanied Israel when they exited Egypt. Jehu wanted the endorsement of this reputable man.) He was also on his way to meet Jehu. Jehu greeted him and said, "Are you as good a friend to me as I am to you?" (Literally, "Is your heart, as my heart?")

Jehonadab answered, "Yes, I am."

Jehu said, "If you are, then give me your hand." So, Jehonadab offered him his hand, and Jehu pulled him up into the chariot (a position of great honor). Jehu said, "Come with me. You can see how strong my feelings are for the Lord." (However, Jehu's ambition was mostly to gain political power.) So, Jehu had Jehonadab ride in his chariot.

When Jehu arrived at Samaria, he killed all of Ahab's family. He did this until he had destroyed all of those who were remaining in Samaria. Jehu carried out what the Lord had told Elijah.

The Worshipers of Baal Are Killed

Then Jehu gathered all the people together and said to them, "Ahab served Baal a little. But Jehu will serve Baal even more.

"Now, summon for me all of Baal's prophets and all of his priests. Call all the people who worship Baal. Don't let anyone miss this meeting. I have a great sacrifice for Baal. Anyone who is not there will not remain alive." (However, Jehu was tricking them, so that he could exterminate the worshipers of Baal.) Jehu said, "Prepare a holy meeting for Baal." So, they announced the meeting. Then Jehu sent word throughout all Israel. All the worshipers of Baal came. Not one stayed home. They came into the temple of Baal. The temple was filled from one side to the other.

Jehu spoke to the man who kept the robes. He said, "Bring out robes for all the worshipers of Baal." So, he brought out the special robes for them. Then Jehu and Jehonadab, the son of Rechab, went into the temple of Baal. Jehu said to the worshipers of Baal, "Look around. Be sure that there are no servants of the Lord with you. Be sure there are only people here who worship Baal." So, the worshipers of Baal went in to offer sacrifices and whole burnt offerings.

But Jehu had 80 men waiting outside. He told them, "Don't let anyone escape. If you let anyone escape, then you must pay with your own life!"

Jehu finished offering the whole burnt offering. (This was only a ruse to dispel any suspicion by Baal worshipers.) Then he spoke to the guards and the captains, saying, "Go in and kill the worshipers of Baal. Don't let anyone come out." So, the guards and the captains killed the worshipers of Baal with the sword. They threw out the bodies of the worshipers of Baal. Then they went into the inner rooms of the temple of Baal. And, they brought out the pillars (the Phoenician pillar idols were simple columns, obelisks, or posts) of the temple of Baal and burned them. Then they tore down the stone pillar of Baal. They also tore down the temple of Baal. They made it into a latrine (a sewage pit), and it is still one today.

So, Jehu destroyed Baal worship in Israel. However, Jehu did not stop practicing the sins of Jeroboam the son of Nebat. Jeroboam had caused Israel to sin. They still worshiped the golden calves in Bethel and Dan.

The Lord said to Jehu (probably by the mouth of Elisha), "You have done well. You have done what is right in My sight. You have done to the household of Ahab as I wanted. Your descendants—as far as your great-great-grandchildren (for more than 100 years)—will

PRAYING FIRST AND SECOND KINGS AND SECOND CHRONICLES

be kings of Israel." But Jehu was not careful to keep the teachings of the Lord, the God of Israel, with all his heart. (Jehu's dynasty was based on military might, not religious principle.) He did not stop doing the same sins that Jeroboam had done. Jeroboam had caused Israel to sin.

Jehu Dies

At that time, the Lord began to make Israel smaller. Hazael defeated them in all the land of Israel. Hazael conquered all the territory on the east side of the Jordan River. This was the entire land of Gilead. It was the region of the tribes of Gad, Reuben, and Manasseh. Hazael captured the land from Aroer by the Arnon Ravine, even Gilead and Bashan.

The other things that Jehu did are written down in the Book of the History of the Kings of Israel. Everything he did and all his victories are recorded there. Jehu died and they buried him in the city of Samaria. Jehu's son, Jehoahaz, became the king in his place. Jehu had been king over Israel for 28 years in Samaria.

My Time to Pray

Heart Obedience

Come out from among them and be separate, says the Lord. Do not touch what is unclean (2 Corinthians 6:17).

Jehu was a moral reformer. He cleansed Israel of the foreign god of Baal, but he allowed the golden calves to remain. Israel continued to worship them as far away as Dan. But God is seeking more than outward moral obedience, God wants obedience from the heart. God wants worship. *Lord, I will obey outwardly, as did Jehu. But, my obedience will also come from the heart. I worship You.*

When I (Elmer) was a youth in Sunday School, my teacher said all the kings of the north were not "saved" men, that I wouldn't see them in Heaven. I asked a question, "What about Jehu?" I understood enough to know Jehu cleansed the land of moral and religious corruption. I forget what answer my teacher gave, but still I have a question, "Will I see Jehu in Heaven?" If only perfect people make it to Heaven, none of us will be there. Who will be in Heaven is God's decision, not ours. *Lord, I'm not perfect, forgive every fault and sin. Lord, give me the righteousness of Jesus Christ. If I have to depend on my own righteousness, I'll not make it. Lord, look at me through the perfection of Jesus Christ.*

We ought to be as hard on compromise as was Jehu. He herded all Baal worshipers together and killed them. That sounds extreme to me. But when I consider that Jesus had to die for every sin and compromise—that was extreme. Right is right, and wrong must be punished. The Lord is extremely thorough in punishing sin. Jesus died for every sin of every person, for all time. *Lord, thank You for being thorough with my sin. Thank You that Jesus went to extreme limits to die for me.*

Too many people live for their children. The influence of King Ahab stopped when all the children in his line were killed. Jehu also eliminated the line of Ahaziah. *Lord, your prophecies about King Ahab's line came true, just as You predicted. Help me study all Your prophecies to see what You are planning for the future of humankind.*

Jehu killed all the Baal worshipers. Jehu did on earth what God will do at the Great White Judgment Throne. *Lord, I will crucify any idols I have in my life (an idol is anything between me and God). Teach me to be as thorough with false gods as Jehu was. I will not mess around with sin. Amen.*

39

JOASH BECOMES KING

Now Ahaziah's mother was Athaliah. She realized that her son was dead. Then she got up and executed all the royal family. (Like her evil, vindictive mother Jezebel, Athaliah was determined to impose her own selfish will upon Judah. Jehu's revolution in Israel affected Athaliah deeply: (1) She no longer had the support of her blood relatives in Israel. (2) Her pagan religious system was isolated. (3) Her direct ties with Phoenicia were severed. (4) And, the death of King Ahaziah, her son, by the hand of Jehu deprived her of her legal status as queen mother in Judea. Therefore, Athaliah attempted to wipe out the entire lineage of King David and start a new dynasty in Judah with herself as its first tyrant. She murdered all of her own remaining grandchildren. She also executed all of her husband's brothers so that his authority could not be challenged [see 2 Chron. 21:4]. In addition, she wanted to establish Baalism as the state religion of Judah [see 2 Chron. 24:7].)

But Jehosheba (the wife of Jehoiada the priest) took Joash, Ahaziah's son, and stole him from among the other sons of Ahaziah who were about to be murdered. Jehosheba was King Jehoram's daughter and Ahaziah's sister. She put Prince Joash and his nurse in a storage room of the Temple. She hid Joash from Athaliah. So, Joash was not killed. He was hidden with his nurse in the Temple of the Lord for six years. During that time, Athaliah ruled over the land.

In the seventh year, Jehoiada sent for the commanders of groups of 100 men. He sent for guards and the Carites, the royal bodyguards. He brought them together to him in the Temple area of the Lord. Then he made a pact with them there, in the Temple of the Lord making them promise loyalty. Then he showed them the king's son, Joash. Jehoiada commanded them: "This is what you must do: One-third of you who come in on the Sabbath will guard the king's palace. Another third of you will be at the Sur Gate. And, another third will be at the gate behind the guard. In this way, you will guard the Temple by shifts. Two of your groups will go off duty on the Sabbath. They must protect the Temple of the Lord for King Joash. All of you must stand around the king. Each man must have his weapons in his hand. If anyone comes near, kill him. Stay close to the king when he goes out and when he comes in."

The commanders over 100 men obeyed everything Jehoiada the high priest had commanded. Each one took his men who were beginning their Sabbath duty. Each one also took those who were ending their Sabbath duty. Both groups came to Jehoiada the high priest. And, he gave spears and shields to the commanders. These things previously belonged to King David and had been kept in the Temple of the Lord.

Then each of the guards took his place. Each man had his weapons in his hand. There were guards from the south side of the Temple to the north side. They stood beside the guards shoulder to shoulder around the altar and the Temple and the king. (Young Joash was positioned next to the altar with soldiers all around him, drawn up several ranks deep across the entire courtyard. Apparently, the boy king was to be carefully guarded by the soldiers as he made his way from the Temple chamber where he had been kept for seven years. A procession would begin to his rightful throne, where he would be proclaimed king.) Then Jehoiada brought out Joash, and he put the crown on Joash. Then he gave Joash a copy of the Torah. They appointed him king and poured olive oil on him. They clapped their hands and said, "May the king live long."

Athaliah heard the noise of the guards and the people. So, she went to the courtyard of the Temple of the Lord (this revolution probably took place on a major feast day, when hordes of people would normally be gathered at the Temple). She looked, and, behold, there was the young king, standing by the platform, as the custom was. (Jewish kings had a special place assigned to them in the Temple courtyard from which they could address the people.) The officers and trumpeters were standing beside him. All the people of the land were very happy and they were blowing trumpets (signifying that a coronation was in progress). Then Athaliah ripped her clothes and screamed, "Traitors! Traitors!"

Jehoiada, the high priest, gave orders to the commanders of the groups of 100 men who led the army, "Surround her with soldiers! Get her out of here! Kill anyone who follows her!" He said this because Jehoiada had said: "Don't put Athaliah to death inside the Temple area of the Lord." So, they caught her when she came to where the horses enter the palace grounds. She was put to death there.

Then Jehoiada made another covenant between the Lord and the king and the people (a renewal of the same covenant that Yahweh had previously made with His people). They agreed to be the Lord's special people. Jehoiada also made a pact between the king and the people. All the people of the land went to the Temple of Baal and tore it down. They smashed the altars and the idol images into small pieces, and killed Mattan, the priest of Baal, in front of the altars.

Then Jehoiada, the high priest, placed guards at the Temple of the Lord. He took with him the commanders of the groups of 100 men and the royal bodyguards. He took the guards and all the people of the land. Together, they took the king out of the Temple area of the Lord. (It was an official procession en route to an ascension to the throne, the final act in the whole ceremony orchestrated by Jehoiada.) They went into the palace through the gate of the guards. Then King Joash sat on the royal throne. So, all the people of Judah were very happy. And Jerusalem had peace, because Athaliah had been put to death by the sword at the royal palace.

Joash was seven years old when he became the king.

My Time to Pray

The Man of God

As unknown, and yet well known... (2 Corinthians 6:9).

The key to spiritual peace and prosperity of any nation is the man of God. Sometimes the king (or the president) was the man of God. But when an unrighteous person rules a nation, then the man by God (usually a preacher) must take leadership not just for the sake of peace, but for the cause of God. Here Jehoiada, the high priest, was used of God to bring righteousness and peace to Israel. *Lord, I pray for a spiritual person to lead my nation. Give me leaders who seek Your glory in everything.*

Did you see how close satan came to destroying the godly line of David? Athaliah thought she was destroying David's line for her selfish purposes, but in actuality, she was doing satan's will. If the devil could cut off David's line, he could annul God's promise that David's son would rule in the coming Millennium—the thousand years of peace when the Kingdom of God rules the earth. Satan could prevent the Messiah—Jesus Christ—from being born. How close did satan come to thwarting God's plan? One baby. *Lord, I thank You for Jehosheba who changed history. In a small way, I can change history. Lord, thank You for Jehoiada the high priest who changed history, use me in the same way.*

When Jehosheba chose one baby to save, all the others were killed. How did she know which one to choose? Who can tell the greatness of a person when they are only a baby in arms? Is it the aggressiveness of a baby? Or a gentle spirit? Or the cute one? No one can tell but God. Yet in the circumstances of life, Jehosheba chose one, perhaps without any thought, but in the providence of God. She knew that boy would be a godly king who would bring revival to Judah. *Lord, I trust my life to Your circumstances. Sometimes when the choice doesn't seem to matter, let Your hand make the right choice behind the scenes.*

There's nothing like preparation behind the scenes to help the prayer go well before the people. Jehoiada the high priest planned carefully, and the revolution worked. Every soldier stood in his place, and everything "clicked." God worked to put Joash on the throne, because Jehoiada planned carefully before the event and behind the scenes. *Lord, help me learn the lesson of details. You work through careful planning, and You work through details.*

Sometimes the greatest punishment of evil is the excess of evil. Even as Cain cried out, "My iniquity is my punishment," so the rebellion of Athaliah earned her a rebellion. Her evil palace politics to secure the throne earned her the palace politics that destroyed her lineage and led her to execution. Don't those who give themselves excessively to alcohol become addicted (a slave) to alcohol, so they have no fulfillment in life? Their sin becomes their evil punishment. *Lord, I am free in Your discipline. I will obey You excessively so that I can become Your slave in dedicated obedience. Then I will find life, and live more abundantly (see John 10:10). Amen.*

40

KING JOASH RULES OVER JUDAH

Second Kings 12

Joash became the king of Judah in Jehu's seventh year as the king of
Israel. Joash ruled for 40 years in Jerusalem. His mother's name
was Zibiah, she was from Beer-Sheba. Joash did what was right
in the sight of the Lord all the time that Jehoiada the high priest
taught him. (According to Second Chronicles 24:15, Jehoiada
lived to be 130 years old.) But the high places were not removed.
The people still made sacrifices and burned incense there.

Joash said to the priests, "Collect all the money brought as sacred
offerings to the Temple of the Lord. This includes the money
that each person owes in taxes. It also includes the money that
each person vows or brings to the Temple of the Lord because
he wants to do so. Each priest must collect the money from the
people whom he serves. Then the priests must repair any damage
that they find in the Temple." (A full century had passed since
King Solomon built the Temple. Therefore, it truly needed repair.)
However, by the twenty-third year of King Joash, the priests had
still not actually repaired the Temple. So, King Joash summoned
Jehoiada the high priest and the other priests, and said to them,
"Why are you not repairing the damage to the Temple? From
now on, don't collect any more money from the people whom
you serve. Instead, hand over the money for the repair of the
Temple." So, the priests agreed not to take any money from the

people, and they agreed not to repair the Temple themselves. (Because of the unfaithfulness of the priests in repairing the Temple, the king relived them of the responsibility of doing any reconstruction.)

However, Jehoiada the high priest took a box and bored a hole in the top of it. Then he put it by the altar. It was on the right side, as the people came into the Temple area of the Lord. The priests guarding the doorway put all the money that was brought to the Temple of the Lord into the box.

Each time the priests saw that the box was full of money, the king's royal assistant and the high priest came and put the money that had been brought to the Temple of the Lord into bags. Then they counted it. Next, they weighed the money. They gave it to the men who were in charge of the work on the Temple. With it, they paid the carpenters and the builders who worked on the Temple of the Lord. They also paid the stone workers and the stone cutters. They used the money to buy timber and to cut stone. The money was used to repair the damage of the Temple of the Lord. It paid for everything.

The money that was brought into the Temple of the Lord was not used to make silver cups, nor was it used for wick trimmers, bowls, or trumpets. And, it was not used for any gold or silver containers. (Those things needed to be replaced because they had been polluted by Baal worship during the reigns of Ahaziah and Athaliah.) They paid the money to the workers, who used it to repair the Temple of the Lord. They did not make the men report how the money was spent, because the men were dependable. (This might be hinting that the priests who were handling the money previously were not honest.) The money from the guilt offerings and the sin offerings was not brought into the Temple of the Lord. It belonged to the priests.

About this time, Hazael, the king of Syria, attacked Gath and captured it. Then he turned to attack Jerusalem. But Joash, the king of Judah, had all the sacred objects gathered together that his ancestors (Jehoshaphat, Jehoram, and Ahaziah) had dedicated. He got together his own sacred objects, and all the gold that was found in the treasuries of the Temple of the Lord, and the gold from the palace. Then Joash sent all of this treasure to Hazael, the king of Syria, so that he turned away from Jerusalem.

Everything that Joash did—all that he accomplished—is written in the Book of the History of the Kings of Judah. Joash's officers conspired against him. (Probably because Joash had executed Zechariah, the son of Jehoiada [see 2 Chron. 24:25].) They assassinated him at Beth-Millo on the road to Silla. The officers who killed him were Jozabad the son of Shimeath and Jehozabad the son of Shomer. Joash was buried with his ancestors in Jerusalem; and Amaziah, his son, became the king in his place.

My Time to Pray

Money Problems

...when he is old, he will not depart from it (Proverbs 22:6).

How is it that a king like Joash can bring revival, yet still allow the high places to remain where some people made sacrifices and burned incense? To answer that question, I should look in my own heart. I am not perfect, and I allow some vestiges of sin to reside in my heart or at least in my life. I wish sin could be completely eradicated in this world and from my life, but it's not. So I can't complain about Joash, nor can I criticize his life. *Lord, I am a sinner; I fall far from perfection. I plead the blood of Jesus Christ to forgive my sins—all of them.*

How could God's representative—his priest—keep back money that was given to God? I would have thought those who served God would be careful with money, with doctrine, and with worship. But I guess I'm an optimist. When I look at the church today, I see preachers who are in it for money. I also see preachers compromising the truth of Scripture, and I see some preachers completely denying the Scriptures. I see greed among preachers. *Lord, forgive me for comparing myself to anyone. When I look to Jesus Christ my standard, I fall far short of perfection. Forgive me, cleanse me, and use me. Even when I'm not perfect, use me.*

It seems money is always a problem in God's service. Even the priests were not faithful stewards of God's money. But then, the workers were faithful. They could be trusted. *Lord, I want to be like these carpenters and stone cutters who could be trusted. I commit myself to honesty. Use me in Your work.*

Even good men have their Achilles' heel. Joash was a revival king, but he had the prophet Zechariah executed who preached against him. It's too bad that his spiritual mentor, Jehoiada, had died. Maybe King Joash would have listened to Zechariah if Jehoiada were still alive. Joash seemed to do right as long as he had good spiritual counsel. *Lord, give me good counsel. I promise to listen to spiritual people and do the right thing.*

Did you see that Joash lived 47 years, yet he ruled 40 years? Then he sinned in his old age. He lived a good life but spoiled it at the last. Remember, Noah got drunk in his old age. Solomon gave himself to sexual sins in his old age. *Lord, I want to live for You all my life. I don't want to spoil a good life with a bad ending. Give me spiritual strength to continue to the end. I will not turn back for any reason. Amen.*

41

Jehoahaz Rules Over Israel

Second Kings 13

Jehoahaz, the son of Jehu, became the king over Israel in the capital city of Israel. And Jehoahaz ruled Israel for 17 years and did what was evil in the sight of the Lord. Jehoahaz did the same sins of Jeroboam, the son of Nebat. Jeroboam had caused Israel to sin, and Jehoahaz did not turn away from these same sins. So, the Lord was angry with Israel, and continually delivered them into the control of Hazael, the king of Syria, and his son, Ben-Hadad.

Then Jehoahaz begged the Lord, and the Lord listened to him. The Lord had seen Israel's troubles, how terribly the king of Syria had been treating the Israelites. So, the Lord provided Israel with a man to save them. (This could have been the prophet Jonah who prophesied the great deliverance. Because of the preaching of Jonah, Assyria [Nineveh] was saved from God's judgment. Then Assyria began to "rescue" Israel from the constant oppression of the Syrians. In 805 B.C., near the end of Jehoahaz's reign, Adad-Nirari III of Assyria led an expedition into Palestine and subdued Syria. He later became king of the Assyrians [810-783 B.C.].) And Israel escaped from the Syrians. So, the Israelites lived in their own homes as they had before.

But the Israelites still did not turn away from the same sins of the household of Jeroboam who had caused Israel to sin. They continued doing those sins. The Asherah idol was also left standing in the city of Samaria.

Nothing was left of Jehoahaz's army except 50 horsemen, 10 chariots (King Ahab once had more than 2,000 chariots), and 10,000 foot soldiers. The king of Syria had destroyed them and had made them like the dust at the time of threshing.

Everything else that Jehoahaz did—all he accomplished and his victories—are written down in the Book of History of the Kings of Israel. Jehoahaz died, and was buried in the city of Samaria. His son Jehoash became the king in his place.

Jehoash Rules Over Israel

Jehoash, the son of Jehoahaz, became the king of Israel in the city of Samaria, during Joash's thirty-seventh year as the king of Judah. Jehoash ruled over Israel for 16 years over the ten northern tribes. He did evil in the sight of the Lord and did not turn away from practicing all the sins of Jeroboam, the son of Nebat. Jeroboam had caused Israel to sin, and Jehoash continued to practice those things. Everything else that Jehoash did—all that he accomplished and his victories—are written down. This includes his war against Amaziah, the king of Judah. Everything is written in the Book of the History of the Kings of Israel. Jehoash died, and Jeroboam II occupied the throne. Jehoash was buried in Samaria with the kings of Israel.

The Death of Elisha

At this time, Elisha became very sick. (It had been at least 63 years since God called Elijah to Heaven. Elisha was approximately 90 years old at this time.) Jehoash, the king of Israel, went down to Elisha and wept over him. Jehoash said, "My father, my father.

(The evil king may have respected this old prophet, and was worried about what the implications of Elisha's death would bring to his kingdom. Elisha was Elijah's successor, but there was no successor to Elisha. Elisha was the last hope of Israel. What would become of them after this man of God was gone?) The chariots of Israel and their horsemen." (This utterance may indicate that Jehoash knew about how Elijah departed this earth [see 2 Kings 2:11]. Perhaps the king was wondering if Elisha would leave in the same manner as Elijah did.)

Elisha said to Jehoash, "Get a bow and some arrows." So he got a bow and some arrows. Then Elisha said to the king of Israel, "Put your hand on the bow." So, Jehoash put his hand on the bow. Then Elisha put his hands on the king's hands. (This represented divine power being imparted to the bow shot through His intermediary, Elisha. Elisha was trying to convince the skeptical king that God's help was quite sufficient to one who places his total trust in Him [compare Isaiah 31:1-9; 8:11-15].)

Elisha said, "Open the east window." (The Syrians had taken the eastern part of the kingdom of Jehoash—Gilead.) So Jehoash opened the window. Then Elisha said, "Shoot." And Jehoash shot. Elisha said, "The Lord's arrow of victory, the arrow of victory over Syria. You will fight the Syrians at Aphek until you destroy them."

Elisha said, "Take the arrows." So Jehoash took them. Then Elisha said to the king of Israel, "Shoot at the ground." ("Hit the ground!" that is, Elisha was directing Jehoash to shoot arrows from the window into the ground outside.) So, Jehoash shot at the ground three times. Then he stopped shooting. (Jehoash clearly did not believe that what he was doing was of any real value. So, because of his limited faith, God limited the number of Jehoash victories.) The man of the one true God was angry with Jehoash. Elisha said, "You should have shot five or six times. Then you would have defeated Syria until they were completely finished off. But now, you will defeat Syria only three times."

So Elisha died, and they buried him.

At that time, marauding bands of Moabites used to raid the land of Israel in the springtime. Once, the Israelites were in the process of burying a man. (Jewish tombs were cave-like, and the mouth of each cave was usually closed up by a heavy stone.) Suddenly, they saw a band of Moabites coming. So, the Israelites tossed the dead man into Elisha's grave. When the man's body touched Elisha's bones, the man came back to life. And, the man stood up on his feet.

During all the days that Jehoahaz was king, Hazael the king of Syria was always attacking Israel. But the Lord was kind to the Israelites and had mercy on them. At this time, He helped them because of His covenant with Abraham, with Isaac, and with Jacob. He did not want to destroy them or throw them out of His presence.

Hazael, the king of Syria, died, and his son, Ben-Hadad, became the king in his place. During a war, Hazael had taken some towns west of the Jordan River from Jehoahaz, Jehoash's father. But now Jehoash took those towns back from Hazael's son, Ben-Hadad. He defeated Ben-Hadad three times, and he took back Israel's towns.

My Time to Pray

A Time to Die

Then Elisha died and was buried (2 Kings 13:20 TLB).

It's sad to read of Elisha's death, yet all must enter that veil. We must all die. King Jehoahaz thought Elisha might go home without dying—Elisha might go to Heaven by a whirlwind and chariots of fire, as did Elijah. But no! Elisha died. *Lord, I will die one day. I don't want to, but that will happen if Jesus doesn't come back to rapture me up. I don't want to die with pain; I'm not good with pain. I look forward to seeing You in death. If not, "even so come, Lord Jesus."*

It's a known fact that sin blocks our prayers from being answered (see Ps. 66:18;John 9:31;Isa. 59:1-2). We have to repent and ask for forgiveness for God to hear and answer us. But what about the person lost in sins? Can an idolatrous man beg God for mercy and will God hear and answer him? Jehoahaz was evil, and God was angry with Israel. Yet Jehoahaz "begged God" and "the Lord answered." God used Assyria to take pressure off of Israel that was coming from Syria. *Lord, I marvel at Your plan for the nations. When I don't realize what Your hand is doing in the world, I will trust Your heart.*

King Jehoash didn't understand what Elisha was telling him with the bow and arrow. It would have been good for Jehoash to obey, even when he didn't understand what God was telling him. *Lord, I will obey blindly, even when I don't understand what You are doing in my life.*

God loves symbols, and still speaks to us today in symbols—the cross, baptism, the broken body, and the cup representing the spilt blood of Christ. The prophet told King Jehoash to shoot the arrow east, symbolizing victory over Syria to the east. Elisha put his hands on the hands of the king symbolizing "God and man working together." *Lord, I will look for symbols in my life. I will learn from these symbols found in Scripture. Help me see—take away my blindness—so I can understand what You are telling me to do in this world. Amen.*

42

JEROBOAM II RULES OVER ISRAEL

Second Kings 14:15-29

The other deeds of Jehoash and his victories are written down, including his war against Amaziah, the king of Judah, in the Book of the History of the Kings of Israel. Jehoash died and was buried in Samaria with the kings of Israel. And his son, Jeroboam II became the king in his place. Amaziah, the son of Joash was king of Judah. He lived 15 years after Jehoash the king of Israel died. Jehoash was the son of Jehoahaz. The rest of the things that Amaziah did are written down in the Book of the History of the Kings of Judah.

The people planned a conspiracy in Jerusalem against Amaziah. So, he ran away to the city of Lachish. But they sent men after him to Lachish and killed him there. They brought back his corpse on horses, and he was buried with his ancestors in Jerusalem, in the city of David.

Then all the people of Judah chose Uzziah to be king in place of his father, Amaziah. Uzziah was 16 years old. Uzziah rebuilt the city of Elath and made it part of Judah again. He did this after Amaziah died.

Jeroboam II Rules Over Israel

Jeroboam II the son of Jehoash, became the king of Israel in Samaria. This was during the 15th year that Amaziah was king of Judah. Amaziah was the son of Joash. And, Jeroboam II ruled for 41 years. He did what was evil in the sight of the Lord. Jeroboam I the son of Nebat had caused Israel to sin and Jeroboam II did not turn away from committing the same sins. Jeroboam II won back Israel's border, from Lebo-Hamath to the Dead Sea. This happened just as the Lord, the God of Israel, had said. He spoke it through His servant, Jonah, the son of Amittai. He was the prophet from Gath-Hepher. The Lord had seen how all the Israelites, both slave and free, were suffering terribly. There was no one who could help Israel. But the Lord had not said that He would completely destroy the name Israel from the world. So, he saved the Israelites through Jeroboam II the son of Jehoash.

Everything that Jeroboam II did is written down—all that he did and all of his victories. He won back Damascus and Hamath for Israel. (They had once belonged to Yaudi.) All of this is written down in the Book of the History of the Kings of Israel. Jeroboam II died and he was buried with his ancestors, the kings of Israel. Jeroboam's son, Zechariah, became the king in his place.

My Time to Pray

Did you notice that Jeroboam II did all the sins of the first king of Israel, Jeroboam I? Did Jeroboam II follow the sins of Jeroboam I because they both followed their evil nature, or did Jeroboam II take his namesake as an idol or hero? It's important that you follow good role models, because five years from now you will be like your hero. Also remember, we do more than mimic their actions, we usually take on their attitudes and values. *Lord, I will choose good role models who live according to Scripture. I will judge my role models by the way they follow Scripture.*

God allows some evil men to win some good victories because those victories fit into God's overall plan. When it seems evil people flourish, it's not always the *blessing* of God on their life, it's God *allowing* them to do good things that fit within His overarching plan. *Lord, help me see beyond the victories of evil men, help me see Your overall plan for things, and help me see Your personal plan for my life.*

Again we see in Amaziah the principle, "What goes around, comes around." When Amaziah became king, the first thing he did was execute the men who assassinated his father. Then Amaziah died by assassination. They who live by the sword shall die by the sword. *Lord, I will give good in life so I will receive good in return.*

Both Amaziah (last chapter) and Jeroboam II were kings of smaller nations when you consider Syria and the other large nations around God's people. Part of their problem was thinking they were great just because they won "minor wars." A man is not the heavy weight champion of the world until he defeats *all* challenges. *Lord, I want to be humble and I want to be used by You. But my ego keeps telling me I am greater than I really am. Honestly, I can't pray for You to "humble" me, because You would send persecution and troubles, and I don't want that. All I can honestly pray is for You to forgive my sins, for I am a great sinner. I humble myself before You. Amen.*

43

AMAZIAH RULES OVER JUDAH

Second Chronicles 25:1-24

Amaziah was 25 years old when he became king over Judah. (King Joash was about 47 years old when he died.) He ruled in Jerusalem for 29 years. His mother's name was Jehoaddin, from Jerusalem. Amaziah did what was right in the sight of the Lord, but not with a complete heart (half-heartedly). Amaziah took strong control of the kingdom, and put to death the servants who had murdered his father, Joash the king. But Amaziah did not put their children to death. He obeyed what was written in the Torah, the Book of Moses. There the Lord commanded: "Fathers must not be put to death when their children do wrong. And, children must not be put to death when their fathers do wrong. Each person must die for his own sins."

Amaziah gathered the people of Judah together, and grouped all the people of Judah and Benjamin by families. He put commanders over groups of 1,000 and over groups of 100. (The soldiers formed a regiment with brothers, relatives, and friends. Thus, the Hebrew troops were closely linked together, and they had strong inducements to remain firm in their ranks.) He counted the men who were 20 years old and older. In all, there were 300,000 soldiers ready to fight. They were skilled with spears and shields. Amaziah also hired 100,000 soldiers from Israel and paid about 7,500 pounds of silver for them. But a man of the one true God came to Amaziah and said, "O king, do not permit the troops of Israel to go with you. (The prophet was urging the king to trust Yahweh God.) The Lord is not with Israel. God is not with the people of Ephraim. You can make yourself strong for war, but the one true God will defeat you in front of the enemy. He has the power to help you or to defeat you."

Amaziah said to the man of the one true God, "But what about the 7,500 pounds of silver that I paid to the troops of Israel?"

The man of the one true God answered, "The Lord can give you much more than that."

So, Amaziah sent the troops from Ephraim back home to Israel. They were very angry with the people of Judah (their "honor" was at stake), and they were furious when they went home.

Then Amaziah became very bold and led his army to the Valley of Salt. There Amaziah's army killed 10,000 men from Edom. The army of Judah also captured 10,000 men. They took those men to the top of a cliff and threw them off. And they were broken to pieces.

At the same time, the Israelite army (who was sent home) was raiding some towns in Judah. These were the troops that Amaziah had not permitted to fight in the Edomite war. They robbed towns between Samaria and Beth-Horon. They killed 3,000 people and took many valuable things as plunder.

Amaziah came home after he had defeated the Edomites, and brought back the idols that the Edomites worshiped. He started to worship them, too, bowing down to them and burning incense to them. The Lord was angry with Amaziah, and God sent a prophet who said to him, "Why have you asked their gods for help? They could not even save their own people from you."

As the prophet spoke, Amaziah said to him, "We never gave you the job of advising the king. Stop now, or you will be killed."

The prophet stopped speaking, but he said, "I know that God has decided to destroy you, because you have done this. You did not listen to my advice."

Amaziah, the king of Judah, consulted with his advisors, and sent a challenge to Jehoash the king of Israel. Amaziah said to Jehoash, "Come, let us meet face-to-face in battle" (a declaration of war).

Then Jehoash the king of Israel answered Amaziah, the king of Judah, "A little thorn bush in Lebanon once sent a message to a big cedar tree in Lebanon, saying, 'Let your daughter marry my son.' But then a wild animal from Lebanon came by and trampled the thorn bush underfoot. You say to yourself: 'I have defeated Edom.' You are proud, and you brag. Stay home. Don't ask for trouble by fighting me. If you do, you and Judah will be defeated."

But Amaziah would not listen. The one true God planned to let Jehoash of Israel defeat Judah. This was because Judah prayed for help from the gods of Edom. So, Jehoash the king of Israel, went up to battle. He and Amaziah, the king of Judah, faced each other in battle at Beth-Shemesh in the territory of Judah. Israel defeated Judah. Every man of Judah ran away to his home. At Beth-Shemesh, Jehoash, the king of Israel, captured Amaziah, the king of Judah. Amaziah was the son of Joash, who was the son of Ahaziah. Then Jehoash brought Amaziah to Jerusalem. Jehoash broke down the wall of Jerusalem, from the Gate of Ephraim to the Corner Gate (about 600 feet long. This was a catastrophic defeat and humiliation for the arrogant King Amaziah. Jehoash left him on the throne of Judah purely out of a sense of contemptuous mercy). Then Jehoash took all the gold and the silver and everything in the Temple of God.

My Time to Pray

Sins of the Fathers

...The fathers shall not be put to death for their children, nor shall the children be put to death for their fathers; but a person shall die for his own sin (2 Chronicles 25:4).

It was comforting to see the compassion extended to the children of Joash's servants. Do you often judge, reward, or punish children because of their parents, or parents because of their children? I'm glad that the Lord judges, rewards, and punishes us according to our individual actions, faith, and personal relationship with Him. *Lord, I will do my best to keep away from the "guilt by association" snare. Thank you for helping me see people individually and as the unique children of God whom you love and cherish. Amen.*

44

Uzziah Rules Over Judah

Second Kings 15

Uzziah, the son of Amaziah, became the king of Judah. This happened
during Jeroboam II's twenty-seventh year as king of Israel.
Uzziah was 16 years old when he became the king, and ruled
for 52 years in Jerusalem. His mother's name was Jecoliah from
Jerusalem. He did what was right in the sight of the Lord, just as
his father Amaziah had done. However, the high places were not
removed, so the people still made sacrifices and burned incense
there.

The Lord struck Uzziah with leprosy. He had this disease until the day
he died. He lived in a separate house. Jotham, the king's son, was
in charge of the palace, and governed the people of the land.

All the rest of the things that Uzziah did are written down in the Book
of the History of the Kings of Judah. Uzziah died, and they
buried him with his ancestors in Jerusalem. And, his son Jotham
became the king in his place.

Zechariah Rules Over Israel

Zechariah, the son of Jeroboam II, was the king over Israel in Samaria.
He ruled for six months during Uzziah's thirty-eighth year as the
king of Judah. Zechariah did what was evil in the sight of the

Lord. He did just as his ancestors had done. Jeroboam I, the son of Nebat, had caused the people of Israel to sin, but Zechariah did not turn away from the same sins.

Shallum, the son of Jabesh, conspired against Zechariah and attacked him in front of the people and assassinated him. And Shallum became the king in Zechariah's place. The rest of the deeds of Zechariah are written in the Book of the History of the Kings of Israel. Now the Lord had told Jehu: "All the way down to your great-great-grandchildren, your sons will be kings of Israel." (For four generations—Jehoahaz, Joash, Jeroboam II, and Zechariah—thus ended Israel's era of peace and prosperity.) And the Lord's word came true.

Shallum Rules Over Israel

Then Shallum, the son of Jabesh, became the king during Uzziah's thirty-ninth year as the king of Judah. Shallum ruled for one month in Samaria, then Menahem, the son of Gadi, came up from Tirzah to Samaria. He attacked Shallum, the son of Jabesh, in Samaria, and killed him and became the king in Shallum's place.

The rest of the deeds of Shallum and his conspiracy are written in the Book of the History of the Kings of Israel.

Menahem started out from Tirzah and attacked Tiphsah (a border city of Solomon's kingdom [see 1 Kings 4:24] on the Euphrates River), and destroyed the city and the area nearby. Why? Because the people had refused to open the city gates for him. So, he conquered them and ripped open all of their pregnant women.

Menahem Rules Over Israel

Menahem, the son of Gadi, became the king over Israel. This happened during Uzziah's thirty-ninth year as the king of Judah. Menahem ruled for ten years in Samaria and did what was evil in the sight of the Lord. Jeroboam I, the son of Nebat, had caused Israel to sin. And, all the time that Menahem was king, he did not turn away from practicing the same sins.

Pul, the king of Assyria, came to attack the land. Menahem gave to Pul about 74,000 pounds of silver. This was so that Pul would support Menahem and make his hold on the kingdom stronger. Menahem raised the money by taxing all the powerful men of Israel. He taxed each man about 1¼ pounds of silver, and gave the money to the king of Assyria. So, the king of Assyria left, and did not stay in the land.

And the rest of the deeds that Menahem did—all that he did—is written in the Book of the History of the Kings of Israel. Then Menahem died, and his son, Pekahiah, became the king in his place.

Pekahiah Rules Over Israel

Pekahiah, the son of Menahem, became the king over Israel in Samaria. This happened during Uzziah's fiftieth year as the king of Judah. Pekahiah ruled for two years. Pekahiah did what was evil in the sight of the Lord. Jeroboam I had caused Israel to sin; and Pekahiah did not turn away from the same sins.

Pekah, the son of Remaliah, was one of Pekahiah's captains. He conspired against Pekahiah—taking 50 men of Gilead with him, he assassinated Pekahiah, along with Argob and Arieh, in the fortress of the royal palace at Samaria. Then Pekah became the king in Pekahiah's place. And the rest of the deeds of Pekahiah—

all that he did—is written in the Book of the History of the Kings of Israel.

Pekah Rules Over Israel

Pekah, the son of Remaliah, became the king over Israel in Samaria. This happened during Uzziah's fifty-second year as the king of Judah. And, Pekah ruled for 20 years. Pekah did what was evil in the sight of the Lord. Jeroboam I, the son of Nebat, had caused Israel to sin; and Pekah did not turn away from practicing the same sins.

Tiglath-Pileser, the king of Assyria, attacked while Pekah was the king of Israel. Tiglath-Pileser captured the towns of Ijon, Abel-Beth-Maacah, Janoah, Kedesh, Hazor, as well as the regions of Gilead and Galilee. He also captured all the territory of Naphtali. He sent the people from these places away to Assyria. (This was the first deportation.) Then Hoshea, the son of Elah, conspired against Pekah, the son of Remaliah. Hoshea attacked Pekah and assassinated him. Then Hoshea became the king in Pekah's place. This happened during the twentieth year after Jotham, the son of Uzziah, was made king.

The rest of the deeds of Pekah—all that he did—are written in the Book of the History of the Kings of Israel.

Jotham Rules Over Judah

Then Jotham, the son of Uzziah, became the king of Judah, during the second year of Pekah, the son of Remaliah, the king of Israel. Jotham was 25 years old when he became the king. He ruled for 16 years in Jerusalem. His mother's name was Jerusha, the daughter of Zadok. Jotham did what was right in the sight of the Lord, just as his father Uzziah had done. But the high places were not removed, and the people still made sacrifices and burned incense there. Jotham rebuilt the Upper Gate of the Temple courtyard of the Lord.

The rest of the deeds that Jotham did while he was king are written in the Book of the History of the Kings of Judah. At that time, the Lord began to send Rezin, the king of Syria, against Judah. He also sent Pekah, the son of Remaliah against them. Jotham died and was buried with his ancestors in Jerusalem, the city of David, his ancestors. And Jotham's son, Ahaz, became the king in his place.

My Time to Pray

Restoring Power and Glory

In the year that King Uzziah died, I saw the Lord sitting on a throne, high and lifted up... (Isaiah 6:1).

King Uzziah had been a powerful king who restored power and glory to Judah. He rebuilt a ring of fortresses around the land, increased the strength of the army, invented new armaments for battle, increased agricultural output, and gave peace to the land. Isaiah was a member of his court, and when Uzziah died, it must have shocked Isaiah's world. Isaiah needed the same thing we need when our government goes through a transition. We need to see the Lord ruling our nation. God sits on the throne, no matter who is president or prime minister here on earth. The Lord sits in majesty, waiting for us to acknowledge His rule. Waiting for us to worship Him. *Lord, You are my ultimate ruler, no matter who sits in power on this earth. I will obey You, follow Your commands, and worship Your majesty.*

God wants to rule us, no matter who is the earthly power. He sits waiting to rule our lives. Will you let the Lord sit on the throne of your heart today? *Lord, come sit on the throne of my life. Whatever Your word commands, I will do. Whatever You want me to say, I will speak. I yield to Your leadership and rule.*

In this chapter we see the assassination of one king after another. In an evil world, men do to others what was done to them. *Lord, I want to live under a stable government where there is no trickery, corruption, or evil conspirators. But I know that will never happen until Jesus Christ sits on the throne in the Millennium. Lord, I pray for Your kingdom to come on earth. I pray for You to rule on earth as You now rule in Heaven.*

Can you imagine living under one of the kings described in this chapter? There seemed to be so much intrigue and instability. We don't know much about those kings, but what we do know, we generally don't like. But you can know the King of your life. You can know King Jesus (see 1 Tim. 1: 17). He lives in your heart, and wants to direct your activities. He is closer to you than anyone on earth. Talk to Him, listen to Him, enjoy His presence. *Lord, I rest in the way You rule this earth. Amen.*

45

AHAZ RULES OVER JUDAH

Second Kings 16

Ahaz was the son of Jotham, the king of Judah. Ahaz became the king of Judah in the seventeenth year that Pekah was the king of Israel. Pekah was the son of Remaliah. Ahaz was 20 years old when he became the king and ruled for 16 years in Jerusalem. He was not like his ancestor, David. He did not do what was right in the sight of the Lord, his God. Ahaz did the same things that the kings of Israel had done. He even sacrificed his own son by burning him in the fire. He practiced the same disgusting sins as the non-Jewish nations had, the ones the Lord had forced out of the land ahead of the Israelites. And, Ahaz offered sacrifices and burned incense at the high places. And, he did this on the hills and under every green tree.

Rezin, the king of Syria, and Pekah, the king of Israel came up to Jerusalem to attack it. Pekah was the son of Remaliah. They surrounded Ahaz, but they could not defeat him.

Ahaz Sins

Second Chronicles 28:5-19

So, the Lord permitted the king of Syria, Rezin, to defeat Ahaz. (This account in Second Chronicles passes over a previous, unsuccessful attempt by Rezin and Pekah to capture Jerusalem.) The Syrians carried them off as prisoners to Damascus.

The Lord also permitted Pekah, the king of Israel, to defeat Ahaz. Pekah's army killed many soldiers of Ahaz, killing 120,000 brave soldiers from Judah in just one day. Pekah defeated them because they had abandoned the Lord, the God of their ancestors. Zichri was a warrior from Ephraim; he killed the king's son, Maaseiah. He also killed Azrikam the officer in charge of the palace and Elkanah second in command to the king. The sons of Israel captured 200,000 of their own relatives as prisoners of war. (The northern kingdom besieged Ahaz, but they could not defeat him completely. This siege of Jerusalem was carried out by Pekah and Rezin with the hope that those who no longer sympathized with the Davidic lineage would get control of the city from within.) They took women, sons, and daughters, and many valuable things from Judah and carried them off to Samaria.

But there was a prophet of the Lord named Oded, who went out to meet the army of Israel when it returned to Samaria. He said, "Listen, the Lord is the God of your ancestors. He is the One who permitted you to defeat Judah because He was furious with those people. But you went too far. In a rage, you slaughtered them without mercy. God saw that, and now you plan to make the men and women of Judah and Jerusalem your slaves. But you have sinned against the Lord, your God. Now listen to me. Send back your Jewish brothers and sisters whom you captured from your relatives in Judah. Why? Because the Lord is very angry with you."

Then some of the leading men in Israel met the soldiers of Israel coming home from the war. These leaders were: Azariah the son of Jehohanan, Berechiah, the son of Meshillemoth, Jehizkiah, the son of Shallum, and Amasa, the son of Hadlai. They warned the soldiers: "Don't bring those prisoners from Judah here. If you do, then we will be guilty of major sin. That will only make our sin and guilt even worse. And, our guilt is already so great that the Lord is furious with Israel."

So, the soldiers left the prisoners and the valuable things there in front of the officers and the entire assembly. The designated leaders took charge of the prisoners who were naked and gave them the clothes that had been seized. They gave the prisoners clothes, sandals, food, drink, and medicine. They put all the weak prisoners on donkeys, and took them back to their families in Jericho, the City of Palm Trees. Then they returned home to Samaria.

At that same time, the Edomites attacked Judah and carried away some prisoners. So, King Ahaz asked the king of Assyria for help. The Philistines also raided the towns in the western mountain slopes and in southern Judah. They captured the town of Beth-Shemesh, Aijalon, Gederoth, Soco and its villages, Timnah and its villages, and Gimzo and its villages. Then the Philistines lived in those towns. The Lord humbled the nation of Judah because of Ahaz, their king. Ahaz had caused the people of Judah to sin and had been unfaithful to the Lord Who Is Always Present.

Second Kings 16:6-20

At that time, Rezin, the king of Syria, took back the city of Elath for Edom. He forced all the Jews out of Elath, then the Edomites moved back into Elath. They still live there today (at the time the Book of Second Kings was written. See Second Chronicles 28:5-8; Isaiah 7:1-2).

Ahaz sent messengers to Tiglath-Pileser, the king of Assyria. Ahaz said: "I am your servant and your son, come up and save me from the control of the king of Syria and the king of Israel. They are attacking me." So, Ahaz took the silver and the gold that was in the Temple of the Lord, and the treasures of the royal palace, and sent these as a gift to the king of Assyria. So, the king of Assyria listened to Ahaz. (The Assyrians wanted to eventually conquer Egypt anyway. The small nation of Judah lay between Assyria and Egypt.) The king of Assyria attacked Damascus and captured it. Then he sent all the people of Damascus to Kir. And, he killed Rezin.

Then King Ahaz went to Damascus to meet Tiglath-Pileser, the king of Assyria. (The Assyrians held court in various cities that they conquered, and demanded that all vassal kings, in this case: Judah, Edom, Ammon, Moab, Gaza, Ascalon, and Tyre, appear before them with monetary payments ready to give to them.) Ahaz saw an Assyrian altar at Damascus. (No doubt, Tiglath-Pileser insisted that Ahaz honor the Assyrian gods by constructing such an altar in Jerusalem.) King Ahaz sent the detailed plans and a model of this altar to Uriah the priest. So, Uriah the priest built that altar, just like the plans that King Ahaz had sent to him from Damascus. Uriah the priest finished the altar before King Ahaz came back from Damascus. When the king arrived from Damascus, he saw the altar, and approached it and offered sacrifices upon it. Ahaz burned his whole burnt offerings and food offerings, and poured out his drink offering. He also sprinkled the blood of his peace offerings on that altar.

Ahaz moved the brazen altar of sacrifice that was in the presence of the Lord at the front of the temple that was between Ahaz's altar and the Temple of the Lord (to a less conspicuous place). He put it on the north side of his altar. King Ahaz gave a command to Uriah the priest, "Burn in the morning the whole burnt offering on this large altar. Also, in the evening, offer the king's whole burnt offering and his food offering. Offer the whole burnt offering for all the people of the land. And, offer their food offering and drink offerings. Sprinkle on this altar all the blood of the whole burnt offering and of the sacrifice. But I will use the brazen altar to ask questions of God." Uriah the priest did everything that King Ahaz commanded him to do.

Then King Ahaz took off the side panels from the stands, and took the washing bowls off the top of those stands. He also took the Golden Laver, which was called "the Pond," off the bronze bulls that supported it. And, he put it on a stone foundation. (These radical steps ordered by King Ahaz were converting sacred Temple objects for the purpose of pagan worship.) And, Ahaz took away the Sabbath canopy for the royal throne that had been built at the Temple. (This seat under a canopy had been originally constructed for the king and his family to attend public worship on the Sabbath day. A private passageway led to it.) He also closed up the outside entrance for the king. He did these things because he wanted to please Tiglath-Pileser III, by making these token alterations in Jewish worship.

The rest of the deeds that Ahaz did as king are written down in the Book of the History of the Kings of Judah. Ahaz died, and was buried with his ancestors in Jerusalem. And, Ahaz's son, Hezekiah, became the king in his place.

My Time to Pray

Compromise

Now in the time of his distress King Ahaz became increasingly unfaithful to the Lord (2 Chronicles 28:22 NLT).

Ahaz was probably the worst king of Judah (the godly line ran through the southern kingdom) and God punished him for his continual compromise. He not only continued idol worship, but he followed the evil kings of the northern kingdom of Israel. Ahaz sacrificed his son like the evil nations around him (see 2 Kings 16:3), then he saw an altar in Damascus and had one built like it and placed it in the Temple of the Lord. It was one thing to worship other gods, but it was a complete rejection of the Lord God to replace His sacred objects in the Temple. Compromise leads to rejection of God. *Lord, I will examine my life to see if I'm compromising my walk with You or my worship of You. Open my blind eyes to see if I have compromised anything at all. I will repent and give You first place in every area of life.*

Ahaz tried to play one evil nation against another, and ended up in slavery to that nation. A believer cannot get protection from evil things, unless he puts God first in everything. God is our best protection. *Lord, I would rather be a slave to You, than a slave to evil. Don't punish me with my sin. I repent. I look to You for victory over sin. I want to be Your slave.*

It was a terrible time when God's people fought against each other. It was just as terrible when some of God's people put their brothers into slavery. *Lord, give me love for all my brothers and sisters in Christ. Keep me from attacking them and fighting them. Teach me how to respond if they attack me. Give me strength to respond as Jesus would respond.*

The life and struggles of Ahaz teach us that a life of sin and compromise is hard. Ahaz seemed to spiral downward politically from one difficulty to another. In parallel, Ahaz seemed to spiral downward spiritually, taking one step away from God after another, and another. *Lord, stop me when I take a first step away from You. Give me ears to hear Your warnings, and eyes to see spiritual dangers, and an obedient heart to follow You. Amen.*

46

HOSHEA RULES OVER ISRAEL

Second Kings 17

Hoshea, the son of Elah, became the king over Israel during Ahaz's twelfth year as king of Judah. Hoshea ruled in Samaria for nine years. He did what was evil in the sight of the Lord. But he was not as bad as the kings of Israel who had ruled before him. Shalmaneser, (who was also known as Sargon) the king of Assyria, came up to attack Hoshea. Hoshea had been Shalmaneser's vassal. Hoshea had made the money payments to Shalmaneser that Shalmaneser had demanded. But the king of Assyria found out that Hoshea had treacherously sent messengers to So, also known as Shebek (730 B.C.), an Ethiopian king who occupied the throne of Egypt for about 50 years. Also, Hoshea had stopped making the money payments to Shalmaneser. In the past, Hoshea had paid him every year. Therefore, the king of Assyria put Hoshea under house arrest (for the rest of Hoshea's life).

The Fall of Samaria and the Exile of Its Inhabitants

Then the king of Assyria (Sargon II may have been the one who actually captured the city of Samaria in 722 B.C.) came up and attacked all the land of Israel. He surrounded the city of Samaria and besieged it for three years. The king of Assyria captured Samaria

(the city fell after it had existed for 356 years) in the ninth
year that Hoshea was king. And, Shalmaneser took Israel away
to Assyria. (It was Assyrian policy to deport their captives in
small groups and disperse them as much as possible, so that
they would mingle with various local populations, thus being
assimilated and losing their ethnic identities.) He resettled some
of them in Halah. Some people were made to settle in Gozan on
the Habor River. Others were settled in the cities of the Medes.

All of these things happened because the Israelites had sinned against
the Lord, their God. He had brought them out of the land of
Egypt. He had rescued them from the control of Pharaoh, the
king of Egypt. Nevertheless, the Israelites honored different gods.
They lived like the ethnic groups that the Lord had forced out of
the land ahead of the Israelites.

They also lived by the customs that the kings of Israel had introduced.
They smugly sinned against the Lord their God, doing things
that were not right. They built for themselves high places in
their cities where false gods were worshiped. They built them
everywhere from the watchtower to the strong-walled city. (This
was a popular idiom, meaning, from shack to mansion.) They set
up for themselves sacred stone-pillars for worshiping false gods.
And they put up Asherah idols on every high hill and under every
green tree. The Israelites burned incense there in all the high
places, as ethnic groups who lived there before them had done.
And, the Lord had forced them out of the land. The Israelites
did evil things that made the Lord very angry. They served those
idols, even though the Lord had told them: "You must not do
such a thing."

The Lord used every prophet and seer to warn Israel and Judah. God
said, "Turn away from your evil ways. Obey My commands
and My laws. Follow all the teachings that I commanded your

ancestors to obey. I sent you these instructions through My servants, the prophets."

But, the people would not listen. They were stubborn, just like their ancestors had been. Their ancestors did not truly believe in the Lord their God. They rejected the Lord's laws and His covenant that He had made with their ancestors. And, they refused to listen to His repeated warnings. They worshiped useless idols— and became useless themselves. They did what the non-Jewish nations around them did. And, the Lord had warned them not to do this.

The people abandoned all the commands of the Lord their God. They made for themselves statues of two calves from melted metal. And, they made an Asherah idol. They worshiped all the stars of heaven and served Baal. They sacrificed their sons and daughters in the fire. And they tried to discover the future by black magic and witchcraft. They always chose to do what was evil in the sight of the Lord. And, this made God very angry.

So, God was very angry with the people of Israel. He removed them from His presence. Only the tribe of Judah was left.

But even Judah did not obey the commands of the Lord, their God. They did what the Israelites had done. So, the Lord rejected all the people of Israel. He punished them and permitted people to plunder them. God drove them out of His presence.

The Lord separated them from the household of David, when the Israelites made Jeroboam, the son of Nebat, their king. Jeroboam led the Israelites away from following the Lord. He caused them to sin greatly. So, they continued to do all the same sins that Jeroboam did. They would not stop practicing these sins, until the Lord removed the people from His presence. This was just as God had said through all His servants, the prophets. So the

Israelites were taken captive out of their land to Assyria. And, they have stayed there until today.

Foreigners Settle in Samaria and Worship False Gods

The king of Assyria brought people from Babylon, Cuthah, Avva, Hamath, and Sepharvaim, and settled them in the towns of Samaria to replace the Israelites. These people took over the region of Samaria and lived in those towns. At first, after they settled there, they did not respect the Lord. And, the Lord sent lions among them. The lions were killing some of them. The king of Assyria was told this: "You sent foreigners into the towns of Samaria. But, they do not know the law of the god of the land. (Polytheists of the day believed that every locality had its own god, which had certain powers over that region. Therefore, they needed to placate that particular god in order to be "blessed." They did not realize that Yahweh God is the one and only true God of all creation—monotheism.) This is why the god of that land has sent lions among them. Look, the lions are killing them, because the people don't know the law of that god."

Then the king of Assyria gave a command, saying, "You took Samaria's priests away. Send back one of the priests to live there. Let him teach the law of the god of that land." So, one of the priests who had been carried away from Samaria returned. He came to live in Bethel, and he taught the people how to respect the Lord.

However, each ethnic group made gods of its own. (Although they gave lip service to Yahweh, they did not think that Yahweh was the only God. Instead, those pagans combined the worship of Yahweh with that of their own gods—syncretism.) They put them in the towns where they lived. They put them in the temples of the high places. These temples had been made by these Samaritans. The men from Babylon made Succoth-Benoth their god. The men from Cuthah worshiped Nergal. The men of Hamath worshiped Ashima (a bald, male goat). The Avvites worshiped Nibhaz (the image of a dog's head) and Tartak. And, the Sepharvites burned their children in the fire, sacrificing them to Adrammelech (the sun god) the gods of Sepharvaim. They also respected the Lord. But they chose priests for the high places. The priests were chosen from among themselves (not of the descendants of Aaron), and they officiated as priests for the people in the shrines of the high places. The people respected the Lord, but they also served their own gods in accordance with the customs of the countries from where they had been deported.

Even today, they still carry on their old customs. They do not revere the Lord only. They do not obey His rules and commands. They do not obey the teachings or the commands of the Lord. He gave these commands to the children of Jacob, whom the Lord had named "Israel." The Lord had made a covenant with them. He had commanded them: "Do not worship different gods. Do not bow down to them or serve them. Do not offer sacrifices to them. Worship only the Lord who brought you up out of the land of Egypt. He did it with great power and with strength. Bow to the Lord and make sacrifices only to Him. Obey the rules, the orders, and the teachings. Obey the commands that the Lord wrote for you. Obey them and always do them. You must not worship different gods. Do not forget the covenant that I made with you. And, do not worship different gods. Instead, worship only the Lord, your God. He will save you from all your enemies."

But the Israelites did not listen. They kept on practicing the same pagan practices that they had done before. So, these non-Jewish nations respected the Lord, but they continued serving their idols. And, to this day, their children and grandchildren do as their ancestors did.

My Time to Pray

As Their Ancestors Did

Do not be deceived, God is not mocked; for whatever a man sows, that he will also reap (Galatians 6:7).

After generations of rebellion, God finally allows an evil nation to destroy the cities and way of life of the Israelites in the north. They had surrendered themselves to the gods of foreign nations, so God gives them into the control of these nations. There's a lesson in this picture of punishment. You become a slave to the thing to which you surrender. To the young people who surrender themselves to alcohol, they become addictive alcoholics. Alcohol controls their desires, controls their life, and cuts short their lives. The same is true for drugs, sex, pleasure, or anything that dominates your life. "You're a slave to anything that masters your life." *Lord, I will be Your slave. Come fill my life with Your presence. Give me more yearnings to know You. Dominate my life, I want to serve You.*

God has a passion for small things. Both Israel and Judah were small nations. The biggest nations were Syria, Assyria, Egypt, and Babylon. God's people were a "speck" on the map of nations. The same is true today. Churches are small, considering the big influences of the world. So, God fills a Christian, a church, or in the past the small nation of Judah or Israel, so the world can see God's power, not the power of His people. Also, the world can see the glory of Christ, and not glorify God's people. *Lord, I'm glad to be a member of a small ministry on this earth. I'm a member of the true Body of Christ. May the world see Your powers in the true Church and may they not focus on the people. May the world see Your presence in my life, and not focus on me. Not I, but Christ.*

God is glorified in His people. If they live holy lives, God is glorified in the holiness of His people. If God's people sin, God will punish them, usually, more severely than He punishes the world. Why? Because God wants the world to know that He is holy. He will not allow His children to disobey Him. *Lord, I will obey Your commands. I will live as holy as possible. Come, live in my heart. Give me the power to live above temptation and sin. Help me live for You.*

This chapter tells us the child of God cannot live like the world. You cannot pursue the religions of the world. You must be different from the world. *"You are a chosen generation, a royal priesthood, a holy nation. His own special people..."* (1 Pet. 2:9). *"Having your conduct honorable among the Gentiles...by your good works that they observe, glorify God..."* (1 Pet. 2:12). *Lord, may the world glorify You because of the things I do. Amen.*

47

HEZEKIAH RULES OVER JUDAH

Second Kings 18:1-8

Hezekiah (means "the strength of Yahweh), the son of Ahaz, became the king of Judah during the third year that Hoshea, the son of Elah, was the king of Israel. Hezekiah was 25 years old when he became the king, and he ruled for 29 years in Jerusalem. His mother's name was Abijah, the daughter of Zechariah. Hezekiah did what was right in the sight of the Lord, just as his forefather David had done. He removed the high places and broke the stone pillars that they worshiped. He cut down the Asherah idols. Also, the Israelites (literally, "the sons of Israel") had been burning incense to the bronze snake made by Moses, called Nehushtan. (The Egyptians and Phoenicians adored serpent gods as emblems of health and immortality. Therefore, this old relic had longstanding, dark associations with satan [see Gen. 3:1-15; Isa. 27:1; Ps. 91:13; Rev. 12:9; 20:2].) Hezekiah knew that this object no longer served the purpose for which it was originally erected [see Num. 21:1-9].) But, Hezekiah smashed it into pieces.

Hezekiah trusted in the Lord, the God of Israel. There was no one like Hezekiah among all the kings of Judah. There was no king like him—either before him or after him. Hezekiah was loyal to the Lord, and did not turn away from following the Lord. He obeyed the commands that the Lord had given to Moses. And, the Lord was with Hezekiah. He had success in everything he did. He rebelled against the king of Assyria (unlike his father Ahaz [see 2 Kings 16:1-4;10-18], he did not pay any homage to Assyrian gods). He stopped serving him. (Hezekiah decided to depend solely on Yahweh God.) Hezekiah defeated the Philistines all the way to Gaza and its borders. He defeated them everywhere, from the watchtower to the strong, walled city.

The Temple Is Cleansed

Second Chronicles 17

Hezekiah reopened the doors of the Temple of the Lord and repaired them. He did this in the first month of the first year that he was king. Hezekiah brought the priests and Levites together in a group. He met with them in the courtyard on the east side of the Temple. Hezekiah said, "Listen to me, you Levites. Consecrate yourselves for serving God now. And, make the Temple of the Lord holy. He is the God of your ancestors. Remove from the sanctuary the things that make it impure. Our ancestors were unfaithful to God. They did evil in the sight of the Lord, our God. They abandoned Him and stopped worshiping at the Temple where the Lord once dwelled. They rejected Him. They also shut the doors of the porch of the Temple and put out the fire of the lamps. They stopped burning incense and offering whole burnt offerings to the God of Israel at the sanctuary. So, the Lord became very angry with the people of Judah and Jerusalem, and punished them. Other people are scared and shocked by what the Lord did to Judah and Jerusalem. They insult the people of Judah. You know these things are true. Listen, that is why our ancestors were killed in battle. That is why our sons and daughters, and our wives were taken away as prisoners.

"So now I, Hezekiah, have decided to make a new covenant with the Lord, the God of Israel. Then He will not be furious with us anymore. My sons, don't waste any more time. The Lord chose you to serve Him. You should be His ministers and burn incense to Him."

These are the Levites who started to work: From the Kohathite clan there were: Mahath the son of Amasai; and Joel the son of Azariah. From the Merarite clan there were: Kish, the son of Abdi; and Azariah, the son of Jehalelel. From the Gershonite clan there were: Joash, the son of Zimmah; and Eden, the son of Joah. From Elizaphan's family there were Shimri and Jeiel. From Asaph's family there were: Zechariah and Mattaniah. From Heman's family there were: Jehiel and Shimei. From Jeduthun's family there were: Shemaiah and Uzziel.

These Levites gathered their brothers together, then consecrated themselves for service in the Temple. They obeyed the king's command that had come from the Lord. They went into the Temple of the Lord to purify it. The priests went into the inner part of the Temple of the Lord to purify it. They got all the unclean things that they found in the Temple of the Lord, and put them in the Temple courtyard. Then the Levites took those things out to the Kidron Valley. (Probably to burn them as did King Asa.) They made the Temple holy for serving the Lord. They began on the first day of the first month. On the eighth day of the month, they came to the porch of the Temple, and sanctified the Temple of the Lord for eight more days. They finished on the sixteenth day of the first month.

Then they went inside to King Hezekiah and said to him, "We have purified the entire Temple of the Lord. We have purified the altar for whole burnt offerings and its objects. We have purified the table for the showbread and all of its objects. When Ahaz became the king, he was unfaithful to God. He removed some objects from the Temple. But we have put all of them back and made them holy for the Lord. They are now in front of the Lord's altar."

Early the next morning, King Hezekiah gathered the leaders of the city and went up to the Temple of the Lord. They brought seven bulls, seven male sheep, seven male lambs, and seven male goats. (Seven was considered God's favorite number.) These animals were a sin offering for the kingdom, for the sanctuary, and for Judah. King Hezekiah commanded the priests to offer these animals on the altar of the Lord. The priests were from the sons of Aaron. So, the priests killed the bulls and caught the blood in big pans. Then they sprinkled some of it on the altar. They killed the rams and sprinkled the blood on the altar. Then they killed the lambs, and sprinkled the blood on the altar. Then the priests brought the male goats into the presence of the king and the congregation. The goats were for a sin offering. The king and the congregation put their hands on the goats and confessed their sins. (They identified their sin with the death of the animal and its blood covered their sins.) Then the priests killed the goats. They made a sin offering, using the blood of the goats on the altar to cover (make atonement for) the sins of the Israelites. The king had ordered that the whole burnt offerings and sin offerings should be offered for all Israel. (Hezekiah invited all the tribes of the northern kingdom to attend this special ceremony [see 2 Chron. 30:5-10]. This demonstrated his heart commitment to the Lord.)

King Hezekiah stationed the Levites in the Temple of the Lord with cymbals, harps, and lyres. He did this as David, Gad, and Nathan had commanded. Gad was the king's seer, and Nathan was a prophet. This command came from the Lord through His prophets. So, the Levites stood ready with David's musical instruments, and the priests stood ready with their trumpets.

Then Hezekiah gave the order to sacrifice the whole burnt offerings on the altar. When the whole burnt offerings began, the singing to the Lord also began. The trumpets were blown, and the musical instruments of David, the king of Israel, were played. All the people worshiped as the singers were singing, and the trumpet players blew their trumpets. They did all this until the whole burnt offerings were finished.

When the sacrifices were finished, King Hezekiah and everyone with him bowed down on the ground and worshiped God. King Hezekiah and his officials ordered the Levites to praise the Lord. They used the words that David and Asaph used. They praised God with joy, and bowed their heads and worshiped.

Then Hezekiah said, "Now you people of Judah have committed yourselves to the Lord Who Is Always Present. Come near to the Temple of the Lord. Bring sacrifices and offerings of thanksgiving to the Lord Who Is Always Present." So, the congregation brought sacrifices and offerings of thanksgiving to the Lord. Anyone who wanted to do so also brought whole burnt offerings. They brought a total of 70 bulls, 100 male sheep, and 200 male lambs. All these animals were sacrificed as whole burnt offerings to the Lord. The offerings that had been dedicated to the Lord totaled 600 bulls and 3,000 sheep and goats. There were not enough priests to skin all the animals for the whole burnt offerings. So, their relatives, the Levites, helped them until the work was finished. Then, more priests were consecrated for serving the Lord. The Levites had been more careful than the priests to make themselves holy for the Lord's service. There were many more whole burnt offerings, along with the fat of the peace offerings and the drink offerings associated with the whole burnt offerings. So, the services in the Temple of the Lord began again. And Hezekiah and all the people rejoiced. They were happy that the one true God had made this event happen so quickly for His people.

My Time to Pray

Everyday Idols

He [Hezekiah] remained faithful to the Lord in everything and he carefully obeyed all the commandments the Lord had given Moses. So, the Lord was with him, and Hezekiah was successful in everything he did (2 Kings 18:6-7 NLT).

An unusual thing happened when Hezekiah took over the throne after wicked King Ahaz. Most of the time an evil king produced a son who was more wicked than his weak and unprincipled father. How could such a turnaround happen? It was the grace of God. God uses people or events to accomplish His purposes. What did He use? First, the godly influence of Isaiah the prophet cannot be ruled out. Then there were the dark political days. Judah paid enormous taxes to Assyria, and sin ran rampant among the priests and idol worship influenced every area of life. The brazen serpent—once used of God—was now even worshiped. The common people were terrorized and worship of God was a sham. When man has nowhere else to turn, he turns to God. That's what happened to Hezekiah. *Lord, remind me that You are the only solution to all my problems. When trouble first comes, I'll turn to You. When trouble gets too heavy to bear I'll turn to You. Remind me, Lord, of Your daily grace.*

We can all make an idol out of a good thing. God used the brazen serpent to save Israel when the nation sinned in rebellion. All the people had to do was "look and live." Perhaps when trouble came to Israel, they took out the brazen serpent, and again "looked to it for a solution." Sometimes old solutions don't solve modern problems, then again sometimes they do. But the old solution didn't work this time because the people looked to a thing, rather than looking to the One (the Lord) who was symbolized in the thing. *Lord, forgive me for trusting in religious symbols, or church services, or music, or anything that takes Your place. Forgive me. Cleanse me by the blood of Christ. I look to You, Lord, for direction.*

But there is a place for the proper use of symbols. When Hezekiah repented and turned to the Lord with all his heart, he returned to the proper use of symbols. The Temple was cleansed, and the sacrifices were properly administered. The people appeared before the Lord to seek forgiveness of sin and to worship. Just so, when we return to God, we must properly use the symbols God has given us today. We must gather in God's house. We must sing worship music to God. We must bring the tithe (symbolic of giving our all to God), and we must bow in His presence. *Lord, I will bow my heart to You, and I will bend my back in humble worship. I will sing to You, I will give my time, talent, and treasure to You. Lord, may my outward life reflect my inner dedication to You.*

When God's people return to Him, the blood must be applied to the sins of His wayward people. Here we read the priests gathered the blood of the animals and sprinkled it before the Lord. The sacrifice of these animals only looked forward to Jesus the Lamb of God (see John 1:29). What must we do? *"If we walk in the light, as He is in the light, the blood of Jesus Christ God's Son cleanses from all sin"* (1 John 1:7). *Lord, touch me with the blood of Christ. Cleanse me. Make me fit for service. Use me. Here am I. Amen.*

48

THE PASSOVER FEAST IS CELEBRATED

Second Chronicles 30

King Hezekiah sent messages to all the people of Israel and Judah. He also wrote letters to the people of Ephraim and Manasseh. Hezekiah invited all these people to come to the Temple of the Lord in Jerusalem. There they could celebrate the Passover for the Lord, the God of Israel. King Hezekiah, his officials, and all the congregation in Jerusalem agreed to celebrate the Passover in the second month. They could not celebrate it at the usual time (approximately our April). This was because not enough priests had consecrated themselves to serve the Lord. And, the people had not yet gathered in Jerusalem. (They did not have enough time to get the notices out, and they did not want to postpone it for another full year.) This plan satisfied King Hezekiah and the entire assembly. So, they decided to make a special announcement everywhere in Israel, from Beer-Sheba to Dan. They told the people to come to Jerusalem to celebrate the Passover for the Lord Who Is Always Present, the God of Israel. Because, for a long time, many of the people had not celebrated the Passover as it was prescribed. So, under direct orders from the king, the messengers took letters from the king and his officers throughout all Israel and Judah. This is what the letters said:

"O people of Israel, come back to the Lord, the God of Abraham, of
Isaac, and of Jacob. Then God will come back to you who
are still alive. You have survived the invasion of the kings of
Assyria. Don't be like your ancestors or your relatives who were
unfaithful to the Lord, the God of their ancestors. So, the Lord
caused other people to be shocked at them. You know this is
true. Don't be stubborn as your ancestors were. Obey the Lord
willingly. Come to His sanctuary (the Passover festival was one of
three annual pilgrim feasts that required attendance at the Temple
in Jerusalem [see Num. 28:9-29]) that He has made holy for His
service forever. Serve the Lord Who Is Always Present, your God.
Then He will turn away His fury from you. If you come back to
the Lord, then the people who captured your relatives and your
children will be kind to them. They will permit them to return to
this land. The Lord Who Is Always Present, your God, is merciful
and kind. He will not turn away from you, if you come back to
Him."

The messengers traveled to every town in the land of Ephraim and
Manasseh. They went all the way to the territory of Zebulun.
(This tribe was the most distant one from Jerusalem.) But
the people laughed at the messengers and made fun of them.
Nevertheless, some men from the tribes of Asher, Manasseh, and
Zebulun were sorry for what they had done. And, they went to
Jerusalem. The one true God also caused all the people in Judah
to agree to obey King Hezekiah and his officers. The command
had come from the Lord.

A very large crowd of people came together in Jerusalem to celebrate the
Festival of Unleavened Bread, in the second month. The people
got up and removed the pagan altars, and they cleared away all
the incense altars to false gods in Jerusalem. They threw them
into the Kidron Valley. (They burned these pagan cult objects at
this designated dump site.)

They killed the Passover lambs on the fourteenth day of the second month. The priests and the Levites were ashamed of themselves, so they consecrated themselves to the Lord. They brought whole burnt offerings into the Temple of the Lord. They took up their places in the Temple, as prescribed by the teachings of Moses, the man of the one true God. The Levites gave the blood of the sacrifices to the priests. Then the priests sprinkled the blood on the altar. (Professor Barnes writes: "According to Mishna, the custom was for the priests to stand in two rows extending from the altar to the outer court, where the people were assembled. As each offerer killed his lamb, the blood was caught in a basin, which was handed to the nearest priest, who passed it on to his neighbor, and he to the next. The blood was thus conveyed to the altar, at the base of which it was thrown by the last priest in the row. While basins full of blood were thus passed up, empty basins were passed down in a constant succession, so that there was no pause or delay."[1])

Many people in the crowd had not consecrated themselves. So, the Levites were responsible for killing the Passover lambs (according to the Law of Moses [see Exod. 12:6; Deut. 16:6], the heads of the families were to slaughter the Passover lambs) for everyone who was not clean. The Levites made each lamb "consecrated" to the Lord. Most of the people from the tribes of Ephraim, Manasseh, Issachar, and Zebulun had not purified themselves for the festival. Nevertheless, they ate the Passover meal, even though it was contrary to what was written. But, Hezekiah prayed for them. He said, "O Lord Who Is Always Present, You are good. You are the Lord, the God of their ancestors. Please pardon each one of them who tried to obey you. Pardon them even though they did not make themselves 'clean,' according to the rules of the sanctuary."

And the Lord listened to Hezekiah's prayers and He did not punish
them. The Israelites who were present in Jerusalem celebrated
the Festival of Unleavened Bread for seven days, and they were
happy. The Levites and the priests praised the Lord every day
with instruments of praise for the Lord. Some of the Levites
were very skillful at conducting the worship service to the Lord,
and Hezekiah encouraged them. The people ate their assigned
portions for seven days, and they offered peace offerings. They
praised the Lord, the God of their ancestors.

Then the entire congregation agreed to celebrate seven more days.
They did celebrate enthusiastically for seven more days. Then
Hezekiah, the king of Judah, donated 1,000 bulls and 7,000
sheep to the congregation. The leaders gave 1,000 bulls and
10,000 sheep to the congregation. Many priests consecrated
themselves to the Lord. The entire congregation of Judah, the
priests, the Levites, all those who came to visit from Israel, the
foreigners from the land of Israel, and those who were living in
Judah were extremely happy. There was much joy in Jerusalem,
because there had not been a celebration like this in Jerusalem
since the time of Solomon, the son of David and king of Israel.
The priests and the Levites stood up to bless the people, and
God heard their voices, because their prayers reached Heaven,
His holy dwelling place.

My Time to Pray

Pardon Them

Did you notice how heart devotion to God overcame the legalistic
keeping of laws? The people were supposed to ritually consecrate
themselves when they came into the Temple. The people from the tribe
of Ephraim, Manasseh, Issachar, and Zebulun apparently were untaught

because the Levites had not properly taught the people. But they ate the Passover anyway. Hezekiah prayed, "Pardon them..." God heard and blessed them anyway. *Lord, when I forget Your commandments, pardon me. Lord, when I break Your law because I am untaught and ignorant, pardon me. Be merciful to me for I know I am not perfect.*

Notice the advertisement (letter) that went out to invite people to come to Jerusalem for the Passover. So it's permissible to invite people to our church services today. Today, just as during Hezekiah's time, there are backslidden believers who must return to fellowship with the Lord, and return to the house of God to worship Him. *Lord, I will go to church on a regular basis, and I will join my sisters and brothers in worshiping You.*

The Jews in Zebulun laughed at the invitation to come to Jerusalem to worship the Lord in celebration of Passover. So nothing is new, today some church members laugh at what is happening in our churches. *Lord, I will pray for those who reject worship at my church.*

It was good to see King Hezekiah involved in worship in the Temple. Usually, worship was led by the Levites and priests, and there was separation between the monarchy and priesthood. But Hezekiah was vitally involved and led in the prayer for forgiveness of those who came to Passover ceremonially unclean. *Lord, I pray for my political leaders as You command (see 1 Tim. 2:1ff). I pray they may make righteous laws and rule with biblical justice. But more than that, I pray for my political leaders to lead in moral reform and biblical worship.*

When Israel couldn't celebrate Passover in the regular time because of circumstances, they met as soon as they could to worship God. That tells me God may overlook when we can't worship at the designated time. But I see Israel worshiping God as soon as they could. *Lord, I will be in church every time I am supposed to be there. When I have to miss, I'll be back in worship as soon as I can. Amen.*

Endnote

1. Albert Barnes, *Barnes Notes on the Old and New Testaments* (Fourteen volumes) (Grand Rapids, MI: Baker Book House, 1983). Because of the many additions to the notes of Barnes, this is referenced to a verse and not a specific page number.

49

THE PRIESTS AND LEVITES
RECEIVE PROVISIONS

Second Chronicles 31

After the Passover celebration was finished, all the Israelites in Jerusalem went out to the towns of Judah. There they smashed the stone pillars that were used to worship false gods. They cut down the Asherah idols. They destroyed the altars and the places for worshiping false gods. They destroyed all of them in the areas of Judah, Benjamin, Ephraim, and Manasseh. They destroyed everything used for worshiping the false gods. Then all the Israelites returned to their own towns and homes.

King Hezekiah organized each shift of priests and Levites for their special duties. They were to offer whole burnt offerings and peace offerings, and were to minister and to give thanks and praise within the gates where the Lord dwells. The king gave some of his own animals for the whole burnt offerings. Whole burnt offerings were sacrificed on the weekly Sabbath days and during New Moons and other set feasts commanded by the Lord's teachings.

In addition, Hezekiah commanded people who lived in Jerusalem to give the priests and the Levites the portion that belonged to them. Then the priests and the Levites could give all their time to the Lord's teachings. So, the king's command went out to the

Israelites, and they gave the firstfruits of their grain, new wine, olive oil, and honey. They gave the first portion of everything they grew in their fields. They brought a large amount—one-tenth of everything. (The tithes [see Lev. 27:31] were intended for the adequate support of the whole Levitical tribe [see Num. 18:8,20,34].) The men of Israel and the men of Judah who lived in the towns of Judah also gave. They also brought one-tenth of their cattle and sheep. And, they brought one-tenth of the holy things that were dedicated to the Lord, their God. They laid out all these things in several big piles. The people began bringing their things in the third month (our June, about the time of the Pentecost). Hezekiah and his officials came and saw the huge piles, and they praised the Lord and the people of Israel. Hezekiah asked the priests and the Levites about those piles. Azariah was the high priest from Zadok's household. He answered Hezekiah: "Since the people began to bring their offerings to the Temple of the Lord, we have more than enough to eat. And, we have plenty left, because the Lord has blessed His people. So, we have all this abundance."

Then Hezekiah commanded the priests to prepare the storerooms in the Temple of the Lord. So, this construction work was completed. Then the priests faithfully brought the extra offerings and the things that were dedicated to the Lord to the storerooms. They also brought the tithes of everything that the people had given.

Conaniah the Levite was in charge of these things. Conaniah's brother, Shimei, was second to him. Conaniah and his brother Shimei were over these supervisors: Jehiel, Azaziah, Nahath, Asahel, Jerimoth, Jozabad, Eliel, Ismachiah, Mahath, and Benaiah. King Hezekiah and Azariah, the officer in charge of the Temple of the one true God chose those men.

Kore was in charge of the special gifts that the people wanted to give to the one true God. He was responsible for giving out the contributions made to the Lord and the consecrated gifts. Kore was the son of Imnah the Levite. Kore was the guard at the East Gate. Eden, Miniamin, Jeshua, Shemaiah, Amariah, and Shecaniah helped Kore. They faithfully helped in the towns where the priests lived. They distributed what was collected to the other shifts of priests. They gave both to the young and the old.

In addition, these men also distributed fairly from what was collected to the males who were 30 years old or older. These were males who had their names in the Levites family histories. They were to enter the Temple of the Lord to perform their daily duties. Each shift had its own responsibilities. The priests were given their part of the collection. This was done by families, as listed in the family histories. The Levites who were 20 years old and older were given their part of the collection (if the individual was on the official list). This was done by their responsibilities and by their shifts.

The babies of the Levites, their wives, their sons, and their daughters— the whole community—also got part of the collection. This was done for all the Levites who were listed in the family histories. This was because the Levites always kept themselves ready to serve the Lord.

Hezekiah also approved that some of Aaron's descendants, the priests, lived on the farmland near the Levitical towns. Some also lived in the towns. Responsible men were designated by name to distribute the food collected to these priests. All the males and those named in the family histories of the Levites received part of the collection.

This is what Hezekiah did throughout all of Judah. He did what was good and right and faithful in the presence of the Lord, his God. Hezekiah tried to obey his God in his service of the Temple of the one true God. He tried to obey God's teachings and commands.

He gave himself fully to his work for God. So, Hezekiah had success.

My Time to Pray

No Other Gods

You shall have no other gods before Me. You shall not make for yourself a carved image—any likeness of anything that is in heaven above, or that is in the earth beneath, or that is in the water under the earth; you shall not bow down to them nor serve them (Exodus 20:3-5).

You can't really be right with God, nor can you expect Him to bless you if you have idols in your life. So what must you do? The same as Hezekiah, *"There they smashed the stone pillars that were used to worship false gods"* (2 Chron. 31:1). And what is an idol? Anything that gets between you and the Lord. False worship is giving the priority of your life to anything but God. *Lord, I repent of allowing anything to take first place in my life. Forgive me. I plead the cleansing blood of Christ. I will rid my life of anything that takes Your place.*

When Israel properly worshiped the Lord and repented of their idolatry, then they rightly brought their tithes and offerings to the Temple that they had neglected. They provided for the needs of the Temple and the priests. *Lord, I will bring my tithes and offerings to my church to take care of its needs, and the needs of Your workers. I will do it because of my obligation. I recognize I can't be spiritual without fulfilling my obligations. Thank You for the privilege of giving to You and Your work.*

"Hezekiah tried to obey his God...Hezekiah tried to obey God's teaching and commandments. He gave himself fully to his work for God" (2 Chron. 31:20). Hezekiah was used of God because of his yieldedness and deep desire to please God. *Lord, Hezekiah is my role model, I will follow his example. I will obey Your teaching and commands to the best of my ability. Amen.*

50

THE ASSYRIANS THREATEN JERUSALEM

Second Kings 18:9-37

Shalmaneser, the king of Assyria, surrounded Samaria, the capital city of Israel and besieged it. This occurred in the fourth year that Hezekiah was king of Judah. And, it was during the seventh year that Hoshea the son of Elah was the king of Israel. After three years, the Assyrians captured Samaria, in the sixth year when Hezekiah was king. And, it was Hoshea's ninth year as the king of Israel. The king of Assyria deported the Israelites to Assyria, and put them in Halah and in Gozan on the Habor River. He also put them in the cities of the Medes. This happened because they did not obey the voice of the Lord, their God. They broke His covenant, not obeying all that Moses, the Lord's servant, had commanded. They would not listen to the commands, nor do them.

During Hezekiah's fourteenth year as king, Sennacherib, the king of Assyria, attacked Judah. He attacked all the strong-walled cities of Judah and seized them. Then Hezekiah, the king of Judah, sent a message to the king of Assyria who was at Lachish. He said, "I have made a mistake. (King Hezekiah faced a menacing, overwhelming Assyrian army. He wanted to avoid an all-out war against his country. Therefore, he hoped that the Assyrians would retreat if they were paid off, and the Jews could still maintain a measure of independence. But Josephus reports: "The Assyrian king took about $10 million, and yet had no respect to what he had promised." Isaiah 36:10 says that Sennacherib's real purpose from the very beginning was the total destruction and devastation of Jerusalem. But Sennacherib's army, which was under this field commander, had to withdraw from Jerusalem to fight against Libnah [see Isa. 37:8; 2 Kings 19:8], because the army of Tirhakah from Ethiopia and some Egyptians were advancing against Sennacherib from the south [see Isa. 37:9-13; 2 Kings 19:9-13].) Turn away from me. I will pay whatever you demand of me."

So, the king of Assyria told Hezekiah how much to pay. It was about 22,000 pounds of silver and 2,000 pounds of gold. Hezekiah gave Sennacherib all the silver that was in the Temple of the Lord. And, Hezekiah gave him all the silver in the royal palace treasuries. At that time, Hezekiah the king of Judah stripped off all the gold that covered the doors of the Temple of the Lord. He also removed the gold from the door posts. He gave it all to the king of Assyria. (Once Sennacherib had his money, he returned to Nineveh, the capital city of the Assyrian Empire. Hezekiah felt bad about his submission to Sennacherib. So Hezekiah began negotiations for an alliance with Egypt [see 2 Kings 18:21,24; Isa. 30:2-6; 31:10]. This implied that Hezekiah was betraying his existing alliance with Assyria. While besieging Lachish, on Sennacherib's way to encounter his main enemy to the south, in Egypt and Ethiopia, Sennacherib sent his representatives to Jerusalem to seek their surrender.)

The king of Assyria sent out his supreme commander, his chief officer, and his field commander. They went with a large army from Lachish to King Hezekiah in Jerusalem. When they approached Jerusalem's waterway from the upper pool, they stopped there. The upper pool is on the road to Bleacher's Field. They called for King Hezekiah. So Eliakim, Shebna, and Joach went out to meet them. Eliakim, the son of Hilkiah, was the palace manager. Shebna was the royal assistant. And Joach, the son of Asaph, was the historian.

The Assyrian field commander said to them, "Tell Hezekiah this:

""The great king, the king of Assyria, says: "What is there that remains that you can trust? You claim that you have battle plans and military strength, but your words are empty. On whom are you trusting for help such that you rebel against me? Look, you are not depending on Egypt to help you. Egypt is like a splintered walking stick. If you lean on it for help, it will stab you and hurt you. Pharaoh, the king of Egypt, will hurt anybody who depends on him. But you might tell me: 'We are depending upon the Lord, our God.' Well, Hezekiah destroyed the Lord's altars and the high places of worship. (This pagan field commander did not understand that Yahweh was very pleased with King Hezekiah's religious reforms. The Assyrian official was only reasoning like a polytheist, not a monotheist.) Hezekiah told Judah and Jerusalem: 'You must worship only at this one altar in Jerusalem.'

"""Now, let's make a deal with my master, the king of Assyria: I will give you 2,000 horses...if you can find enough men to ride them. You could not defeat even one of my master's least important officers. So, why do you depend on Egypt to give you chariots and horsemen? I have not come to attack and destroy this place without an order from the Lord. Why, the Lord Himself told me (this was an outright lie!) to come to this country and destroy it."""

Then Eliakim, the son of Hilkiah, Shebnah, and Joach spoke to the field commander, saying, "Please speak to us in the Aramaic language. We understand it. Do not speak to us in Hebrew, because the people on the city wall can hear you."

But the field commander said to them, "No, my master did not send me to tell these things only to you and your king. My master sent me to say them also to those people sitting on the wall. (The field commander wanted to deliver his boastful taunt directly to the Jewish populace to intimidate them and demoralize them. His intent was to drive a wedge between King Hezekiah and his people, hoping that the inhabitants would self-destruct and surrender.) Like you, they will have to eat their own dung and drink their own urine." (The Assyrian field commander was arrogantly projecting the dreadful extremes to which the people of Jerusalem would be reduced after a very long siege. Compare Second Kings 6:25.)

Then the field commander stood up and shouted loudly in the Hebrew language, saying, "Listen to the word from the great king, the king of Assyria. The king says that you should not let Hezekiah fool you. Hezekiah cannot save you from my power. Don't let Hezekiah talk you into trusting the Lord. Hezekiah says: 'The Lord will surely save us. This city won't be given over to the king of Assyria.'

"Don't listen to Hezekiah. The king of Assyria says: 'Make a peace treaty with me. Come out of the city to me. Then everyone will be free to eat the fruit from his own grapevine and his own fig tree. Everyone will be free to drink water from his own well. (This was a total lie! The Assyrians were some of the most brutal conquerors that the world has ever seen.) Then I will come and take you away to a land similar to your own land. It is a land with grain and new wine. It is a land of food and vineyards. It is a land of olive oil and honey. Then you can choose to live and not die.

"Don't listen to Hezekiah. He is fooling you when he says: 'The Lord will save us.' No god of any other nation has saved his people from the power of the king of Assyria. Where are the gods of

Hamath and Arpad? Where are the gods of Sepharvaim, Hena, and Ivvah? They did not save Samaria from my power. (Samaria had been the capital city of Israel; it was completely destroyed in 722 B.C.) Not a single one of any of the gods of these countries has saved his people from me. Therefore, the Lord cannot save Jerusalem from my power."

The people kept silent. They did not answer the field commander at all. (This was because King Hezekiah had ordered them, "Don't answer him.")

Then Eliakim, Shebna, and Joach tore their clothes. (They knew that a lengthy siege was certain and imminent.) Eliakim, the son of Hilkiah, was the palace manager. Shebna was the royal assistant. And Joach, the son of Asaph, was the historian. The three men went to Hezekiah and told him what the field commander had said. (The insulting Assyrians were demanding unconditional surrender. This was one of the darkest moments in the history of God's people. See Isaiah 36:21-22.)

My Time to Pray

Depending on God Alone

For if we sin willfully after we have received the knowledge of the truth, there no longer remains a sacrifice for sins, but a certain fearful expectation of judgment, and fiery indignation which will devour the adversaries (Hebrews 10:26-27).

The child of God cannot continually sin without God's punishment. If you have idols in your life, don't you realize God is jealous? When you give your love and worship to an idol, how can you be so dumb to think God will not punish you for your rebellion to Him by worshiping idols? The ten northern tribes had sinned so deeply and so long that they exhausted God's patience. Finally, He judged them. *Lord, I know You will judge me for any idol in my life. I will search them out and destroy them. I repent of ignorant sin and thoughtless idolatry. Open my blind eyes to see where I am doing wrong.*

This chapter tells me not to rely on the world for spiritual protection. The world will lie to me, deceive me, and in the end it will not protect me spiritually. The world, the flesh, and the devil want to destroy me completely and devastate all I do for God. *Lord, I trust You for spiritual protection. I claim the promise, "Greater is He who is in you, than he who is in the world" (1 John 4:4). When I have to work with, or for people of the world, teach me how to relate to them, while I put You first in my life. Lord, I'm ignorant to a lot of politics and "dealings" that go on behind my back. Protect me when I can't protect myself. Protect me when I don't know the evil around me.*

There are many in the world who claim to know God and to know God's will for my life. There are those who claim they have a "word" for me from God. Remember what Jesus said, "Let no man deceive you, for many will come in My name." *Lord, I will search Your Scriptures to find Your will for my life. I will find Your will and do it. I will not listen to those who are ignorant of Scripture or who advise me contrary to Scripture. I will listen for the voice of the Holy Spirit when He speaks to my heart from Scripture.*

Some will come to tell God's children that their God will not help them, nor can He save them. Because they do not know God, they do not know how God will save His people or what method God will save His people. *Lord, I claim the promise, "Yea though I walk through the valley of the shadow of death, I will fear no evil..." (Ps. 23:4). Amen.*

51

KING HEZEKIAH
SEEKS ADVICE FROM ISAIAH

Second Kings 19

When King Hezekiah heard the message, he tore his clothes. And he put on some sackcloth and went into the Temple of the Lord. Hezekiah sent Eliakim, Shebna, and the older priests to Isaiah. Eliakim was the palace manager, and Shebna was the royal assistant. The men were all wearing sackcloth when they came to the prophet Isaiah, the son of Amoz. These men told Isaiah: "This is what Hezekiah says: 'Today is a day of sorrow and punishment and disgrace. Why? It is sad, like when a child should be born, but the mother is not strong enough to give birth to it. The king of Assyria sent his field commander to make fun of the living God. Perhaps the Lord, your God, will hear what the field commander said. Perhaps the Lord, your God, will punish him for what he said. So, pray for the remnant who are left alive.'"

When Hezekiah's officers came to Isaiah, he said to them, "Tell your master this: The Lord says: 'Don't be afraid of what you have heard. Don't be scared by the words that the servants of the king of Assyria have spoken against Me. Listen! I am going to put a sense of dread in the king of Assyria. He will hear a report that will cause him to go back to his own country. And, I will cause him to die by the sword there.'"

The field commander heard that the king of Assyria had left Lachish. So, the field commander left Jerusalem and found the king fighting against the city of Libnah.

Sennacherib received a report that Tirhakah (an Ethiopian dynastic name, like "Pharaoh") was coming to attack him. Tirhakah was the Cushite king of Egypt. When the king of Assyria heard this, he sent messengers to Hezekiah. The king of Assyria said: "Do not let your god, upon whom you depend, deceive you by promising that Jerusalem will not be delivered in to the hands of the king of Assyria. Listen, you have heard what the kings of Assyria have done. They have completely defeated every country. Do not think that you will be spared. The gods of those nations did not save them. My Assyrian predecessors destroyed them. My ancestors defeated the cities of Gozan, Haran, and Rezeph. They defeated the people of Eden living in Tel-Assar. Where are the kings of Hamath and Arpad? Where is the king of the city of Sepharvaim? Where are the kings of Hena and Ivvah?"

King Hezekiah Prays to God

Hezekiah received the letter from the messengers and read it. Then he went up to the Temple of the Lord. Hezekiah spread the letter out in front of the Lord, and prayed: "O Lord Who Is Always Present, God of Israel, Your throne is between the golden Cherubim. Only You are the one true God of all the kingdoms of the earth. You made the heavens and the earth. Hear, O Lord Who Is Always Present, and see. Listen to the words that Sennacherib has spoken to insult the living God.

"It is true, O Lord Who Is Always Present, that the kings of Assyria have destroyed these countries and their lands. These kings have thrown the gods of these nations into the fire. But they were not gods—they were only wood and rock statues that human beings made. So, the Assyrian kings have destroyed them. But now, O Lord Who is Always Present, our God, save us from the king's power. Then all the kingdoms of the earth will know that You, O Lord Who Is Always Present, are the only God."

Isaiah Reassures King Hezekiah

Then Isaiah, the son of Amoz, sent a message to Hezekiah, saying, "The Lord, the God of Israel, says this: 'I have heard your prayer to Me about Sennacherib, the king of Assyria.' So, this is what the Lord has said against Sennacherib:

'The sacred people of Zion hate you and make fun of you, The people of Jerusalem laugh at you, as you run away.

You have insulted Me and spoken against Me,

You have raised your voice against Me.

You have a proud look on your face;

You opposed Me, the Holy One of Israel. You have used your messengers to insult the Lord; You have thought: "I have many chariots. With them, I have gone up to the tops of the Mountains;

I have climbed the highest mountains of Lebanon.

I have cut down its tallest cedar trees;

I have cut down its best pine trees.

I have reached its farthest places;

I have gone to its forests, no matter how dense.

I have dug wells in foreign countries;

I have drunk water there.

By the soles of my feet

I have dried up all the rivers of Egypt."

"'O king of Assyria, surely you have heard

Long ago, I, the Lord, planned these things.

Long ago, I planned them;

Now I have caused them to happen.

I allowed you to turn those strong, walled cities

into piles of rocks. The people living in those cities were weak;

They were scared and put to shame.

They were like grass in the field;

They were like tender, young grass.

They were like grass that grows on the housetops;

It is burned by the wind before it can grow.

"I know when you relax, and when you come and go;

I know how you speak against Me.

You speak strongly against Me

And, I have heard your proud words.

So, I will put My hook in your nose

and I will put My bit in your mouth.

Then I will force you to leave My country

the same way that you came.'

"Then the Lord said, 'Hezekiah, I will give you this sign:

This year you will eat the grain that grows wild

And, the second year, you will eat what grows wild from that.

But, in the third year, you should plant grain and harvest it;

Also, plant vineyards and eat their fruit.

Some of the people in the household of Judah

will be saved.

Like plants that take root downward,

they will grow strong and have many children.

A few people will come out of Jerusalem alive;

There will be a few from Mount Zion who will survive.

The strong love of the Lord of the armies of Heaven

will cause this to happen.

"So, this is what the Lord says about the king of Assyria:

'Sennacherib will not enter this city;

He will not even shoot an arrow here,

He will not fight against it with shields;

He will not build a ramp to attack the city walls.

He will return to his own country the same way he came;

He will not enter this city,' says the Lord. 'I will defend this city and
    save it;

I will do this for Myself and for David, my servant.'"

185,000 Assyrians Die

That night, the Angel of the Lord went out and killed 185,000 men in the Assyrian camp. (This judgment could have been a direct supernatural work of God, just as the Death Angel killed the firstborn of every family in Egypt. Or, God could have used secondary means. The Greek historian, Herodotus, mentions an attack by mice at Pelusium. This might suggest that the bubonic plague might have wiped out all of them.) The Jewish people got up early the next morning, and saw all the dead bodies. So, Sennacherib, the king of Assyria, left and went back to Nineveh and stayed there.

One day, Sennacherib was worshiping in the temple of his god Nisroch. While he was there, his sons, Adrammelech and Sharezer, killed him with a sword. Then they escaped to the land of Ararat. So, Sennacherib's son, Esar-Haddon, became the king of Assyria.

My Time to Pray

Doing the Right Thing

There is no wisdom, nor understanding, nor plans against the Lord that will prevail (Proverbs 21:30 AMP).

When a great spiritual attack came against Israel, King Hezekiah did the right thing. He sought counsel from a godly person, Isaiah. *Lord, I will listen to those who know Your Word and do Your will. I will listen to those who will pray for me and have my best interests at heart. Lord, speak to me through the godly counsel of Your servants.*

Hezekiah believed in *geographical praying*—going to the place the Lord delights to reveal Himself, the place where there is a history of God working in that place. Hezekiah went into the Temple and spread the letter out before the Lord. *Lord, I will go to the church altar for prayer, or any place where You have spoken to me. I will seek Your presence. Then, I will make my petition to You. Hear me and answer when I pray with a sincere heart.*

Hezekiah spread the letter out before the Lord. He didn't do that to tell God what the letter said. God knows everything; He knew what was in the letter. Also, God didn't need to see the letter to know the credibility of Hezekiah's prayer, or the critical nature of the circumstance. *"Your Father knows what things you have need of before you ask Him"* (Matt. 6:8). No, you bring your bills, or "threatening letters," or any evidence of your trouble into the presence of God to remind you of the threatening nature of your intercession. *Lord, I come into Your presence, I hold my hands up to You as an outward evidence of an inward act of recognizing You and worshiping You. I hold up my trials and problems. See them and see the concern of my heart. Lord, I hold them up to You because there is no one else who can help me. Help me, Lord, now.*

You must recognize the absolute power of God when you pray to Him. Did you see what Hezekiah prayed? *"You are the only one true God...save us from the king's power"* (2 Kings 19:16,19). *Lord, I recognize Your sovereignty over all the earth and the kingdoms of the earth. Lord, You have power to punish sin and save Your people. Deliver me today, help me now.*

The Lord answered Hezekiah's prayer in an unusual way. God's people didn't have to fight—or do anything but trust the Lord. God sent His angel to destroy 185,000 enemy soldiers. God could have killed them directly, as He did when the death angel passed over Egypt. God could have used the bubonic plague to kill them. With the large amount of evil and dirty lifestyle of soldiers living so closely together, and with a large amount of human waste and feces and rats scavenging the filth, they could have spread the disease among the soldiers, just as the black plague (bubonic plague) destroyed almost half of the population of Europe in the Dark Ages. *Lord, I'm amazed when You work directly in supernatural ways to intervene in my life. I'm also amazed when You work supernaturally through circumstances to accomplish Your will. However You do it, Lord, work in my life. Protect me, guide me, fill me, and use me. Amen.*

52

YAHWEH HEALS KING HEZEKIAH

Second Kings 20

At that time, Hezekiah became very sick and almost died. The prophet Isaiah, the son of Amoz, went to visit him, and told him, "This is what the Lord says: You are going to die. So, you should set your house in order. You will not get well."

Hezekiah turned his face toward the wall (for the sake of undisturbed privacy and to concentrate on his thoughts) and prayed to the Lord, saying, "O Lord Who Is Always Present, please remember that I have always obeyed You and have given myself completely to You. I have walked in Your presence with faithfulness and with a complete heart. I have done what is right in Your sight." And, Hezekiah wept bitterly. (Hezekiah knew that he was childless, and that he was leaving his kingdom with no heir. If Hezekiah did not have a son, the Messianic line for David to Jesus Christ would have been broken.)

But before Isaiah had left the middle courtyard of the royal palace, the Lord spoke His word to Isaiah: "Go back and tell Hezekiah, the spiritual leader of My people: 'This is what the Lord, the God of your ancestors David, says: I have heard your prayer. And, I have seen your tears. Listen, I will heal you. Three days from now, you will go up to the Temple of the Lord. I will add 15 years to your life. I will save you and this city from the king of Assyria. And, I will protect the city for Myself and for My servant David.'"

Then Isaiah said, "Make a paste from figs." So, they made it and put it on Hezekiah's tumor. And, he got well.

Hezekiah asked Isaiah, "What will be the sign that the Lord will heal me? What is the sign that I will go up to the Temple of the Lord on the third day?"

Isaiah said, "The Lord will do what He says. This is the sign from the Lord to you: Do you want the shadow to go forward ten degrees, or do you want it to go back ten degrees?"

Hezekiah answered, "It is easy for the shadow to go forward ten degrees. No, let it go back ten degrees."

Then Isaiah the prophet prayed to the Lord, and He brought the shadow backward ten degrees. It went back up the stairway of Ahaz that it had gone down (a large sun dial that told time by points in a garden or courtyard).

Hezekiah Shows Off His Wealth

At that time, Berodach-Baladan, the son of Baladan, was the king of Babylon. (No doubt, Merodach-Baladan was proposing a defensive alliance against the Assyrians, their common enemy. Hezekiah was flattered, and thus, he ventured into a vain display of his own riches. Much of it would have come from the corpses of the Assyrian army. And, perhaps Hezekiah recovered all the silver and gold that he had previously paid to Sennacherib [see 2 Kings 18:14-16].) The Babylonian king sent letters and a gift to Hezekiah, because he had heard that Hezekiah had been very sick.

Hezekiah was happy to see the messengers, so he showed them everything that was in his treasury—the silver, the gold, the spices, and the expensive perfumes. He also showed them his armory. He showed them all of his wealth. He showed them everything in his palace and his kingdom.

Then Isaiah the prophet went to King Hezekiah and asked him, "What did these men say? Where did they come from?"

Hezekiah said, "They came from a faraway country. They came to me from Babylon."

So, Isaiah asked, "What did they see in your palace?"

Hezekiah said, "They saw everything in my palace. I showed them all of my wealth."

Then Isaiah said to Hezekiah, "Listen to the word of the Lord: 'In the future, everything in your palace will be carried off to Babylon. (It is very significant that the prophet Isaiah predicted that it would be Babylon, not Nineveh, their present enemy. This was fulfilled in 606 B.C., 597 B.C., and 587 B.C.) Everything that your ancestors have stored up until this day will be carried away. Nothing will be left,' says the Lord. 'Some of your own descendants will be taken away (Manasseh, see 2 Chron. 33:11). Those who will be born to you will be taken away, and become eunuchs in the palace of the king of Babylon.'"

Hezekiah told Israel, "The word from the Lord is good." He said this because he thought: "There will be peace and security while I am king."

King Hezekiah Dies

Now, the rest of the deeds of Hezekiah—all of his victories and his work on the pool and his work on the tunnel (this famous conduit can still be seen in Jerusalem in the twenty-first century; the ancient inscription that described its construction is now in a museum in Istanbul) to bring water into the city is recorded—they are all written in the Book of the History of the Kings of Judah. Then Hezekiah died. And, his son Manasseh became the king in his place.

My Time to Pray

Prayers and Tears

And the prayer of faith will save the sick, and the Lord will raise him up. And if he has committed sins, he will be forgiven. Confess your trespasses to one another, and pray for one another, that you may be healed. The effective, fervent prayer of a righteous man avails much (James 5:15-16).

God is just as concerned with our physical bodies as He is with our spiritual life. So why do some believers deny physical healing by God, or are surprised when it happens? Perhaps it's ignorance of Scripture. The Lord is Jehovah-Rapha; He heals. In this occasion, it seems intercession is the tool God honored to heal Hezekiah. God heard the king's prayer instantaneously. Before Isaiah was out of the palace, God sent a message to Isaiah that He was going to heal Hezekiah. *Lord, I'm in good health today; use preventative medicine to keep me in good health. When I need it, use therapeutic healing to return my health. And, if it's Your will that I die, I pray with Paul, "For I am hard-pressed between the two* [life and death], *having a desire to depart and be with Christ, which is far better"* (Phil. 1:23). *Lord, I yield my body to You today. Heal me when I need it, but always glorify Yourself through my body.*

What do you think about the "fig paste" that Hezekiah put on a "boil" or inflamed portion of his body? Was the "fig paste" medicine to draw poison or threatening bacteria out of the body? Was God using medicine to heal Hezekiah? You know, that's one way God heals. Or, was the "fig paste" only an outward symbol of an inner working of God. When Hezekiah obeyed and applied the "fig paste" in faith, then God saw his faith and healed him. Was the "fig paste" only a symbol like *anointing with oil* (see James 5:14) that we use today? You know God loves symbols. *Lord, I will not look to medicine, therapy, surgery, or any other human prescription for healing. I look to You—Jehovah-Rapha. But, Lord, I will listen to the diagnoses of doctors, and will follow their prescriptions; I will do as much as I can to be healthy. I have only one body, and I will take care of it as best I can. I will live healthy, eat healthy, and keep myself from bacteria, germs, and exposure to life-threatening diseases.*

God worked sovereignly to preserve the Messianic line leadings to Jesus Christ. What would have happened to God's plan of salvation if satan could have prevented the birth of Jesus Christ? The point is, satan didn't prevent it. Throughout Scripture there is an eternal battle between satan and God—but God triumphs to bring salvation to the human race. *Lord, I rejoice to see Your plan that has overcome satan. Amen.*

53

Manasseh Rules Over Judah

Manasseh was 12 years old when he became the king (Manasseh was probably born three years after Hezekiah's recovery), and he was king for 55 years in Jerusalem. His mother's name was Hephzibah. He did what was evil in the sight of the Lord. (King Manasseh was doing idolatrous practices, no doubt, influenced by his guardians who were hostile to King Hezekiah's reforms.) Manasseh did disgusting things, just like the non-Jewish nations had done, whom the Lord had forced out of the land ahead of the Israelites. Manasseh's father, Hezekiah, had destroyed the high places where false gods were worshiped, but Manasseh rebuilt them. He built altars for Baal. And, he made an Asherah idol just as Ahab the king of Israel had done. Manasseh even worshiped all the stars of heaven and served them.

The Lord had said about the Temple: "I will put My Name in Jerusalem." But Manasseh built altars inside the Temple area of the Lord. Manasseh built altars to worship all the heavenly bodies in the two courtyards of the Temple of the Lord. And, he burned his own son as a sacrifice. He practiced sorcery and used fortune-telling. (All of these abominable practices were forbidden by Moses [see Lev. 19:31; Deut. 18:10-11].) He got advice from mediums (necromancy) and spiritists. He did so many things that were evil in the eyes of the Lord that he made the Lord very angry.

Manasseh carved an Asherah idol and put it inside the Temple area. The Lord had spoken to David and his son Solomon about the Temple, saying: "I will put My Name in this Temple and in Jerusalem permanently. I have chosen Jerusalem from all the tribes of Israel. I will never again cause the Israelites to wander out of the land that I gave to their ancestors. However, they must obey everything I have commanded them. And, they must obey all the teachings that My servant Moses gave to them." Nevertheless, the people did not listen. Manasseh seduced them to do wrong. They did more evil than the ethnic groups that the Lord had destroyed ahead of the Israelites.

The Lord spoke through His servants the prophets (such as Hosea, Joel, Nahum, Habakkuk, and Isaiah). He said, "Manasseh, the king of Judah, has done these disgusting abominations. He has done more evil than all the Amorites before him ever did. With Manasseh's idols, he also caused Judah to sin. Therefore, this is what the Lord, the God of Israel, says: 'Listen, I will bring much trouble upon Jerusalem and Judah. Anyone who hears about it will be shocked. I will stretch out the measuring line of Samaria over Jerusalem. And the plumb line (a lead weight tied to the end of a string that was suspended to see how truly perpendicular a wall was, used to check how straight up and down a building or a wall was) that was used against Ahab's household will be used on Jerusalem. I will wipe off Jerusalem just as one wipes a dish, and turns it upside down (washing both sides of a dish is a metaphor for a complete and thorough judgment by God). I will abandon the rest of My people who survive. I will deliver them to their enemies. They will become prey to all their enemies; they will be plunder. Why? Because My people have done what is evil in My sight. They have made Me very angry ever since the day their ancestors left Egypt until now.'"

Manasseh also killed many innocent people. (Many believe that the prophet Isaiah was sawn in two by Manasseh [see Heb. 11:37].) He filled Jerusalem from one end to the other with their blood. This was in addition to the sin that he caused Judah to do. He caused Judah to do what was evil in the sight of the Lord.

The rest of the deeds that Manasseh did as king—including his sin that he sinned—are written down in the Book of the History of the Kings of Judah. Manasseh died and was buried in the garden of his own palace. It is the garden of Uzza. Then Manasseh's son, Amon (Manasseh named his son after an Egyptian god [see Nah. 3:8]) became the king in his place.

Amon Rules Over Judah

Amon was 22 years old when he became the king. He was king for two years in Jerusalem. His mother's name was Meshullemeth, the daughter of Haruz. She was from Jotbah. Amon did what was evil in the sight of the Lord. He did just as his father Manasseh had done. Amon lived in the same way that his father had lived. He worshiped the same idols that his father had worshiped, bowing down in front of them. Amon rejected the Lord, the God of his ancestors. He did not follow the ways of the Lord.

Amon's officers made a conspiracy against him and assassinated him in his own palace. Then the common people of Judah executed all those who had plotted to kill King Amon. (The people did not want the Davidic lineage of the Messiah to be interrupted.) So, the common people made his son Josiah king in Amon's place.

The rest of what Amon did is written down in the Book of the History of the Kings of Judah. Amon was buried in his grave in the garden of Uzza and, his son Josiah became the king in his place.

My Time to Pray

The First Generation

And these words which I command you today shall be in your heart. You shall teach them diligently to your children, and shall talk of them when you sit in your house, when you walk by the way, when you lie down, and when you rise up (Deuteronomy 6:6-7).

It is said, "God has no grandchildren, only children." That means every generation must be born again into God's family. Christianity does not automatically pass from fathers to children. Every new generation must experience the same new birth as their parents, and they must learn the same spiritual lessons as their parents. Just because Manasseh was the son of Hezekiah, does not guarantee that Manasseh would serve the Lord as did his father. *Heavenly Father, I look to You, and You alone for salvation and spiritual growth. I will not depend on anyone who went before me for my spiritual growth. Thank You for the possibility of a "first" generation relationship with You.*

There are certain places on this earth that are special to God. The Temple Mount is one of those places because God chose to "put My name" there. That place continues to be special to God, even throughout the coming Millennium. The top of Mount Sinai where God spoke to Moses and Elijah is another spot. In my life, Bonnebella, Georgia, is special because I was saved there; also Columbia Bible College where I first grew in Christ. Probably your home church is special to you because you meet God there on a regular basis. *Lord, I will come regularly to my church "sanctuary" to meet You on a weekly basis. I will seek You in the place where Your presence has been revealed to me in the past.*

God measures every generation with His "measuring line," which is a true standard. When we are punished, we cannot blame our parents or anyone else. We must measure up to God's standard. *Lord, forgive me when I don't measure up to Your perfect standard. Forgive me by the blood of Christ. I know I deserve punishment, but I cry out for mercy.*

There was a great revival under Hezekiah, yet one generation later the people willingly gave themselves to idolatry under the influence of Manasseh. This tells us the power of sin in the lives of God's people. *Lord, I know the deception of my evil heart, so be faithful to "pull" me toward righteousness. Don't give up on me when I am tempted to sin. Capture my soul and make me pure. Amen.*

54

JOSIAH RULES OVER JUDAH

Second Kings 22

Josiah was 8 years old when he became the king. He ruled for 31 years in Jerusalem. (The prophet Zephaniah, circa 630-624 B.C. [see Zeph. 1:1-3] and part of Jeremiah's ministry [627-561 B.C.] coincide with Josiah's reign.) His mother's name was Jedidah, the daughter of Adaiah. Adaiah was from Bozkath. Josiah did what was right in the sight of the Lord. He did good things, just as his ancestor David had done. Josiah did not stop practicing what was right.

In Josiah's eighteenth year as king, he sent Shaphan to the Temple of the Lord. Shaphan was the son of Azaliah, who was the son of Meshullam. Shaphan was the royal assistant. Josiah said, "Go up to Hilkiah, the high priest. Have him make ready the money that the gatekeepers have collected from the people. This is the money that they have brought into the Temple of the Lord. The workers are the carpenters, the builders, and the stonemasons. Also, use the money to buy timber and stones that have been cut for repairing the Temple. They do not need to report how they use the money that is entrusted to them, because they are honest."

The Book of the Law Is Found

Hilkiah, the high priest, said to Shaphan, the royal assistant, "I have found the Book of the Teachings of Moses. It was in the Temple of the Lord." (This ancient book was the Temple copy that had been put beside the Ark of the Covenant in the Holy of Holies mentioned in Deuteronomy 31:25-26 about 900 years earlier. Somehow this precious book had survived the ungodly reigns of Manasseh and Amon.) Hilkiah gave it to Shaphan, who read it.

Then, Shaphan, the royal assistant, went to the king and reported to him, "Your officers have paid out the money that was in the Temple of the Lord. They have given it to the workers and supervisors at the Temple." Then, Shaphan, the royal assistant, told the king, "Hilkiah the high priest has given me a book." Then, Shaphan read to the king from the book.

When the king heard the words of the Book of the Teachings, he ripped his clothes. He gave orders to Hilkiah the high priest and Ahikam, the son of Shaphan. He also gave these orders to Achbor, the son of Micaiah, Shaphan, and Asaiah. Shaphan was the royal assistant. And, Asaiah was the king's servant. These were the orders: "Go and ask the Lord about the words in the book that had been found. Ask for my sake and on behalf of all the people and for all Judah, because the Lord's anger is burning against us, because our ancestors did not obey the words of this book. (Josiah understood the conditional nature of God's warnings.) They did not do all the things written for us to do."

So, Hilkiah the high priest, Ahikam, Achbor, Shaphan, and Asaiah left and went to talk to Huldah the prophetess. She was the wife of Shallum, the son of Tikvah, the son of Harhas. Harhas took care of the king's clothes. Now Huldah lived in Jerusalem, in the new area of the city.

She said to them, "This is what the Lord, the God of Israel, says: Tell the man who sent you to me: 'This is what the Lord says: "Listen, I will bring trouble to this place and to the people living here. It is found in all the words of the book that the king of Judah has read. Why? Because they have abandoned Me, and burned incense to different gods. They have made Me very angry by all the idols that they have made. Like a fire, My anger burns against this place. It will not be put out.'"

"Tell the king of Judah who sent you to ask the Lord: 'This is what the Lord, the God of Israel, says about the words you have heard: "Because your heart was tender and you humbled yourself before Me, when you heard what I said against this place and its people, that they would become desolate and a curse, and you tore your clothes and wept before Me; I have heard your request. I will gather you to your fathers and to your grave in peace. Your eyes will not see all the calamity that I will bring upon this place."'" They brought this word back to the king.

My Time to Pray

The Book

And it shall come to pass afterward, that I will pour out My Spirit upon all flesh (Joel 2:28).

It's amazing how the work of God is influenced by the godly man of God. Hezekiah was a revival king, yet his son and grandson were evil kings. Then in the next generation, God raised up Hezekiah's great grandson to be a revival king. Then the people turned back to God and sought the Lord. The depth of revival is tied to the dedication of the spiritual leader to God. *Lord, I pray for You to raise up spiritual leaders to bring revival in our time. Lord, use me to revive Your people. Pour out Your Spirit on me and on Your Church.*

God uses His Word to revive His people and bring them back to spiritual renewal. When King Josiah had the priest clean out the Temple, they found the Book of Deuteronomy. It was the copy Moses placed near the Ark of the Covenant. God's Word contains the life of God, and when the

Scripture finds its way into the hearts of God's people, it brings revival. *Lord, I want revival in my life. I will seek Your presence in Your Word. I will read it to know You. I will memorize it to lodge Your presence in my life. I will follow its teachings to live for You. Lord, live Your life in me as I hide Your Word in my life.*

Only as we learn God's Word do we realize God's anger burns against His people when they don't do all the things God has required of them. *Lord, I will study carefully Your Word to find out everything I am supposed to know. I want to please You, so I will live according to Scripture. Speak to me from Your Word for I am listening to know Your will.*

God hears and postpones judgment when we humble ourselves before God. *Lord, I humbly bow before You; forgive my sin and revive Your church. Heal my land where I live and turn the heart of the people back to seek Your mercy. Lord, it's important that I touch You, but it's more important that You touch me. Amen.*

55

KING JOSIAH ENFORCES GOD'S LAWS

Second Kings 23:1-30

Then King Josiah summoned to him all the elders of Judah and Jerusalem together. He went up (this was a solemn procession of the king and the most important leaders; they were determined to do what was right) to the Temple of the Lord. All the men from Judah and Jerusalem went with him. The priests, the prophets, and all the people—from the least important to the most important—went with him. He read to them (Deut. 31:10-13 stated that the Law of Moses was to be read aloud once every seven years; but about 75 years had passed since "the Bible" had been publicly read to the people) all the words of the Book of the Covenant that was found in the Temple of the Lord. The king stood by the pillar. He made a renewed promise in the presence of the Lord. He agreed to follow the Lord and obey His commands, rules, and laws with his whole being. He agreed to do whatever was written in this book. Then all the people agreed to live by the covenant.

The king gave a command to Hilkiah, the high priest, to the priests of the next rank, and the gatekeepers. He told them to bring out of the Temple of the Lord everything made for worshiping Baal, or Asherah, and for worshiping all the stars of Heaven. Then Josiah burned them outside Jerusalem in the fields of the Kidron Valley (where water would help wash their ashes). And, he carried the rest of the ashes to Bethel. The kings of Judah had chosen idolatrous priests, but Josiah removed those priests. Those priests had burned incense on the high places where false gods were worshiped. These shrines were in the cities of Judah and the villages around Jerusalem. The priests burned incense to Baal, to the sun, and to the moon. And, they burned incense to the planets and all the stars of heaven. He took away the Asherah idol from the Temple of the Lord, and took it outside Jerusalem to the Kidron Brook, where he burned it and ground it into dust. And, he threw the dust on top of the graves of the common people (that is, upon the graves of those who had sacrificed to false gods [see 2 Chron. 34:4]). Then he tore down the tents of the cult prostitutes (many Canaanite fertility shrines employed temple prostitutes, both male and female) who were in the Temple of the Lord. This was where the women did weaving for Asherah.

King Josiah brought all the false priests from the cities of Judah to Jerusalem (where their activities could be monitored). He polluted the high places where the priests had burned incense. These shrines were everywhere, from Geba to Beer-Sheba. Josiah destroyed those pagan places of worship at the entrance to the Gate of Joshua, the ruler of the city. This gate was on the left side of the city gate. ("The Gate of Joshua" may have been a gate in the inner wall.) These priests of the high places were not allowed to serve at the Lord's altar in Jerusalem, but they could eat bread made without yeast with their Levite brothers. (They were disqualified from returning to the priesthood.)

Topheth (the Hebrew word for drum is "toph;" many scholars believe that drums were beaten loudly to drown out the cries of the terrified little children who passed through the fire into the red-hot arms of the god Molech) was in the Valley of the Son of Hinnom. Josiah polluted it so that no one could sacrifice his son or daughter to Molech. Judah's kings had placed horses at the front door of the Temple of the Lord. They were in the courtyard near the room of Nathan-Melech, an officer. Those horses were for the worship of the sun. (In special processions, the horses were probably used symbolically to draw chariots filled with idolatrous images of the sun.) However, Josiah removed them, and burned the chariots that were used for sun worship.

The kings of Judah had also built altars on the roof of the upstairs room of Ahaz. Josiah broke down those altars, too. He also broke down the altars that Manasseh had made. Those altars that were in the two courtyards of the Temple of the Lord were smashed to pieces. Then he threw their dust into the Kidron Brook. King Josiah polluted the high places that were east of Jerusalem, south of Olive Mountain. Solomon, the king of Israel, had built these places. One was for Ashtoreth, the hated goddess of the Sidonians. One was from Chemosh, the disgusting god of Moab. And, one was for Molech, the disgusting god of the Ammonites. Josiah smashed into pieces the stone pillars that they worshiped. He cut down the Asherah idols. And, he covered those places with human bones. Josiah also broke down the altar at Bethel. This was the high place that Jeroboam the son of Nebat had made, when he caused Israel to sin. Josiah burned that high place. He smashed the stones of the altar to pieces, then ground them into dust. And, he burned the Asherah idols. When Josiah turned around, he saw graves on the mountain. He had the bones taken from the graves, and he burned the bones on the altar to pollute it. This happened just as the Lord had said it would happen, through the man of the one true God. (See the prediction of First Kings 13:1-3;11-32.)

Josiah asked, "What is that monument to the dead that I see?"

The people of the city answered him, "It is the grave of the man of the one true God who came from Judah. This prophet announced the things that you have done against the altar at Bethel."

Josiah said, "Leave that grave alone. No person may move this man's bones." So, they left the bones of the prophet who had come from Samaria.

The kings of Israel had built temples on the high places that were in the cities of Samaria. That had caused the Lord to be so angry. Josiah removed all those temples. He did to them the same things that he had done at Bethel. (King Josiah extended his sovereignty up into Samaria because of the weakened condition of the Assyrian Empire.) Josiah executed all the priests of the high places, killing them next to the altars. And, he burned human bones on those altars (for the specific purpose of defiling them forever). Then Josiah went back to Jerusalem.

The king gave a command to all the people: "Celebrate the Passover to the Lord, your God, as it is written in this Book of the Covenant." No Passover Festival like this one had been celebrated since the time the judges led Israel. Not even during the time of the kings of Israel and the kings of Judah had a Passover Feast like this one been observed. This Passover was celebrated to the Lord in Jerusalem, in the eighteenth year of King Josiah's rule.

Josiah destroyed the mediums, fortune-tellers, household gods, and the idols. He destroyed all the disgusting gods that were seen in the land of Judah and in Jerusalem. He did this to obey the words of the teachings that were written in the book that Hilkiah the high priest had found. Therefore, whatever was found in the Temple was included in the Temple of the Lord.

There was no king like Josiah before or after him. (His four successors—Jehoahaz, Jehoiakim, Jehoiachin, and Zedekiah—were all very evil kings [see Jer. 20-39]. The nation went past the point of no spiritual return after Josiah's time.) He obeyed the Lord with all of his heart, soul, and strength. He followed all the teachings of Moses.

Even so, the Lord did not turn away from His strong and furious anger. His anger burned against Judah. (Though they were outwardly purified, their hearts were not cleansed.) It was because all that Manasseh had done to make Him so angry. The Lord said, "I have taken Israel away; I will do the same thing to Judah. I will take them out of my sight. I will reject Jerusalem—this city that I chose. I will take away the Temple about which I said: 'I will put My Name there.'

And the rest of the deeds—all that Josiah did—are written down in the Book of the History of the Kings of Judah.

While Josiah was king, Pharaoh-Necho (Necho II [609-595 B.C.], the second Pharaoh of the twenty-sixth dynasty, the king of Egypt) went to assist the king of Assyria against the Babylonians (see 2 Chron. 35:20-27). Necho was at the Euphrates River when King Josiah marched out to fight against Necho. (So, Josiah attempted to prevent the Egyptian army from going through the pass at Megiddo. Necho tried to get Josiah and his army to retreat, but when Necho's efforts failed, Josiah was killed. Later, Pharaoh-Necho and the Babylonians clashed at Carchemish, one of the decisive battles of all time. Egypt was defeated and never again became a world power.) But at Megiddo, Necho faced Josiah and killed him. Josiah's servants carried his corpse in a chariot from Megiddo to Jerusalem and buried him in his own grave. Then the people of Judah chose Josiah's son, Jehoahaz, and poured olive oil on him to appoint him as king in his father's place.

My Time to Pray

A Pure Heart

If My people who are called by My name will humble themselves, and pray and seek My face, and turn from their wicked ways, then I will hear from heaven, and will forgive their sin and heal their land (2 Chronicles 7:14).

There can be no revival among the people of God until the leaders of God lead them to seek God. So it was when Josiah called the leaders into the Temple to hear the reading of Scripture, that God began His work again. *Lord, I pray for the leaders of my generation; revive them so they will lead the church in revival. Lord, revive me, so I can revive the people I lead. May my life be an example to them and may my words touch their hearts. Lord, make me a spiritual leader of those I influence.*

There can be no revival until God's people deal honestly with their sin. They must repent in their hearts, then make outward changes in their actions to seek God. They must cleanse their surroundings of sin and separate themselves from things that stand for sin. A true heart revival always leads to a moral change in our lifestyle and a cleaning of our outward life of sinful practices. *Lord, I repent; I'm sorry for my sin and careless attitude. I'm sorry for not being more diligent in prayer and witnessing. I rid my life of sin's symbols; I cleanse my life of everything that saps my spiritual strength. I want to be clean inwardly so I will get rid of outward things that compromise my testimony.*

A true leader of God must also be a reformer for God. Josiah didn't just sit on his throne to direct reforms and mandate change. He went to the places of sin and got rid of idols, and cleansed the land of shrines and altars and false gods. Josiah got his hands involved in the work of reform. *Lord, I will get involved. I will personally get rid of evil things in my life. I will no longer do them, but will throw them out. Lord, give me strength to be a reformer.*

Even good people make mistakes. King Josiah was a good king—a revival king—but he made one mistake. He went to battle against Egypt. Josiah didn't listen to Pharaoh who was battling the king of Assyria, and in return King Josiah was killed. Did Josiah die needlessly, or was his military involvement the extension of his religious revival? Did Josiah die following the dictates of his inner nature? We don't know. *Lord, may I not die needlessly, and may I not get involved in battles that are not necessary. Give me wisdom to know when to fight, and to know when to not get involved. Lord, be my conscience and be my guide. Amen.*

56

THE PASSOVER OBSERVED

Second Chronicles 35

King Josiah celebrated the Passover to the Lord in Jerusalem. The
Passover lambs were killed on the fourteenth day of the first
month. Josiah chose the priests to do their duties, and he
encouraged them as they ministered in the Temple of the Lord.
The Levites taught the Israelites, and they were consecrated for
service to the Lord. Josiah said to them: "When David's son,
Solomon, was the king of Israel, he built the Temple and put the
Ark of the Covenant in that Temple. Do not carry it back and
forth on your shoulders anymore. (Scholars have speculated that
the Ark of the Covenant may have been temporarily removed
from the Holy of Holies while Josiah's Temple repairs were going
on. King Josiah was relieving them of this daily duty; the Ark of
the Covenant would again remain undisturbed inside the Holy
of Holies.) Now serve the Lord, your God, and His people, the
Israelites. Prepare yourselves by your clans according to shifts.
Do the jobs that David the king of Israel and his son Solomon
instructed you to do.

"Stand in the holy place with a group of the Levites. Do this for each
subdivision of the families of your people, so that you may help
them. (The people were admitted into the courtyard in groups
of several households at a time. When each group entered to
full capacity, the gates would be shut and the slaughtering of the

offerings would be made. (See Second Chronicles 30:16-18.)
Kill the Passover lambs. Make yourselves holy to the Lord. And,
prepare the lambs for your Jewish relatives. Do everything that
the Lord commanded us to do through Moses." (They were to
instruct the people specifically how to partake of the Passover
meal. Because of the previous lapses, many of the people were
ignorant of the requirements of the Law of Moses.)

Josiah donated to the poor Israelites 30,000 sheep and young goats to
kill for the Passover sacrifices. He also gave them 3,000 cattle.
All of them were King Josiah's own animals.

Josiah's officials also donated willingly to the people, to the priests, and
to the Levites. Hilkiah, Zechariah, and Jehiel were the officials in
charge of the Temple of the one true God. They gave the priests
2,600 lambs and goats and 300 cattle for Passover sacrifices.
Also Conaniah, and his brothers Shemaiah and Nethanel, and
Hashabiah, Jeiel, and Jozabad gave animals to the Levites.
They gave 5,000 sheep and goats and 500 cattle for Passover
sacrifices. These men were leaders of the Levites.

When everything was ready for the Passover service, the priests and the
Levites went to their places in shifts. This is what the king had
commanded. The Passover lambs were killed. Then the Levites
skinned the animals, handing the containers of blood to the
priests who sprinkled the blood on the altar. Then they removed
the parts of the animals for the whole burnt offerings (these
parts were given to the offerers who were supposed to take them
up to the altar and hand them to the officiating priests) to the
different clans of the people. This was done so that the whole
burnt offerings could be offered to the Lord as the Law of Moses
taught. They did this with the cattle, too. The Levites roasted
the Passover lamb over the fire, just as they were commanded.
And, they boiled the holy offerings in pots, kettles, and pans.
Then they promptly gave the meat to all the people. After this

was finished, the Levites prepared meat for themselves and for the priests. (Because the priests were so busy the entire day they had no leisure to provide any refreshments for themselves.) The priests were the direct descendants of Aaron. The priests worked until nightfall, offering the whole burnt offerings and burning the fat of the sacrifices. That is what the Levites did.

The Levite singers were descendants of Asaph. They stood in the places that were prescribed by King David, Asaph, Heman, and Jeduthun the king's seer. (These shifts of singers were chanting Psalms 113-118 over and over again, as each large group came into the courtyard.) The gatekeepers at each gate did not need to leave their posts, because the fellow Levites had prepared everything for them for the Passover Festival. So, the entire Passover ceremony for the Lord was completed on that day. (If each Passover lamb was distributed to ten people, that would mean that far more than 300,000 pilgrims were served in a single day at the Temple.) And, it was done according to King Josiah's orders. The Passover Feast was celebrated, and the whole burnt offerings were offered upon the Lord's altar. The Israelites who were there at that time celebrated the Passover and the Festival of Unleavened Bread for seven days. The Passover Festival had not been celebrated like this in Israel since the prophet Samuel was alive. None of the kings of Israel had ever celebrated such a Passover like this. King Josiah, the priests, and the Levites celebrated it. All the people of Judah and of Israel who were there with the people of Jerusalem celebrated it, too. This Passover was celebrated in the eighteenth year that Josiah was the king.

King Josiah Dies

So, Josiah did all this for the Temple. After this, King Necho of Egypt led an army to attack Carchemish, a town on the Euphrates River.

And, Josiah marched out to fight against Necho. But Necho sent messengers to Josiah, "King Josiah, there should be no war between us. I did not come to fight you, but my enemies. God told me to hurry, and He is on my side. So, don't fight God, or He will destroy you."

But Josiah did not go away. He wore different clothes, so that no one would recognize who he was. ("He disguised himself." Some scholars think it means: "He equipped himself.") He refused to listen to what Necho said. Josiah led his army into battle. He went to fight at the plain of Megiddo. During the battle, King Josiah was shot by arrows. He told his servants, "Take me away; I am badly wounded." So, they took him out of his chariot, and put him in his other chariot. Then they took him to Jerusalem where he died. He was buried in the graves where his ancestors were buried. All the people of Judah and of Jerusalem were very sad because he had died.

Jeremiah wrote some funeral songs about Josiah. Even to this day, all the male and female singers remember and honor Josiah with those songs. It became a custom in Israel to sing those songs. Look, they are written in the collection of lamentations (this "Book of Dirges" is now lost).

The other things that Josiah did as king—from the beginning to the end—are written down in the Book of the Kings of Israel and of Judah. It tells how he loved God and obeyed the Lord's teachings.

My Time to Pray

The Blood of the Lamb

But if we walk in the light as He is in the light, we have fellowship with one another, and the blood of Jesus Christ His Son cleanses us from all sin (1 John 1:7).

E very time there is a revival, it always can trace its roots to the cleansing of the blood of The Lamb. In Josiah's day, the people killed the Passover lamb and renewed their pledge to God. Passover was a yearly responsibility because sin was a constant experience of God's people. *Lord, I need constant cleansing from sin by the blood of Christ. I try to live a perfect life, but I don't. Forgive me by the blood of Christ. I will continually come to You because sin is ever with me.*

The singers were necessary for worship and revival. Why? Because music is the window of the soul. What's really in the heart comes out through the songs we sing. So to prepare for worship, the musicians took their place. *Lord, I will sing the song of my heart to You. I love You and will tell You in the music of my soul. There are many who sing much better than I; so I will listen and worship You. I need Your music when I go about making money, or taking care of my family, or doing the things required of me. When I lie upon my bed, I will sing to You; when I rise in the morning I will thank You for the challenge of a new day. I will worship You through music all the day long.*

Every generation has had its songwriters. *Lord, I thank You for new music to express my soul.* And music is forgotten or lost it seems with every generation. *Lord, I will sing to You with today's music.* Just as the songs composed about Josiah were lost, so there is always a need to write new songs to express our hearts. *Lord, I sing a new song to You from my heart. Amen.*

57

JEHOAHAZ RULES OVER JUDAH

Second Kings 23:31,37,24

Jehoahaz was 23 years old when he became the king. And, he was king
in Jerusalem for three months. His mother's name was Hamutal.
She was the daughter of Jeremiah (not the prophet Jeremiah)
from Libnah. Jehoahaz did what was evil in the sight of the Lord.
He did just as his ancestors (not including Hezekiah or Josiah)
had done.

Pharaoh-Necho took Jehoahaz as a prisoner at Riblah in the land
of Hamath. He did this so that Jehoahaz could not rule in
Jerusalem. Necho forced the people of Judah to pay about 7,500
pounds of silver and about 75 pounds of gold.

Pharaoh-Necho made Josiah's son, Eliakim, the king, in place of Josiah,
his father. Then Necho changed Eliakim's name to "Jehoiakim."
But Necho took Jehoahaz to Egypt, and he died there. Jehoiakim
gave to Pharaoh-Necho the silver and the gold that he demanded.
Jehoiakim taxed the land, so that he could pay Pharaoh-Necho.
He took silver and gold from the people of the land. The amount
that he took from each person depended on how much each one
had.

King Nebuchadnezzar of Babylon attacked Jerusalem. (After the
battle at Carchemish [see Jer. 46:2], Jehoiakim was forced to
become a vassal king for his new masters, the Babylonians

[see 2 Kings 24:1]. But at the end of three years, Jehoiakim threw off the Babylonian yoke in favor of a renewed alliance with the Egyptians, who planned a new military expedition against Carchemish. However, the king of Egypt was completely vanquished by Nebuchadnezzar, who stripped the Pharaoh of all his possessions between the Euphrates River and the Nile River [see 2 Kings 24:7]. Then Nebuchadnezzar marched against Jerusalem.) He bound Jehoiakim with bronze chains. Then Nebuchadnezzar planned to take him away to Babylon. (He was allowed to remain in his tributary kingdom, but he was later killed ignominiously at Jerusalem [see Jer. 12:18-19; 36:30; Ezek. 19:8-9].) Nebuchadnezzar took some of the sacred objects from the Temple of the Lord. He took them away to Babylon and put them in his own palace.

Jehoiakim Rules Over Judah

Jehoiakim was 25 years old when he began to rule. And, he ruled for 11 years in Jerusalem. His mother's name was Zebidah, the daughter of Pedaiah of Rumah. And, Jehoiakim did what was evil in the sight of the Lord, just like all his ancestors.

In Jehoiakim's days, Nebuchadnezzar the king of Babylon came up. (This was the first year of Nebuchadnezzar's rule and the beginning of the fourth year of Jehoiakim's tenure. The 70 years of Jeremiah's prediction [see Jer. 25:11] actually begins here. This invasion occurred in 605 B.C.) And, Jehoiakim became Nebuchadnezzar's servant for three years. Then Jehoiakim turned and rebelled against him. And the Lord sent against him bands of the Chaldeans, and bands of the Syrians, and bands of the Moabites, and bands of the Ammonites, and sent them against Judah to destroy it, according to the word of the Lord, which He spoke by His servants, the prophets. Surely this came upon Judah at the command of the Lord, to remove them out of His sight, for the sins of Manasseh, according to all that he had done, and also for the innocent blood that Manasseh had shed, because he filled Jerusalem with innocent blood, and the Lord would not pardon it.

Now the rest of the deeds of Jehoiakim—all that he did—is written down in the Book of the Chronicles of the Kings of Judah. So, Jehoiakim died. (Nebuchadnezzar captured Jehoiakim and had him executed. After the Babylonians withdrew, Jehoiakim's remains were finally collected and buried where Manasseh had been buried.)

And, Jehoiachin, his son, ruled in his place. And the king of Egypt (Pharaoh-Necho) did not come out of his land again, because the king of Babylon had taken all that belonged to the king of Egypt, from the Brook of Egypt to the Euphrates River.

Jehoiachin Rules Over Judah

Jehoiachin was 18 years old when he began to rule; and he ruled in Jerusalem for three months. His mother's name was Nehushta, the daughter of Elnathan. She was from Jerusalem. Jehoiachin did what was evil in the sight of the Lord just as his ancestors had done.

At that time, the officers of Nebuchadnezzar, the king of Babylon, came up to Jerusalem and surrounded the city and besieged it. (The siege lasted from December of 598 B.C. to March of 597 B.C., according to Babylonian records.) And, Nebuchadnezzar, the king of Babylon, came against the city while his officers were attacking it. Jehoiachin, the king of Judah, surrendered to the king of Babylon. Jehoiachin's mother, servants, leaders, and officers also surrendered. Then the king of Babylon made Jehoiachin a prisoner. This was in the eighth year when Nebuchadnezzar was king.

Nebuchadnezzar took all the treasures from the Temple of the Lord. He also removed the treasures from the royal palace. He broke up all the gold objects that Solomon, the king of Israel, had made for the Temple. This happened just as the Lord had said it would happen. Nebuchadnezzar took away all the people of Jerusalem. This included all the officers and all the leaders. (The intelligentsia, including Daniel and his three Jewish friends; see Daniel 1-3.) He also took all the craftsmen and the metal workers. There were 10,000 prisoners in all. Only the poorest people in the land remained.

Nebuchadnezzar carried away Jehoiachin to Babylon. He took the king's mother and his wives. He also took the eunuchs and the leading men of the land. They were taken captive from Jerusalem to Babylon. The king of Babylon also took all 7,000 soldiers. These men were all strong and able to fight in war. And 1,000 craftsmen and metal workers were taken away, too. The king of Babylon took them as prisoners to Babylon. The king of Babylon made Mattaniah the king in Jehoiachin's place. Mattaniah was Jehoiachin's uncle. He also changed Mattaniah's name to "Zedekiah."

Zedekiah Rules Over Judah

Zedekiah was 21 years old when he became the king. And, he was king in Jerusalem for 11 years. His mother's name was Hamutal, the daughter of Jeremiah. She was from Libnah. Zedekiah did what was evil in the sight of the Lord just as Jehoiakim had done. All of this happened in Jerusalem and in Judah because the Lord was angry with them. Finally, God threw them out of His presence.

Zedekiah turned against the king of Babylon.

My Time to Pray

Sins Punished

*Thus saith the Lord..."Now have I given all these lands
into the hand of Nebuchadnezzar, the king of Babylon, My
servant..." (Jeremiah 27:2,6).*

D id you see that God called Nebuchadnezzar His servant? How
could Jehovah call a mean, sadistic killer His servant? How could
God use a man who ruthlessly destroyed Jerusalem and the Temple? The
answer is in the plan and nature of God. God is more concerned with the
sins of His people than He is with the sins of the heathen. God expects
the unsaved to sin, that's their nature, but the children of God have a new
nature that was created by God in righteousness. They should not sin. So,
God called Nebuchadnezzar His servant who will punish the sin of His
people. *Lord, I fear You. I know You punish the sin of Your people, so I fear
Your punishment when I sin. I repent. I turn from my sin to You. Cleanse
me of all my sin by the blood of Christ. I will serve You in holiness. Lord, I
claim Your promise, "God is faithful [to His Word and to His compassion-
ate nature], and He [can be trusted] not to let you be tempted and tried
and assayed beyond your ability and strength of resistance and power to
endure" (1 Cor. 10:13 AMP).*

The history of the world swirls around the head of Nebuchadnezzar,
the first man to rule the known Western civilized world. Yet, God has a
purpose for Nebuchadnezzar to punish His people Israel. What the world
counts as a footnote on the pages of history, God counts it as the head-
lines of history. *GOD PUNISHES HIS PEOPLE BY THE HAND OF NEBU-
CHADNEZZAR. Lord, I will read the history books with Your eyes, I will
look for Your plan for Israel. I do not understand why You chose the Jew, but
they are the secret to understanding history. Lord, I need insight.*

The nation of Israel fell because of weak leadership. The kings had no
spiritual foundation to stand against the world; so they became servants

of the ungodly. *Lord, if I don't stand for You, I will become the slave of the ungodly. I will stand. Amen.*